D0321678

WITHDRAWN FROM STOCK

THE BOOK THIEF

THE BOOK THIEF

The True Crimes of Daniel Spiegelman

Travis McDade

 PRAEGER

Westport, Connecticut
London

Library of Congress Cataloging-in-Publication Data

McDade, Travis.
 The book thief : the true crimes of Daniel Spiegelman / Travis McDade.
  p. cm.
 Includes bibliographical references and index.
 ISBN 0–275–99331–0 (alk. paper)
 1. Book thefts—New York (State)—New York. 2. Columbia University. Rare Book
 and Manuscript Library. 3. Spiegelman, Daniel. 4. Thieves—New York
 (State)—New York. I. Title.
 Z733.C7243bM33 2006
 025.8′209747—dc22 2006025930

British Library Cataloguing in Publication Data is available

Copyright © 2006 by Travis McDade

All rights reserved. No portion of this book may be
reproduced, by any process or technique, without the
express written consent of the publisher.

Library of Congress Catalog Card Number: 2006025930
ISBN: 0–275–99331–0

First published in 2006

Praeger Publishers, 88 Post Road West, Westport, CT 06881
An imprint of Greenwood Publishing Group, Inc.
www.praeger.com

Printed in the United States of America

The paper used in this book complies with the
Permanent Paper Standard issued by the National
Information Standards Organization (Z39.48–1984).

10 9 8 7 6 5 4 3 2 1

To
PWM

Contents

Acknowledgments

Obviously this book would not have been possible without the help of a great many people, almost all of them strangers to me when I called upon them. First of all, both Jean Ashton and Consuelo Dutschke spoke with me numerous times in order to help me better understand the world of rare books and the Rare Book and Manuscript Library at Columbia. Consuelo, in particular, made heavy edits on parts of a late draft of the book and corrected a number of misunderstandings. She also paved the way for me to speak with several folks who offered their own valuable information. My interviews with both Jean and Consuelo in March 2005 not only gave me great information but also very much personalized this story.

Other librarians I spoke to also very much helped me shape several parts of the book and offered various pieces of encouragement along the way. I cannot thank them enough for the help they offered me or the service they provided to their communities. I was continually surprised at how personally many of the librarians I spoke with took the thefts that occurred at their libraries and how dogged they were in seeking a resolution. Each of the thefts deserves its own separate account and I'm only sorry I couldn't do that in this book. So thanks to Henry Yaple, Lisa Speer, Ester Sanchez, Karen Smiga, Shaner Magalhaes, Laurel Best, Nancy Davenport, and Robert Dunkelberger. Also, thanks to Rudolph Ellenbogen, Bernard Cristol, Patrick Lawlor, Fred Schreiber, and Sandra Hindman who really offered me some interesting details of the book world and help with understanding the RBML. Cathy Begley, who does terrific work on our behalf at the FBI, helped me a great deal when she sat for an interview. Bob Goldman, who does terrific work on our behalf as a United States Attorney, also gave me some valuable insight into the current world of federal criminal law.

Both Basil Panagopulos and Sebastian Hesselink deserve immense thanks, not only from me for their interviews, but from both Columbia and the book community as a whole, for going way above and beyond the call of duty to apprehend Spiegelman. Finally, numerous people gave me valuable tips and information during the course of my research and writing. There are too many of these people to mention for fear that I would leave someone out. And some have asked to remain anonymous. I appreciate all the help in the form of information I have received and am only sorry that I can't offer a more comprehensive thanks than this.

Along the way, but particularly near the end, various people read the manuscript and offered great advice about what was missing and what wasn't. Emery Lee, in particular, did a very thorough copy edit and provided deep analysis. Chris Maynard, too, gave a late version of the book an exceedingly close read and offered some great suggestions. I thank them both very much for their efforts. I took at least one suggestion from almost everyone who read the thing and each deserves more thanks than this. But this is about all I can give. So thanks to Dick and Kay McDade, Pam Manselle, Traci Yingling, Amy Goudschaal, Stephanie Hoffer, and Aaron Kearns. Any flaws or mistakes that remain in the text are my own, in spite of their advice.

I imposed upon three other individuals to see if they'd be willing to read a late draft of the book and offer a blurb if they liked it. Two of these folks were strangers to me so it was particularly gracious of them to read the pre-bound manuscript of a pushy stranger. So thanks very much to Will Manley and Nicholas Basbanes, both terrific authors who were generous with their time. Also thanks to Doug Berman. Not only did he read the manuscript, but, in the early stages when this was just a research paper, he was the first person to confirm that this was a unique federal sentence I was looking at. Lynne Curry, another busy professor, first encouraged me to turn what was going to be a research paper into a book.

I also would not have been able to complete this work without the support of my colleagues at the Jenner Law Library at the University of Illinois at Urbana-Champaign. Janis Johnston and Paul Healey, in particular, have offered tremendous encouragement and advice at various stages of the project. The institutional support I received both from Jenner and, in particular, from the UIUC Library system was (and remains) indispensable. I very much appreciate the assistance in the form of a grant I received from the Research and Publication Committee of the University of Illinois at Urbana-Champaign Library. This grant got the ball rolling allowing me to go to New York and begin my research; such support is one of the reasons I enjoy working for the University of Illinois so much.

Thanks to everyone at Praeger. In particular, many thanks to Suzanne Staszak-Silva who read my initial proposal and saw it through to a contract. She also remained very patient with me throughout the process, answering the small questions of a first-time author. I cannot thank her enough for what she's done. Also, thanks to Saloni Jain for the very fine copyediting and prompt replies.

This book is partially the result of interviews, discussions, e-mails, books, and articles. But the lion's share of the information contained within was culled from more than a thousand pages of documents that I got from two sources: the Southern District of New York and the Federal Bureau of Investigation. Many thanks to the people who work in the documents areas of these institutions and the folks, throughout our history, who have fought to keep these documents available.

Finally, thanks to Judge Kaplan for getting it right.

Introduction

It may have seemed strange in the late evenings of the spring of 1994 to see a small man in his early thirties carrying a duffel bag almost as big as he was through the front doors of Columbia University's Butler Library. By 10:30 p.m. the various component libraries that made their home in the large building had been closed for five hours and the circulation staff—the only operation still open—was getting ready to shut down their concern. This included closing the stacks. It was true that the reading rooms would be staying open the whole night, but usually the sorts of people who would be studying that late had started well before the time when Daniel Spiegelman and his large bag wandered in.

But living in Manhattan tends to put a damper on one's interpretation of strange, so the unusual man easily escaped notice. Even his age wouldn't have turned any heads: He could convincingly have passed for one of the many graduate students populating the library late into the night. In truth, so intent were most students on their studies that Spiegelman probably could have walked into the main portico on horseback, gone up the stairs that went either left or right to the third floor, down the hall, and into the main reading room and only gotten a few stares, meeting his gaze to tell him to keep the racket down.

So it happened that no one noticed when he walked past the circulation desk and disappeared into the stacks, quickly jetting left, and then up the narrow stairs a few flights. Lots of people came in late to gather last minute books. And though the stacks would be closing shortly, for a person who knew what he was doing, a book could be grabbed off its shelf, checked out, and opened on a table in the reading room in less than ten minutes. Hurried and erratic behavior might even be considered the norm late at night in

Butler. In fact, the only thing missing from Spiegelman's demeanor to betray the fact that he was not a student was the look of slight panic. By this time even so much as a raised pulse was in his distant past. The risk was minimal. He was into a routine; a practiced procedure that through repetition had become as easy to him as passing a bad check.

The difference was, he had been caught at that. But he would not be caught at this. It was too easy. And no one was paying attention because he wasn't doing anything that seemed to involve money. In the beginning he had been skittish and worrisome—he was naturally that way. But by that point, more than ten trips in, he never worried at all. In fact, he was already thinking about the next step. He had so much loot accumulated he was starting to figure on how he could get rid of it. It filled several storage lockers in the city and was starting to get to the point where he just couldn't take any more. Besides, this was no crime of passion—he was ready to get paid.

He knew that there were plenty of people who would be interested in what he had but there were just as many who would turn him in. Especially if he tried to unload the stuff in New York. Or, in truth, anywhere in the United States. But he had lived in Europe. He spoke Russian and Dutch. He could get by in Germany. His disappearing to the Continent for a few months would raise no suspicions at all, not even with his mother.

He walked through the heavy, close air of the stacks. The lighting only sometimes reached down the lanes of books. It always seemed like nighttime in those stacks but the late spring air weighed even more heavily than usual. The bag, even mostly empty, was unwieldy in the tight quarters. He sat the duffel down on the tile floor and kicked it behind a book shelf. He walked around the dark floor to see if anyone was there. Then he went back to his shadowed corner and pulled a random book off the shelf. If anyone checking the stacks before closing were to come by here he would feign that he was engrossed in reading. But he knew no one would come by. The sorts of people working at the circulation desk that late at night weren't going to go through the rows looking for stragglers or potential thieves; the most that anyone ever did was call out that the stacks were getting ready to close.

What that meant to Daniel Spiegelman at this point in the year was that the Rare Book and Manuscript Library collection, sitting almost directly above him, was about to open.

CHAPTER 1

A Vault Laid Open

Consuelo Dutschke, the curator of the medieval and Renaissance collection, was back from a long weekend. It was July 5th, the Tuesday after the holiday and she was itching to get to work. She and her husband had entertained out-of-town friends for the 4th and the time off had given her a burst of energy. She was aiming to clean off the accumulated piles on her desk.[1]

It was amazing how quickly things had gotten that way. She had only started working at Columbia's Rare Book and Manuscript Library (RBML) a year earlier, relocating from the other side of the country. Jean Ashton, the director of the RBML, had been there slightly less long. They were the two new people on staff and so developed a particular kinship.

They had both been drawn to Columbia for similar reasons: it was an amazing, almost unparalleled collection that resided in an Ivy League school in the best American city for books. But while Ashton was from the east coast and had spent most of her career in the northeast, Dutschke had just moved to New York from California. So she was getting acquainted with the collection and the city at the same time.

The collection of medieval and Renaissance manuscripts in the RBML was impressive in depth and breadth. (The term "manuscript" is from the Latin word *manu scriptus*, meaning written by hand and essentially means a hand-recorded document of any length, as opposed to something produced by moveable type or other means of reproduction.) Included in the collection were items dating from the eighth century but the majority of the material was from the fifteenth century, just before mass reproduction and printed materials broke across Europe. The collection represented almost all of the countries of western Europe—even Iceland—and the subject matter of the manuscripts ranged from literature to liturgy to law.[2] As it would be for most people who appreciate beautiful and one-of-a-kind artistry, it was a fantastic job for Dutschke. She had worked extensively with the catalogue of the superb Huntington Library and so knew her way around such fine materials, but to work so closely with the Columbia collection was quite a treat.

She walked through the public area of the RBML—first through the glass doors at the entrance and then past the tables and glassed-in display cases that lined the walls—toward her office. Now an expert in her area who is called upon to teach seminars and courses at places like the University of Virginia's Rare Book School, she was just beginning to make a name for herself in the profession.

With that accumulated energy she decided to first finish some cataloging of manuscripts she'd been working on in the previous two weeks. So, as she had done on most days during her time at Columbia, she went into what was known as "the vault"—a special secured area within the already secured area of the closed stacks, the place behind the RBML circulation desk that patrons would see the librarians disappear into when they requested a book. This vault was strictly off limits to all but a few of the professionals who worked there; Columbia faculty members were sometimes chagrined to discover that they, too, were excluded. But those were the rules in a place where an item grabbed at random off the shelf could be sold at auction for several hundred thousand dollars. It was not a good idea to have too many people wandering around the rare stacks—it was sheer idiocy to have any but a few people ever go into the vault.

She had planned on consulting a particular manuscript housed in the vault. Since she knew herself to be the only one working with the thing, she assumed it would be right where she left it.[3]

Dutschke was in the process of cataloguing what she thought was a Spanish manuscript. She had been working on a different manuscript— the one she was about to get from the vault—a few weeks prior to that and she *knew* it to be Spanish. She planned to compare the two for similarities; if the one she thought was Spanish had many of the same markings as the one she knew was Spanish, it would confirm her initial speculations about the mystery manuscript. It was the sort of work that provided a jolt of ex- citement every day: comparing the markings on two rare codices, neither of which had been touched in modern times by more than a handful of people, let alone opened in the same room together. It was the sort of work that few people are qualified to do and that fewer still ever get the opportunity to do.

She opened the locked door and went through into the vault. As soon as she was back there she went right to the shelving unit housing the preservation case in which the manuscript was kept. Preservation cases are, essentially, tailor-made boxes—usually cloth over pasteboard—that house individual books and manuscripts. They fit snugly to each item when closed to prevent rubbing against the inside of the box itself. Not only do these boxes prevent the rare liquid spill or pen damage but they also lessen the day-to-day wear that would come from a book being routinely dragged across the shelf or rubbed against the cover of an adjacent book. In other libraries, the cases keep the book out of any sort of direct light when they are not in use; in the RBML there are no windows from which to protect the books. Also, the cases enclose the book in its own microenvironment, diminishing the fluctuations in temperature and humidity that are so threatening to parchment over a long period. These boxes are not made of titanium, but as a simple means of preservation, they can't be beat.

In the RBML the different donated collections are housed in different colored cases (the Plimpton mansuscripts in blue, the Smith Western manuscripts in green, and so on), so even if she couldn't always remember exactly where something was she could identify it roughly by looking for the cases with the same color. In this instance she knew exactly where it was since she had just had it out. Dutschke located the preservation case on the shelf where she had left it and reached to pick it up. Even while pulling it off the shelf, the thing felt light, like the difference between scooting an empty and a full soda can across a countertop. She looked around on the shelves to see if the manuscript was just lying outside of its box, a nearly impossible occurrence at the RBML, to be sure, but possibly a habit of careless or hurried librarians. Given the strict procedures set up in the RBML for transferring books in and out of the vault, in and out of the reading room, and in and out of the hands of readers, the idea of misplacing a book was highly improbable but, at the time, it seemed like the only explanation.

At the same time that she was looking for the manuscript on the surrounding shelves she noticed that there were several call number "flags"—essentially, bookmarks inserted into the cases of the rare materials that contain the cataloguing information that ordinarily is adhered to the outside of library books—scattered about. Since these flags are the only piece of cataloging information attached to particular books, they would never ordinarily be separated from their item. There would be no reason why the flags would be away from the books, unless the book was getting recatalogued (and even then the flag would probably stay with the book). Or, of course, unless the person who was stealing the individual books from the library thought that these flags contained sensors of the sort that would set off the alarm when he walked out of the place with them.

Dutschke felt almost immediately sick. This was all extremely out of the ordinary routine, and the safe upkeep of a library of any valuable or perishable asset demands strict routine. She opened the box, just to confirm that it was empty.

The piece that she had gone in to look at, Western MS 29, contained gospel readings for the Mass: the text on its opening leaf appears as if in a frame hung against a tapestry of flowers and fruits. The style of the script of the sixteenth-century book was influenced by the printing that was going on all over Europe, but its decoration harkened back to the Flanders of the end of the previous century; it is elegantly bound in calf stretched over wooden boards, gilt stamped with gilt edges.[4] It had been a gift from John Crawford in 1971 and, like most such gifts, was now to be permanently housed at Columbia so that scholars of the period could use it in their teaching and research. But Western MS 29, which had already traveled much further than any of its creators could have imagined, was on the move again. As Dutschke stood with preservation box in hand that Tuesday morning, it was nearer to its point of origin than it had been in a long while.

Dutschke, of course, had no idea of this. She was still of the mind that it was somewhere within the confines of the RBML. It was clearly not where it was supposed to be—and this was an almost unthinkable breach of procedure—but she could not imagine that it had been taken outside the threshold of the library. There was just no way for that to happen. Still, in the buildup to the ultimate revelation of the massive theft, this was the first laid brick.

With the hope of someone who had absentmindedly misplaced her keys, she went to her supervisor at the time, Rudolph Ellenbogen, and described what she had seen. Ellenbogen had preceded both Dutschke and Ashton at the RBML by more than twenty years, starting there in 1973. He had been at Columbia since 1970. So he had seen the collection grow and knew the place intimately. There was a lot of territory in the RBML stacks and he thought it was likely that the manuscript was somewhere in the area.[5]

Ellenbogen asked her when last she had seen Western MS 29. Dutschke mentioned that she had had it and several other manuscripts out for a class she was teaching some weeks earlier. Ellenbogen recommended she get a list of all the books she had had out for that class and check to see if by chance the book had gotten put in the wrong case.

Dutschke thought that this would be fruitless—there was little chance that she had put the book back in the wrong case since each case is individually constructed for its particular book, and even if she had done so, the empty case should contain a different item, not nothing. Still, it was a place to start and she knew that Ellenbogen was right that there had to be a simple explanation for the missing item. The best course of action was to not panic and to simply go back over the territory of her last interactions with the manuscript. And since she had an increasingly bad feeling about the situation, it would give her something to do. Her list was at home. She left RBML and walked back to her apartment a few short blocks away, all the time thinking about the emptiness of the case and the troubling mystery it presented.[6]

When she came back with the list she checked out all of the other manuscripts that were on it; they were all in their boxes where she had left them weeks earlier. Once that explanation, however feeble it had been, was disproved she asked Ellenbogen for some help again. He suggested a simple shelf read in that area of the vault. This was simply to scour the immediate location to see if the thing had accidentally been left out somewhere. Again, this wasn't very likely but it was the next logical step in the process. With a couple of other members of the staff they began the same search that she had done earlier in the day, each of them going through the same mental steps. An item as important and valuable as Western MS 29 was not the sort of thing that could be allowed to just go missing. There would be serious consequences if it did not turn up somewhere, not least for the last person who admitted to having had it in her possession. But what that search revealed was not the news she was looking for. In fact, it revealed a truth far worse than she could have imagined: Western MS 29 was but the opening sentence in a larger horror story. Preservation cases all over that area of the stacks were, when picked up, heart-rendingly light.

Dutschke thought to herself on the matter for a few moments before talking to senior members of the staff. It was afternoon by that point and the workday was disappearing along with the hope that this could all be some sort of misunderstanding. Had there been a break-in over the long weekend? It was starting to seem almost possible that that was the truth. But before anyone left for the day she wanted to make sure that there was not some entirely explainable and legitimate reason for these manuscripts not to be in their proper places. Ordinarily, of course, the preservation box would accompany the manuscript wherever it went both for protection of the article and so that the catalogued information stayed with the manuscript. And yet, at that point the staff had a number of empty cases in front of them and no plausible explanation as to why.

The next step was to broaden the circle and ask if anyone else knew of an explanation for the missing books. No one did. No one knew why Western MS 29 wasn't with its counterparts in its proper place. And aside from the manuscript Dutschke had been working on in the not-too-distant past, her colleagues noticed things missing that they had worked on within the past couple of weeks. At least one staff member got down on her knees to look underneath the shelves on the off chance that this was all a hoax or that something had slipped down there. It was at that point that Dutschke realized that there was simply no way that that many books had accidentally fallen out of their cases and into some hidden place. It was at that point that she knew that the books were simply gone.

"It's just not possible," she said to herself. The small group of colleagues dragged themselves to the office of Jean Ashton, director of the RBML.[7]

No one knew what to say once they got there, no one could understand at all how so many things could be missing unless someone with ready access to the place had simply walked in, grabbed the stuff, and walked out. So maybe Ashton knew something that no one else did. Dutschke walked in and laid it out for her hoping that was the case. She was disappointed again. Ashton had no special knowledge about anyone taking any of the books out of their boxes. The hollow feeling in the stomach that had plagued Dutschke since earlier that morning had now infected all of the librarians at the RBML, right up to the director.

Asthon made the necessary decisions: put a padlock on the vault door; no one should discuss this with anyone yet. The next day they would begin a major shelf read in all areas. She would also present the situation to the Columbia University librarian, security, legal, and public relations. And they would go from there.[8]

The vacation of the previous few days would be the last real rest most of them would get for a good long while.

Books have four natural enemies: age, fire, water, and theft. Though the aging process cannot be stopped, rare books of the sort that have survived this long tend to be made of sturdy stuff. Absent careless handling or much circulation, small efforts of preservation go a long way. Extreme temperatures and swings in humidity, direct light (particularly sunlight), and rough handling are all detrimental, but even private collectors or libraries without great financial means can fairly easily avoid these dangers. In truth, the major battle for the survival of most old books took place long ago in the hands of the people who created them. Everything that comes after is essentially upkeep.

Fire can also be overcome. A scourge on books throughout history—no one knows how many great manuscripts and printed books have been lost to both random and targeted fires—this force now can be essentially controlled. Rooms equipped with mechanisms to suck the air out in case of fire or to douse books in fire-resistant and nondamaging chemicals all reside inside double-sealed, fire-proofed walls. It is testament to our society's progress, in fact, that today a shelf of books on the tenth floor of a large stone building is more likely to be damaged by water now than by fire.

The prevalence of pipes or low-level rooms exposed to rising waters are their own hazard, of course. For those collections of rare materials housed in rooms without special protections, the damage of a random fire sprinkler or a frozen pipe can have catastrophic consequences. But, again, with the right precautions (and funding) the question of accidental water damage can be almost completely controlled.

But thievery is a more delicate matter. Simply by nature of their scarcity—and hence, value—rare books are a target of theft. The true value of rare books, however, is not their market price but their usefulness to researchers. So unlike oil paintings or gold bullion, keeping even treasured rare books completely out of human hands is not practical. Rare book collections—particularly libraries—are only as valuable as they are accessible. If no one can get to a book, it might as well not exist. So exposure to theft for working libraries is something that can be reduced but never eradicated.

As with the other three major threats, there are plenty of ways to keep the likelihood of thievery to a minimum. Simple locked doors, surveillance systems, and human patrols all have their places in the modern library complex. On top of that, most stolen rare materials—like works of art— are as difficult to unload onto the market as uncut diamonds. These facts taken together tend to keep most rare collections safe. Still, there are failures (including some spectacular failures), particularly with pieces of a collection that are coveted. Fortunately, these thefts typically involve only small bits of a collection.

Since book aging is impossible to prevent, and happens to all books at a fairly uniform rate, it is easy to come to terms with. Accidental fire and water damage are scourges that, with the right preparation, can be almost completely controlled today. Only thievery has the continued *potential* of devastating a large chunk of a collection regardless of precaution, but the happy fact of poor logistics makes taking a large portion of a collection nearly impossible: A stranger taking a cartload of books out of a rare collection after hours would require a breakdown in security on a scale that is almost impossible to imagine.

Moreover, even if someone were to steal a large number of books in one fell swoop, it would not escape notice. For a working academic rare book collection, at least, someone would notice in pretty short order if a great swath of the collection were missing. There would be instantaneous attempts both to track the person down and to kill his market, meaning that not only would he be hiding with a valuable yet unwieldy prize, but there would also be almost no safe way for him to get rid of it. That means that the only ways for a person to steal wholesale from a heavily used and patrolled rare book library would be either to work there for a great number of years and steal a bit at a time or to make a number of undetected return visits.

An employee with access to the library has a number of advantages. He has knowledge of the collection and so can determine, over time, which books are most used. He also has continuing access to the books, allowing for an ongoing appraisal of the available material. In addition, he would have access to the sorts of people who would be interested in buying such books. While none of these things guarantee a successful theft of large amounts of material—there are very many things that can go wrong—these are certainly advantages the employee-thief has over a regular thief.

It happened that in the 1970s the RBML was struck by just such a thief. A graduate student at Columbia who often worked in the rare stacks stole a number of items before he was caught—as it turned out—by an alum who ran a local gallery and happened to recognize one of the items offered to him for sale as a Columbia letter. The student had been taking thin, uncatalogued items and sliding them under a door in the stacks that led to an empty hallway. After leaving the RBML he would go to the hallway and collect his loot. In a way that would presage the Spiegelman thefts, he was able to steal a range of materials from manuscripts to presidential letters to a Matthew Brady photograph.

This thief was caught, of course, but he was not charged with a crime—he was simply kicked out of Columbia. The curator of manuscripts collected the stolen materials from a safe deposit box and the student's house.[9]

For an outsider to pull off a similar theft, he would have to be far more skilled and very lucky. Not only would he have to be familiar with the collection, but would also have to be able to gain recurring access to it. Since even the least regarded rare book libraries have some form of security, repeat thefts are very unlikely.

Given the physical location of Columbia's RBML, daunting would seem to turn to impossible. Six floors up in a heavily used and nicely secured location, the idea that anyone not associated with the library could gain continued, long-term access to the place and not be discovered was unthinkable.

But Spiegelman had three things in his favor. He wasn't in a hurry because the library wasn't going anywhere. He wasn't stealing particular books to fill an order, so he could afford to take whatever he wanted, including things that may not have been of the highest value but that were convenient to carry or easy to hide. And the Butler Library had one serious security flaw that is endemic to most older libraries, even those that, like Butler, have modernized their security systems in this era of high-end rare book markets.

And one flaw was enough.

The way the RBML came about, through a combination of donations, acquisitions, and luck, is generally the way with rare book collections. While some libraries have always maintained separate special collections for rare materials, a great many libraries simply housed their rare books in the general collection. Since many libraries did not have any specified circulation practice for any of their books, housing rare materials in the general shelves was not a particularly cavalier approach. It was just what was done with all books. And until the mid-nineteenth century the market for rare books was such a limited one that there was not really a great need for most libraries to be concerned with security.

By the twentieth century, however, many librarians became concerned with preservation of older works. While there still was little concern for protecting books from theft, there began to be pangs of concern for protecting the books from the wear and tear of ordinary use. This led first to special areas in larger libraries being deemed to house rare books and then, finally, for the largest libraries to allow for separate special collections departments.

In truth, many libraries to this day have books that ought to be in their special collections departments shelved in their general collections. One reason for this is that no hard and fast criteria exist for what constitutes a rare book. While many special collections libraries have policies for inclusion, they are far from comprehensive and usually err on the side of exclusion.

In addition, even when libraries recognize that they have rare or delicate materials housed within the general collection they often simply do not have ample space to preserve it elsewhere. This is particularly true of specialized academic libraries like those in the legal and medical fields. And until the age of online library catalogues, it didn't matter much that some older and valuable books were out in the general collection. The physical location of many libraries—away from the great book markets—kept many valuable items accidentally safe. While the most committed book thieves could—and in the 1980s and early 1990s did—travel from one library to the next looking for targets of opportunity, this was an impractical and time-consuming activity.

Like most horrific events, the changes that could have prevented the event itself weren't seriously considered until after the thing happened.

In 1994 the Butler Library was, essentially, open to the public. With roughly 2 million volumes comprising the bulk of the university's holdings in the humanities, there was no practical way to keep tabs on all the people coming and going; even a security desk at the front was but little inconvenience: Spiegelman had an ID that he showed when asked. (Today's front door security at Butler is tighter. Columbians must swipe their cards through an electronic sensor and show it to a security guard. Visitors are admitted only for specific purposes and must check in at a special office. The RBML also has electronic locks opened by swipe cards. But nothing like this technology was widely employed by libraries in the early 1990s.) This was the perfect environment for a would-be book thief: a confusing population of people milling about in a large and complex building.

At the time, there was even more confusion. The Butler Library was undergoing a substantial renovation and, throughout that summer, workmen were moving all around the building.[10] Nobody noticed a single man taking note of particular architectural structures of the building. Nor did they notice when he spent extra time in some hallways and open areas—the sorts of places that didn't contain books and so were not anyone's responsibility. If anyone had noticed him they might have assumed that he was like the hundreds of other people who sometimes wandered the library seemingly absentminded, admiring the workmanship, looking for particular shelving ranges, or simply taking a walking break from studying.

At first, Spiegelman would have had some trepidation about wandering around the library. He had an ID that he could show if anyone stopped him but he was by nature taciturn and his interactions with others had a way of going south. Still, he was a slight man, short and inconspicuous. He wasn't the sort of person who was going to attract attention even if he wore a path in the floor by constantly going over the same territory.

In his wandering he took note of much that was going on around the Butler Library. While he certainly toured the whole system, he took a special interest in what was housed on the south side of the sixth floor of the Butler Library: the Rare Book and Manuscript Library. By the time in the early 1990s that Spiegelman began haunting the Butler Library's sixth floor, the collection would have seemed to have had all of the incumbent security that would ordinarily go along with a library whose simple monetary value at auction stretched easily into the hundreds of millions of dollars. There were wires conspicuously threaded along the top of the thick glass front doors, librarians were very careful about who could have access to certain areas, and people who used any of the rare items had to abide by a series of rules designed to prevent both damage and theft. Taken together, small traits like these would demonstrate to a would-be thief that the staff at the library took the security of the collection very seriously, and that these measures were probably just the tip of the iceberg.

But the security of the RBML wasn't, in fact, very impressive at all. Nor was it high-tech. No motion detectors or ubiquitous small cameras were scattered throughout the library, no round-the-clock guard was posted at the entrance. There had been lip service paid to reducing the amount of entrances and exits from the place and adding some more state-of-the-art technology, but nothing had been seriously considered, let alone implemented.[11] The simple fortress-like location of the remote library coupled with the vigilance of the staff had always seemed to do the trick. The RBML was well protected against any sort of frontal assault or the sort of backdoor break-in that the staff members could imagine.

Unfortunately, that was far from enough. The RBML was known to lock its doors at 5 p.m. on weekdays and turn into a ghost town—no one patrolling the stacks and no one even working there after hours.[12] A person who managed to stick around after closing time or somehow make his way in would have an undisturbed run of the place.

When Spiegelman walked into the RBML in the early 1990s he was presented with a one-stop shopping center of almost infinite value. He had no real experience with rare books nor did he have any way to fence the items—an oversight that would eventually be his downfall—but he saw a target that was rich and not protected near enough in proportion to its value. Not that extra security measures would have much mattered; the way he eventually gained access to the RBML would not have been prevented with any measures under consideration.

Spiegelman was no experienced burglar, but he was very smart. He knew that he would never be able to get into the RBML head on—aside from the locks, there could be a host of other security measures guarding the entrance. And even if he could somehow defeat the locks and possible surveillance, what would be the sense in it? There would be no going back. It would have to be a one-time trip: a quick, rare-book equivalent of a smash-and-grab.

Since he had no real knowledge of books he would have to be lucky enough to grab the right things on that one trip. And he'd have to take only those things that he could discretely carry down six floors and hope that there was a market for them. And there was no possibility at all that he would have a chance to get back behind the RBML desk, into the area where the librarians disappeared to when a person ordered a certain book. Back there where all of the most valuable items rested night after night. That would remain off limits to him with a one time hit.

So he would have to think of something else. He would have to come up with another way to get in this place besides the front door—another, less clumsy avenue than simply barging in and smashing the place up. Some way befitting the precise and reasoned skills that he thought he brought to the table.

If he was patient enough, he knew he would think of something.

In the six months prior to the discovery of the thefts by Dutschke, Spiegelman had been particularly busy. His first step had been to scout out the library.[13] From this he had learned a few things. While the main library reading room of the Butler Library was open all night, the departmental libraries above were closed. On the sixth floor, the RBML closed at 5 p.m. The outer glass doors of the RBML looked in onto a public display that, to the knowing eye, was breathtakingly valuable. While Spiegelman couldn't be said to have had a knowing eye, he certainly knew that even what he could see through the door would be more valuable on the market than anything he'd ever had his hands on before. But he also knew that the stuff might as well have been behind steel bars. Outside those doors was as close as he was going to get after hours.

The public areas of the RBML certainly held many valuable and worthy pieces for Spiegelman, but this route presented two major problems. First, this was the most highly secured area. Getting into the RBML after hours this way promised to be almost impossible, especially for a lone man without high-tech burglary experience. Second, even if he were successful, his thefts would be discovered almost as soon as anyone came into the place the next morning. This would leave him no time to leave the city, let alone attempt to sell the books abroad.

But his wandering had given him another idea. The Butler Library is essentially a large rectangular space organized around a smaller, core rectangle. The outer rectangle on most floors contained departmental libraries, lockers, reading rooms, rest rooms, stairwells, and elevators. Inside that outer rectangle were the stacks. In the middle of the stacks was an even smaller rectangular area that housed several vertical avenues that allowed patrons, librarians, and books to traverse up and down between the numerous floors of stacks. In this innermost rectangle were two elevator shafts large enough to carry several people, two small stairwells with room for one person to walk up or down, one electronic book lift, and a tangle of wires and pipes. Like the crowded stacks of most large research libraries, there was a claustrophobic feel to the areas immediately surrounding this inner rectangle: the ceilings were low, the rows of books were close together and full, two people didn't so much pass each other as turn and squeeze by, and the lighting never seemed to reach all the way down the corridors. In short, stacks.

In addition, the stacks at Butler had different numbered floors than those on the main floor. So, for instance, floor 6 of the Butler Library corresponded with floors 12 and 13 in the stacks. There were roughly two stack levels per regular level.

Also in this inner area there were places where people almost never went. In the nooks and crannies of these floors of stacks there were places that seemed unused and caged off; other places had librarians coming in and out of them, and they were caged off, too. These places were easy enough to look into and everyone could see what was behind them; the caging cordoning off these areas was mostly just a heavy chain link fencing. Mostly, at that point in the Butler Library history, what these cages were protecting was nothing. Almost every floor of stacks had at least one area cordoned off this way and all that seemed to be protected were old book carts and various library supplies. Nothing that anyone—least of all Spiegelman would want to steal, just discarded or broken supplies that didn't fit anywhere else.

But on one of the stack floors that corresponded with the sixth floor of Butler—stack 12—there was no such wired off area. The parts of this floor that were blocked off from the regular stacks were done so with solid metal walls instead of cages. Though there was no sign indicating such, anyone could tell through simple deduction that just on the other side of those metal walls was the RBML secured stacks area. And if simple deduction wasn't enough, just a few minutes time spent sitting next to the walls would confirm the fact.

The public area of the RBML was on the southernmost side of the outer rectangle of the Butler Library. Spiegelman knew that when someone requested a book from the locked stacks the librarians who got the thing disappeared into an area immediately north of the RBML public area. It made sense, then, that that was where the rare stacks were. He also knew that the areas to the northeast of the RBML were open to the public: a hallway, bathrooms, reading rooms, lockers, an elevator, and a stairway. That meant that the rare stacks must be to the northwest of the RBML public area. But when he walked around the corridor that ran through the outer rectangle of the sixth floor he eventually came to another locked door (and another elevator and stairway and more reading rooms) over on that side. Simple mapping, therefore, would dictate that to the northeast and northwest of the RBML, there were no areas of stacks. So the stacks had to be immediately in a small area to the north of the circulation desk on that floor, exactly where the librarians disappeared to when requested a book.

To confirm this he could simply go to the southernmost wall in the inner rectangle of the open stacks—the wall that was the back of the RBML—and then walk immediately west. He would quickly come to that metal wall. It was as simple as that. For confirmation of his suspicions, he just had to wait for a few minutes in the row of books abutting the metal wall.

While this metal wall was certainly far more solid than the cages that could be seen on the other floors, there were gaps at the top where it didn't quite reach the ceiling and two quarter-inch holes about seven feet up from the floor. The gaps at the top were there to allow pipes and ductwork from one side of the wall to the other. The holes didn't appear to serve any purpose and must have simply been part of the manufacturing process of the solid metal piece. None of these small fissures were really useful to Spiegelman other than to allow him one thing: confirmation that on the other side of the 1/8-inch wall of metal, a treasure of rare books lay. He could sit in the row of books just on the stack side of the wall and listen to librarians from the RBML go about their work. If he were feeling like he wanted to take a small risk, he could even grab one of the many step stools lying around the stacks that were used to retrieve high books, scoot the thing over to the metal wall, stand on it, and peer through one of the small holes. It would only allow him a small view into the rare stacks but enough to see that mostly what was on the other side of that wall were a bunch of shelves, stocked full of identical looking gray boxes.

At the other end of the shelf that lined this wall with the rare stacks there was another three-foot wide area, similar to the metal wall, that didn't quite reach all the way up to the ceiling. This one appeared to be made of concrete. And though this, too, offered the sounds of the RBML stacks, there were no holes in that more solid wall for him to look through. Still, there was a several inch gap at the top, larger than above the metal wall, so that if he got up high enough and craned his neck just right, he could see into the stacks at a slightly different angle. The scene on the inside wasn't much better but at least it was a new view. He could get a sense of the dimensions of the place.

By simply standing there long enough—pretending to browse the shelf of books that lined this wall on the other side of the rare stacks—he could even hear the librarians' discussions, hear them crumple the paper on which were written notes or call numbers, hear them slide a preservation box out of its place and lay it down on a table. He was within a few feet of his destination, breathing its air and hearing its sounds. It simply remained for him to defy the laws of physics and walk three feet west, through a solid sheet of metal.

But there was no getting through the wall, that was for certain. Even the wall that was simply a metal sheet was directly impervious without a blow torch or a large mallet. In the dim and quiet atmosphere of the Butler Library, even after hours, neither of those was an option. Simply getting either of those things up to that floor, not to mention the damage that would be seen the next day, made such a clumsy route unthinkable. Spiegelman was a forgery expert who was attempting to steal rare and delicate materials; those sorts of overt techniques were not the solution.

But Spiegelman could learn one other important thing from that metal wall: it was temporary. Not temporary in the sense that it was going to be moved any time soon, but temporary in the sense that it had not been in the original design of the place. It was an afterthought, a piece that was bolted on to the surrounding concrete structures at some point after the original construction. And any thing that could be attached to a structure could be detached from it.

In this case, the metal was affixed to the surrounding concrete by screws—large screws that had been painted over. No normal screwdriver was going to do the trick. Not even a very large power screwdriver could probably handle the job. And even if he could get the thing unscrewed, the metal wall itself would be very heavy, and he would be alone. The chances of it falling and creating a loud noise or him not even being able to budge it at all were high. On top of that, even if he were to jar it loose and lean it against the wall, that whole production would take place at the end of a long corridor in the open stacks. While it's likely that no one would see him, it would simply take one person walking past to hear noise or notice the metal wall out of place to ruin the whole job. What he needed was a way in that was both discrete and repeatable.

So the metal wall wasn't the way in, but its existence would have set his mind in motion. Some of the walls were temporary; that didn't make them easy to dismantle, but it certainly didn't make them impossible to dismantle, either. It simply remained for him to find the right one. He also knew that he couldn't get in from the front, the back and, now, from the side. That left two options: above and below.

Any quick check of the stack level below showed that that route was fruitless. Short of drilling through the floor, he wasn't going to get into the rare stacks that way. Coming in from above was probably equally pointless. But he couldn't even get up to the next floor up to check. There was no public access.

Even the dimmest bulb could have put two and two together at that point: A collection as impressive as Columbia's couldn't simply be housed in that one small area on stack 12. There had to be another stack level above the one on 12 that housed more rare materials; that meant that there were two stack levels of rare treasures to be plundered.

It turns out that was only half right.

Old libraries of the sort that Butler was were built with many traits that have been made obsolete by technology. One of those technological improvements that made life easier for librarians for the first half of the twentieth century was the dumbwaiter. Also called a book lift or vertical conveyor or book dummy, depending on your taste, this minielevator had been an essential part of construction for most multitiered libraries for almost a century, but for much of that time they had gone unused. Essentially they are a shaft, like a small elevator, running vertically through a library that delivers a set of books from one floor to another by a manual pulley system or, like an actual elevator, using electricity. Smaller than a regular elevator shaft, most have simple brick walls and either the sorts of ropes and tethers that we all know from elevators or a greasy track that runs along the back side of the system on which the individual cars run. Also, unlike an elevator shaft, there is no internal lighting. No one will ever get caught in the shaft in an emergency and no repairmen will spend a bunch of time in the shaft making repairs.

By the 1940s library designers were realizing that the chimney effect of the system required particular fire prevention steps to be taken—fire, at the time, was still a worse threat to libraries than thieves.[14] By the mid-1960s, library consultants found more mundane reasons to recommend against the dumbwaiters. Thought to be a cheap alternative for elevators, dumbwaiters were "a snare and a delusion," according to Keyes Metcalf, librarian at the Widener Library, flagship of the Harvard University system.[15] Unless you had a person at each end of the system, the "librarian will not be saved from climbing stairs, and the books will be subjected to an unnecessary handling at each end of the line." On top of this, if the lift was too small to fit a full book cart—as almost all of them were—there was extra work and wear and tear on the books. Many libraries at the time rarely used the book lifts they had. Metcalf said that they had not used their book lift system since the 1920s.[16] The Butler Library system had itself been mostly abandoned for many years—though certain supplies, like light bulbs, were sometimes still hauled up on the thing. In six months spanning late 1993 and early 1994, however, it would get more heavy use.

Though the book lifts in Butler were not in heavy use they were yet to be properly sealed off. In the spirit of the fact that imaginative crimes are only thought to have been inevitable after they are committed, few thought that the shaft of an obsolete book lift could be used to get a *person* vertically from floor to floor. The doors to the stack floors, like regular elevator doors, didn't open without the carriage being in place. Certainly no person older than a child could ride one of the book lift carriages.

Besides, the ongoing construction would soon seal them off permanently (as has been done now). Most of the entrances were already sealed off or only accessible to librarians and the book lift doors were checked by librarians at night to make sure they were closed. This was mostly just for fire prevention. The idea that someone would climb up the inside of the shaft and then be able to flip a switch to get the doors to open from the inside was not one that crossed anyone's mind.[17] Most of the employees at RBML assumed to be true what Patrick Lawlor had been told when he started working there in 1987: the shafts were sealed off. No person could get from floor to floor that way.[18]

That people assumed or were told that the book lift was secure may not have been simply recklessness. The shaft itself was quite small. If the idea that someone could ride up the book lift carriage seemed remote, that idea that someone could climb up the shaft seemed preposterous. Anyone who climbed into the thing would have to be very, very small. And he would have to not be afraid of clinging to the inside of an unlit shaft that went six stories straight down. Spiegelman, a man who had emigrated from the Soviet Union when he was a boy, had done time in federal prison and was then paroled to live in Yonkers with his mother, had seen worse. It would have been hard for anyone at RBML to anticipate Daniel Spiegelman.

So it happened that on stack 11 there was one of the many caged off areas full of excess supplies and future junk that also contained an unsealed entrance to the book lift shaft. It was behind one of the locked cages, of course, but he had already seen that those things could simply be unscrewed. But a clear understanding of the physical layout of the place showed that it was not below the sealed-off area of the rare stacks. Climbing up that thing would only deliver him to a place on stack 12 where he could easily walk to, anyway. But he knew now that he could get from floor to floor that way, and maybe there was something of value on stack 13.

The stacks closed at 11 p.m. but it was easy enough to hide out there. No one did a thorough search of all the floors before they closed the place up; there were just too many stacks in the library. And a person accidentally locked in could get out simply enough, particularly since the main reading rooms and the library entrances were open all night. Once Spiegelman was in, he was not going to be detected.

After waiting a sufficient amount of time after the stacks closed he could set about his work. Climbing into the abandoned dumbwaiter on stack 12 he would shinny up the shaft to the next set of doors, roughly ten feet above. From the inside of the shaft he would be able to get the doors to open with a mechanical lever. Once he did this he would climb out and find himself on stack 13, right in the heart of the RBML collection. The combination of his cramped and dangerous egress with the serene and undisturbed feel of the silent rare stacks must have seemed to him like the treasure room at the end of dark tunnel.

The first night he had some decisions to make. It was his first time in the stacks and so he didn't yet know the layout. He didn't know that the RBML stacks reached from stack 12 below him to stack 15, two levels above. He also didn't immediately know that the most valuable items in the collection were behind caged areas, known as vaults. One of the caged areas was there on stack 13 but another was one flight up.

"Value" is, of course, a relative term. Most of the items in the RBML stacks outside the vault would be worth more than just about anything else he had ever touched—and he would certainly avail himself of many of these items. But within the vault were items that were astoundingly valuable, if only he could get to them.

He, of course, had no way at all of knowing how much most of the items on the shelves—in or out of the vault—could fetch in the open market. He knew they all would have some sort of significant monetary value but he wasn't near knowledgeable enough about rare books and manuscripts to be discerning. For that reason he did what most people would do: when in doubt, he took what looked prettiest. Particularly with the Arabic manuscripts, Spiegelman stole those that seemed to have the finest calligraphy or richest illustrations. Other similar Arabic manuscripts that were rarer or could fetch a higher price on the market were bypassed for the prettier ones. He did this with maps, as well.[19]

With many of the manuscripts he was just as selective, but for a different reason. Often when collectors purchase a rare book they clip the description of the item from the purchase catalogue and put it in the book. This provides a lot of information to the average user and may be a reminder to the person who bought it what his interest was. This was particularly true of one of the greatest contributors to the RBML, George A. Plimpton. He included these descriptions in almost all of the books he bought and gave to Columbia. Spiegelman, presumably so that he could be an informed seller, took a great many items from those manuscripts that had such descriptive tags and, for that reason, the Plimpton manuscripts were very hard hit. Rare book libraries now often take those clippings out of books because they were mostly printed on acid paper. Libraries conscientious about thefts, like Columbia is now, do it for security reasons as well. On the off chance that a burglar has the time and ability to systematically go through a collection, he would most likely be drawn to those items that he could learn the most about.[20]

At the time of the Spiegelman theft, Dutschke was doing just that. She knew that, even if the clippings weren't made of acid paper, just the fact that they were stuck in the book made them hard on the bindings. Besides, the loss of the pieces of paper, many of which weren't anchored to the book in any way, presented its own problem. The slips of paper contained information sometimes not available anywhere else. So from each manuscript that Dutschke would work with, she would remove the slip of paper and put it in a bibliographic folder that she had made for all of the medieval and Renaissance items. Without knowing it, she had saved many of those early Plimpton manuscripts. Spiegelman stole heavily from the ones that she had not gotten to, but left the ones without the slips of paper in them there on the shelves.[21]

The vault on stack 13, of course, had a lock on it and Spiegelman didn't have any real way of getting through it. He could see inside the vault because it was simply heavy caging, but he couldn't directly get through that lock.

So he would eventually bypass the lock altogether in a fairly ingenious way. Looking around he noticed that abutting the caged vault on one side was a wood cabinet about four feet wide and three feet tall. Each time he entered the vault he moved this cabinet aside—no small task for a man of his humble stature—and then unscrewed the panel of the cage that was behind it. In that way he could gain entrance to the vault fairly easily with just a little heavy lifting and a screwdriver. By returning the cabinet to its rightful location before he left he could also cover his tracks. It was unlikely anyone would notice if one of the panels of the cage had been unscrewed, but it would be almost impossible to notice if the cabinet were covering what evidence there was.

The whole procedure, from getting from the stack floor below to inside the vault, took about a half hour. But there was still plenty of very valuable material outside of the vault. Some of the Edison materials he stole were housed in preservation boxes sitting on the shelves. Items like a first edition John Steinbeck book would be simply sitting out on the stack shelves. On stack 14 there was a row of map cases that held many of the historical maps in the RBML collection. He would have access to these and he would not neglect them.

But perhaps the greatest tragedy of the whole Spiegelman episode surrounded another collection of maps. The RBML had a Bleau atlas that was, in an incredible collection of unique and priceless materials, the crown jewel. So valuable was the atlas to the collection that it had been taken out of the glass display cases in the RBML area that was open to the public for fear that something would happen to it.[22] The irony, of course, is that the items in the glass cases were untouched by Spiegelman because there was no way for him to get to them. The Bleau atlas, which had been moved to the stack in order for it to be sufficiently protected, was destroyed.

Once Spiegelman knew on that first night in the stacks the sort of access he had and the sort of time it would take him to get in and out, he could make a more informed decision about his future. He could do the rare book spree and simply take as much stuff as he could carry or he could make several return visits. That first option was appealing in the sense that there would be relatively little chance that he'd get caught since the hardest part was over and he'd only have to risk the dumbwaiter shaft once more to be free of it. But this option proved unappealing since it wouldn't allow him to carry very much with him and any attempts at overloading himself were not only dangerous but also threatened to notify the first person who came into the stacks the next morning. Besides, the reward seemed feeble in comparison with the planning and execution and imaginativeness of the whole scheme.

Another option seemed better. The relative ease of the crime coupled with the fact that he really didn't know much about which books to take led him to think that return visits would be best. By taking just a bit at a time he could better transport his loot (and transport it in the way befitting delicate materials) and better conceal that he had been there. If his plan really was to sell this stuff without getting caught, a bit of discretion might prove to be the most valuable thing of all. On top of that, a simple one-time break-in would be a clumsy job, almost amateurish. He was a professional who thought himself gifted at being subtle and precise in his crimes. He was going to take his time.

So the first night he took just a few selections. His plan for return visits would prove extremely wise for Spiegelman and bad news for Columbia. Not only did this allow his persistent thievery but his attempts at concealing his thefts were what led to his greatest destruction: taking a razor blade to the Blaeu atlas for the sake of individual maps. Since maps are both extremely valuable and, absent their being attached to an atlas, hard to trace, this destruction made perfect sense to him. The fact that rolled-up maps were also easier to carry out sealed the deal.

The amount of material that Spiegelman was able to steal is staggering. It is, in fact, a kind of testament to the breadth of coverage at RBML that he was able to steal as much as he did and have it go unnoticed for as long as it did. But this is also an indication of Spiegelman's attention to detail. He knew to take only those things whose disappearance would be difficult to detect. He never took preservation boxes and was careful to leave everything just as he found it. Any cursory glance around the rare stacks after a Spiegelman visit would show it looking exactly the same as it did before he was there.

As the medieval manuscripts were the first discovered—and the hardest hit—it was originally assumed that that was all he had taken. But as the accounting inventory of the rare book stacks progressed, it became clear that he had wandered through classes and eras of materials, from the ancient maps and manuscripts to the more recent correspondence and patents. The only items of the collection that weren't vulnerable to him, ironically, were those things on display in the public area.

It was another bit of luck for Spiegelman that the RBML was rich in those items such as maps and letters that are valuable in almost inverse proportion to their heft. This was an advantage because these items were not only easier to carry but they were also the sort of things whose theft is more easily concealed. An atlas with a few maps missing is not easy to spot. And while an empty preservation box on a shelf looks exactly like a full one, an empty preservation box that is supposed to contain a letter *feels* the same as a full one.

The same way that the inclusion of the clipped catalogue descriptions—a piece of paper that was supposed to aid the book user—actually worked in Spiegelman's favor, the universal use of the preservation boxes also very much aided him. It is undoubtedly the case that had the RBML not used preservation boxes the crime would have been discovered well in advance of when it was. Even a faraway eye at a glance will notice a missing volume or two from a bookshelf; no one at all can notice anything missing from a preservation box unless he or she takes it down and opens it. (This is obviously not an argument against the use of preservation boxes, a resource that is invaluable to the preservation of old books.)

But even with his attention to surreptitious detail, Spiegelman had to get very lucky in his selection. It was this luck, more than anything else, that allowed so many return visits. He could, by definition, only take those things that would be least likely to be used; since he had no real way of knowing what items would be requested from day to day, he had to get lucky. Even if he knew it was his final visit, the fact that he still had to market these items required maintaining the illusion that there had been no theft. And, of course, the only way his crime was ever found out was when Consuelo Dutschke discovered the missing Western MS 29.

In the end, he took an astounding amount. The first order of business was to find out just what this included. A list needed to be compiled and, ideally, distributed to all of the dealers who might be in the market for the things Spiegelman had taken. Though no one knew it at the time, this list would be extremely important. It helped snag Spiegelman in Europe when he was selling some of what he'd stolen.

Then, five years later, it got him again.

NOTES

1. Consuelo Dutschke's interview with author, March 4, 2005.

2. Columbia Rare Book and Manuscript Library Web site, available at http://www.columbia.edu/cu/lweb/indiv/rbml/collections/medieval_renaissance.html.

3. Dutschke interview.

4. RBML Web site, available at http://www.columbia.edu/cu/lweb/eresources/exhibitions/treasures/html/130.html#description.

5. Rudolph Ellenbogen interview with author, April 7, 2006.

6. Dutschke interview.

7. Dutschke interview.

8. Jean Ashton interview with author, March 4, 2005.

9. Bernard Cristol interview with author, March 14, 2006.

10. Ashton interview.

11. Ellenbogen interview.

12. Dutschke interview.

13. Cathy Begley interview with author, February 10, 2006.

14. Joseph L. Wheeler, *The American Public Library Building* (Chicago: ALA, 1941), 422.

15. Keyes Metcalf, *Planning Academic and Research Library Buildings* (New York: McGraw-Hill, 1965), 151.

16. Keyes Metcalf, *Planning the Academic Library* (Newcastle: Oriel Press, 1971), 79.

17. Ellenbogen interview.
18. Patrick Lawlor interview with author, April 13, 2006.
19. Rudolph Ellenbogen e-mail, April 10, 2006.
20. Ibid.
21. Consuelo Dutschke e-mail, April 11, 2006.
22. Ellenbogen interview.

CHAPTER 2

Smart Thief, Bad Crook

Mimi Meyer wasn't in it for the money. She just stole books to get back at the University of Texas for firing her friend. She later claimed that, having fallen into a financial predicament, she was forced to sell one of the books. Over the course of ten years, Meyer managed to unload at auction ninety of the books she had stolen to the tune of about $400,000.[1] More than enough, it would seem, to get a person out of all but the most serious of financial predicaments.

Meyer volunteered at the Harry Ransom Center at Texas from 1989 to 1992 when she was fired for suspicion of book theft. Since the people at the Ransom Center had no concrete evidence, however, no charges were filed. But they kept their eye out for the books. In 2001 serious evidence of her thefts came to light. When Swann Galleries in New York listed Il Petrarcha as an item in its auction catalog, the library took note. The FBI investigated and found out from the gallery that the book had been provided by Meyer. Further investigations made it clear that during the 1990s she had been in business with several New York auction houses to sell books she had smuggled out of the library.[2]

The Meyer episode illustrates perfectly one of the major problems of patrolling the modern American rare collection: who to trust. Functioning libraries need to be open to patrons or else they aren't really libraries at all, just warehouses for old books. So, functioning rare book libraries have to have staff members. Unfortunately, it is becoming clear that staff members who can be trusted are themselves an increasingly rare commodity. While there are certainly ways of limiting access of volunteers like Mimi Meyer, in a library with an entrance there will be ways for employees to gain access.

Even the most sound security and surveillance systems can't prevent theft by a person with a key to the place and after-hours access.

Although David Breithaupt did not actually have keys to the special collections at Kenyon College where he worked as the library night supervisor, he was friendly with the custodial staff and other people with the right keys. Trading on his position at the library—he had worked there about seven years before he actually started to take things—he was able to convince maintenance and cleaning staff to let him in to otherwise secure areas.[3] In 2000, a Georgia librarian noticed a Flannery O'Connor letter for sale on Ebay that belonged to Kenyon. The librarian had seen the letter in the *Kenyon Review* and called the head of special collections to see if it was a duplicate or a legitimate close copy.[4] It wasn't. It was the actual letter she had seen in the *Review*.

Over the course of two years, Breithaupt and his girlfriend Christa Hupp managed to sell about 50 of the 250 or so items they stole for a total of around $26,000. He would steal the things (what Hupp called the "acquisitions" part of the operation) and she would take care of sales. The two worked the scheme at Kenyon for about three years though it's clear that they had been in the book theft business for quite a bit longer, hitting many other libraries in the Ohio region before they started in at Kenyon. Both Breithaupt and Hupp worked at Caves Curve Books, which allowed them not only entrée into the book trade but also easy access to the value of rare materials.[5] Particularly hard hit, outside of the special collections, were the materials from the older versions of the *Review*.

If library volunteers and paraprofessionals make up the backbone of the academic library trade, student workers surely comprise the less glamorous rest of the skeleton. Jake Oelerich, a student library worker at Whitman College in Washington, was neither thoughtful about his thefts nor very bright. He simply took advantage of his position by stealing hundreds of back copies of *Harper's Weekly* and *Harper's Bazaar*.[6] Oelerich had been a troublesome employee almost from the beginning, checking out piles of books, CDs, and DVDs on his account and keeping them well past their due date. At one point, largely through his use of the library consortium of which Whitman is a member, he had racked up almost $2,000 in fines. After numerous warnings about this habit, he was fired.[7] In order to get back at the school—and make some good money to boot—he took the whole collection of the magazines, originally valued at $225,000.

Henry Yaple, the library director, had some suspicions but could not prove anything about Oelerich. But three days before graduation, a campus police officer saw Oelerich walking across campus with several large parcels. Knowing of Yaple's suspicions, the officer followed Oelerich to the post office where he then called the local police. They showed up, seized the packages, and discovered the magazines. Oelerich was arrested right there, a few days before he would have been gone for good. Upon investigation of his room the police discovered "half a pickup load" of magazines waiting to be sent around the country.[8] He had simply smuggled them out of the library in his back pack, several issues at a time.

When 22-year-old Benjamin Johnson began stealing books from Yale's Beinecke Rare Book and Manuscript Library he wasn't even a student there—he was just working at Yale for the summer. But back in Madison, Wisconsin, where he *was* a student, he started selling the things to dealers. When one became suspicious at the fact that a college kid was selling such well preserved and unique items out of his dorm room, she contacted authorities in Madison. A search of Johnson's dorm room eventually yielded more than $2 million worth of rare books and letters.[9]

Of course, it's not just volunteers and student workers at small colleges and universities doing the bad work. Librarians on a grander scale and much greater access to materials are part of the problem as well. The Library of Congress saw one of its former librarians arrested, indicted, and sentenced in federal court in 1998 after attempting to sell eight rare books to a Boston antiquarian bookseller. The librarian had taken about two dozen books with him when he had left the library earlier in the year.[10]

James Gilreath had attempted to sell books estimated at about $30,000 to the bookseller, including one of the only five remaining copies of a first edition *Leaves of Grass* printed in French.[11] Up until that point, his long and distinguished career at the LOC had no real blemishes. At least on the surface.

"Insider theft has been a problem for libraries, particularly for libraries with rare material, for quite sometime," said Susan M. Allen, chief librarian at the Getty Research Institute in Los Angeles.[12] This seems to be true for two important reasons. First, people who work with the material often know its value more than anyone. Second, they have unprecedented access to the stuff. As long as libraries need knowledgeable and independent staff, neither of these things can be much ameliorated.

"With anyone that's been hired to work in a facility that houses rare materials, people have to do their assignment and there's often a certain amount of unsupervised time in which they could go astray," Allen said.[13]

Because of this, the librarians themselves are often the first ones suspected. So, aside from the actual physical toll of theft on a library, there is an equally mentally frustrating period during which everyone in the place becomes a suspect and trust built up over years of service can suddenly be destroyed.

"They even asked if we would take a lie-detector test," said Hilary Cummings, the curator of manuscripts at the University of Oregon when it was discovered that some twenty linear feet of papers from Oregon's territorial days were gone. The library staff was placed under such heavy suspicion that within a couple of years the four staffers of the collection had left their positions; Cummings left the profession entirely.[14]

It was the insider route that first made the most sense to the people at Columbia. Due to their relative ease and the steady clip with which reports of them appear in *American Libraries* and *Library Journal*, (and in absence of an upfront job with smashed windows and strewn books) inside jobs are the natural assumption. Particularly at Columbia, where the security was already very tight, there was little thought given to the idea that an outsider could have done such a thing. First, the sheer volume of the thefts indicated that the person (or persons) had had plenty of time to do the work. This suggested thefts that took place over the course of months or years.

Second, there was no evidence that any of the security measures had been defeated. The front doors had not been visibly broken into and the lock to the stacks had not been disturbed at all. This didn't entirely rule out the possibility of a very skilled burglar, but it worked against the possibility. Recent high-profile rare book thefts had weighed heavily on the minds of librarians and so they had been very circumspect about a frontal attack. Guarding against a person wandering from library to library, stealing bits and pieces had become the main priority. Most librarians also knew that, despite their precautions, they were always very vulnerable to insider jobs. From there, Occam's razor took over.

Consuelo Dutschke, who had been at Columbia for only a short time, felt immediately that some eyes were on her.[15] Not only was she new to the RBML but it was her area that appeared to be hardest hit. And it was she who originally discovered the thefts. As the magnitude of the crime became known, the police and the FBI began to systematically interview everyone at RBML. When the presumption was that it was an inside job, no one knew whom to trust. That made for an especially tense work environment; in fact, it sometimes brought work to a halt. The RBML had long limited access of librarians to the locked stacks to a select few; while this certainly helped make the place more secure, after the thefts it actually focused suspicion on those people who had access.

Until it became clear that Spiegelman had not only taken the books but also broken in to the place without assistance, the suspicion on the people who worked there was palpable.

Even after a theft, most of the steps taken to keep thieves out are not effective against insiders. Motion detectors and electronic locks are great, but they are best at keeping out strangers, not people who know their locations or weaknesses.

Still, much can be done to limit the exposure of rare books to nonprofessionals. The Ransom Center at Texas now takes a more active approach to security with its employees and doesn't let volunteers in the stacks. Yale, after its theft, took a page from Columbia's RBML and began limiting access to its most rare items to the librarians. The Library at the State Historical Society of Iowa now bans spiral bound notebooks and the like after a man was caught stealing photographs and documents that way.

The simple fact is a collection that is only accessible to a few, known people is a lot easier to protect from the public and, generally, from the inside job. The fewer people who have access, the smaller the pool of potential criminals. When Southeast Missouri State University was robbed of some of its collection of John Steinbeck letters, the librarians could immediately narrow the suspects down to those few people who had access to the letters: two librarians with keys and two people who had been allowed to use the collection by appointment. While a limited pool of suspects wouldn't have helped to find Spiegelman—a man who was not in the inner circle—it can also be used to rule out suspects. If only four people had had access to the RBML secured stacks and all four could be acquitted of suspicion, the authorities could more quickly have gotten on to the task of finding out how the theft was perpetrated from the outside.

Often, however, the police are only incidental to the resolution of the crime. It is the community of librarians, book collectors, and dealers that does most of the work.

When Robert Hardin Smith sat for almost six hours poring over the collection of William Faulkner materials owned by Southeast Missouri State, he told the collection's archivist, Dr. Lisa Speer, the name of the town he was from, the name of his employer, and his personal interest in Faulkner. "It made it pretty easy to track him down," Speer would later say of the man who even used his own name when setting up the appointment.[16]

The Faulkner collection had just recently come under Speer's aegis and so she was still getting to know it. One of the quirks of the thing that she quickly discovered was that the original donor reserved the right to take out materials from the collection and sell them with the purpose of adding other items to the collection. So anything that was missing wasn't automatically assumed to have been stolen. On top of this, the collection was not yet indexed. So when Speer received a call from a man in Connecticut interested in buying a letter he knew had once been apart of their collection, she wasn't immediately sure if it had been purloined or not.

"Wm. Faulkner: Doing his bit for fox hunting," was the title of item #729965525, originally listed on October 30, 2002. Described as a May 3, 1961 note to a Mrs. Chapman concerning a subscription for a fox hunting list, Faulkner had written "Thank you for the chance to subscribe and do my bit to support fox hunting in our country; I would want to subscribe even if I didn't hunt." The letter was described as in good shape with letter folds and a small area of paper loss on the verso in a blank area toward the bottom.[17] In other words, the letter could have been described as library quality with a blemished area where said library's information was stripped off.

It wasn't Robert Smith who had listed the letter on Ebay—in the long series of mistakes leading up to his third stint in jail, listing his loot on an internet auction site was not among them. Rather, the letter had been listed by a Texas documents seller with whom Smith had dealt. Selling to the Texas dealer had simply been a clumsy and naïve move for Smith, who seemed to be a clumsy and naïve man. He had already lost his law license (and narrowly escaped a prison sentence) in the early 1990s for bilking clients. In 1996 he was convicted of stealing rare letters from the University of Kansas and manuscripts from the University of Arkansas, a sentence he served concurrently in an Arkansas jail.[18] To then steal from SEMO while using his own name and to sell the items to a dealer who had his cell phone number was the work of a man begging to get caught.

Once it became clear to Speer the that letter in question belonged to her library it wasn't long before the police contacted Noble Enterprises, the small autograph dealer in Rowlett, Texas, that had bought the letter from Smith. (Smith had claimed that the letters had been willed to him—the same line used by many documents' thieves who can't otherwise explain how they came across their items.) Noble's very large presence on Ebay practically sealed the deal for Smith, who might well have gotten away with the whole thing if only he had sold the letters to a dealer with a more local market.

In the end, all six of the letters stolen from SEMO were returned to the school. Though Smith could have gotten up to twenty years in prison, considering his legal track record, he was eventually only sentenced to seven years. After his third spell in prison, he claims that he won't ever go back.

"He is a smart thief, but a dumb crook," said Robert W. Hamblin, director of the Center for Faulkner studies at SEMO.[19] Smith was good at getting the letters out of their rightful place but not good at the back end, the part that really counts: getting money for the crime.

This is another frequent aspect of most modern rare book crimes—and one that is a bright spot in an otherwise dim corner of the book industry: the Book Community makes it hard to unload stolen items. Most people who steal the material don't have a trustworthy or reliable fence for their goods. And like uncut diamonds or Van Gogh paintings, the loot is very valuable in an abstract sense but hard to turn into money. So the corollary of this is that the crimes are often discovered through the network of the Book Community. And not only is the Book Community successful at detecting the crimes but also at leading to the capture of the thief, and, ultimately, the recovery of the stolen goods. It is this community of book sellers, collectors, and librarians that, almost without exception, has been responsible for what successful captures there have been in the past couple of decades. Very rarely are there clues left at the scene of the theft that lead the authorities to the criminal; in successful captures, the criminal almost always makes himself known when he tries to unload his goods.

It is members of the Book Community who notice small things about suddenly available rare books, and ask questions. Why is there a worn spot where a bookplate or library stamp would ordinarily be? Why is a book that could fetch several hundred thousand dollars on the open market being offered for a third of that? These small things can make all the difference when it comes to catching thieves.

In a strange twist, the Book Community has been forced to take greater notice of where the book came from not due to a rash of thefts but rather a rash of forgeries. In the past twenty-five years, the Book Community has become very concerned with provenance. While the trail of ownership is no guarantee to authenticity, coupled with standard validations it goes a long way toward guaranteeing that a book is genuine.

The rare book market is a closed and finite universe. The people who deal in particular eras or authors—and the collectors of those genres—know most of what is in existence and where it is. When an item comes to market out of the blue, suspicions are automatically raised. The thieves themselves are almost never tuned to the market so they have no idea—aside from a rough appraisal—of how much what they are selling is worth. They also usually have little idea about the availability of such items. So when they try to unload an item that is known to exist in only a couple of places, it is easy enough for the Community to check and see if any of those places have been robbed.

Thieves who sell on the open market of Ebay have an added worry; even if the item is not particularly rare, the exposure to the Community on such a public site is immense. There are bound to be one or two people out there who recognize the item in question. It is these people who most frequently ferret out the thieves. Librarians who spot suspicious materials on Ebay have no real stake in the matter other than being a member of the community of librarians. But librarians are a protective bunch and aren't afraid of asking questions of their colleagues when they think something is amiss.

Booksellers, on the other hand, have both their reputation and their bottomline to protect: selling hot merchandise makes them not only unpopular but also on the hook for the selling price if they get caught. So there are only two safe options for the amateur book thief once he steals rare materials: keep it or sell to a private party. (Use of the pronoun "he" in these pages is not only generic but also due to the fact that the great majority of the rare book thieves the author mentions are, in fact, male.)

Keeping the book offers its own reward. Aside from the relative security of knowing he'll almost never get caught, a collector who steals for his own collection commits the crime for more than money. He enjoys having such a unique item in his possession. He is probably a member of the Community and just chooses to go about his collection in a way outside the scope of normal channels.

This is the sort of person that James Gilreath was. It was noted after his arrest that he was known to be quite a book collector himself. It is likely that the books he took from the Library of Congress were not a means of enriching himself financially but rather a way of adding to his collection. There is no indication as to why he eventually tried to sell some of the material in Boston, but it is thought that he simply forgot which books were a part of his proper collection and which had been stolen from the Library of Congress. One of his defenses after his arrest was that he had suffered from some brain trauma that had encouraged memory loss. (Whether it was the memory loss that made him steal from the LOC or simply made him forget that he had stolen from LOC is a question that will remain unanswered.) But his memory loss defense certainly wasn't aided by the fact that he managed to steal only uncatalogued material that would be hard to trace.

There is little chance that a man like him would not have known that trying to sell the books to an antiquarian bookseller was a very risky endeavor. In fact, Gilreath had published extensively in the area of authenticity of forged books (most notably in particular about an episode involving forgeries of *The Oath of a Freeman*, the first thing printed in North America). He certainly would have known the peril of simply waltzing in to a bookshop with stolen material and putting it up for sale.

Another federal employee, Shawn Aubitz, had stolen hundreds of documents from his employer, the National Archives. In March 2000 a National Park Service employee spotted a document for sale on Ebay that he thought belonged to the archives.[20] After an almost three-year investigation, the FBI confronted Aubitz, who had worked at the Archives for sixteen years, and he admitted to stealing nearly 500 items from August 1996 to July 1999. Among the missing items was a cache of presidential pardons valued at roughly $100,000. Aubitz pleaded guilty to the crime, saying that he had a "mental illness, a compulsive need to amass collections for self-esteem and approval."[21] And, he also admitted, a need to pay off his credit card.

Gilreath would have at least known that fencing rare books is far more difficult than stealing them. The market for the items is so dependent on the Community that there is no chance of unloading a large amount of the stolen things without raising alarms. The whole history of book theft is paved with stories of people who, once they had the books in their possession, did not know how to convert their loot into cash. A perfect illustration of this point is a recent incident at Transylvania University in Kentucky. In December 2004, a man made an appointment with the rare books librarian there to look at some books. Using a stun gun—and the help of an accomplice— he subdued the librarian, grabbed some books, and ran into a waiting minivan.[22]

The story was news in the library community for the simple fact of its brazenness. Rare book thefts are usually quiet affairs. Not only is the crime itself better executed without creating a disturbance but the ability to sell the books on the back end is also severely hindered by publicity. But 20-year-old boys with money problems and little criminal experience are not known for their subtlety—this was a rare book joyride. Aside from the sloppiness of the crime itself—several books were dropped by the boys in haste as they left the library—the follow up was textbook idiocy. Knowing the approximate value of what they had but not how to go about selling it, the boys drove to New York. Four days before Christmas they showed up at Christie's claiming to represent a mystery man who wanted to sell some Audobon prints and a first edition *On the Origin of the Species*. By February, all four of the boys were in FBI custody.[23]

Those boys could have known what lay in their future if only they had read the newspaper more. Central Kentucky had only recently dispensed with another rare book thief of the armed bandit sort. On October 7, 2000, Ross Vince Brewer posed as a rare book scholar and dealer in order to get access to some 168-year-old prints of Indian chiefs at Centre College. The books were called the *History of the Indian Tribes of North America* and contained engraved plates made in the 1820s. Brewer made an appointment to see the three books that are housed in the Grace Doherty Library's rare book room and that are only brought out by appointment and accompanied by a librarian. When the librarian turned to help a student with another matter, Brewer grabbed the three books and ran.[24]

Centre was but one of the many colleges and universities—and a total of thirty-seven libraries—the man hit, but it was by far his most bold move. When he arranged to sell the books over the internet—books that been reported stolen almost as soon as he had left Centre College with them—to a man in Texas, the authorities were there to pick him up on delivery.[25]

Benjamin Johnson, the Wisconsin student who stole from his summer employers at Yale, was captured because an astute autograph collector noticed that the signatures he offered were in museum-quality shape instead of the rather poor shape she would have expected signatures sold out of a dorm room to be in. David Breithaupt, who took the stuff from Kenyon, was found out by a librarian paying attention to Ebay. Except for the two Kentucky smash-and-grab cases, none of the libraries in question knew that anything had been stolen until their stuff turned up for sale.

That's the significant bright spot in the universe of rare book crime. Someone out there is paying attention. If a rare book thief manages to steal a few books undetected, he might well be able to sell his goods privately without raising many alarms. But the more public a person is with his stolen items, the more opportunities for a random librarian in Florida or book collector in Connecticut to make a connection and place a phone call. And if a library staff is aware that something of theirs has been stolen, the opportunity to unload the material not only on public sales sites but also at reputable booksellers nationwide is foreclosed.

Even the children of the Book Community get in on the act. Another insider of the James Gilreath sort was found out by the son of a prominent art dealer. When Ohio State University Art History professor Anthony Melnikas invited Akron collector and rare book dealer Bruce Ferrini down to his Columbus-area house to see if the dealer would be interested in selling a couple of items for him, Ferrini brought his 14-year-old son along. The younger Ferrini—then a freshman at Western Reserve Academy—had been very much interested in learning the trade from his father. During the meeting the boy had a hunch that the items for sale didn't actually belong to Melnikas and, when he got home, did some research in his school library. After telling his father what he found the elder Ferrini—skeptical but still intrigued—contacted a more august rare book resource: Princeton's James Marrow. He confirmed that the leaves Melnikas offered for sale belonged in the Vatican; they were two pages from a work once owned by Petrarch.[26]

In this respect, Daniel Spiegelman was again an exception to the general rules of book thefts. He was slightly smarter than most (though it must be allowed that his sales spree took place several years before internet auction sites came into their own) so he was quiet with his thefts and left the country with his loot. His plan was to take his materials to Europe, to places unlikely to be in contact with Columbia or have any need to know provenance. As far as plans for unloading stolen rare materials go, it was better than most. And if Consuelo Dutschke had not discovered the thefts when she did, it is likely that Spiegelman would have sold just about every item he brought with him to Europe.

But shortly after Dutschke told Jean Ashton about the thefts they set about getting the materials back. When it became clear how much Spiegelman had stolen Ashton was pretty sure that he would sell the stuff; there was too much and in far too eclectic categories for this to be the work of a man stealing for his own collection. On top of that, atlases with maps razored out of them were the hallmark of a man who cared more about money than the item itself.

The community of booksellers and librarians was about to come up big for Columbia as they had done (and continue to do) in countless cases.

The final link that binds most modern rare book thefts is sadder still than the incidence of inside jobs, because this problem is so prevalent as to be almost universal: lack of punishment. Punishment for book crimes is a sad joke. Even when a thief is caught red-handed, he is treated as less a major criminal than a person who simply has overdue library books. (This image is further fomented by lame newspaper accounts whose titles often work in the overdue book angle. For example, the *Daily Record* of Baltimore, Maryland, had this headline for the resolution of the David Breithaupt affair: *Books Overdue, Fine $250K.*)[27]

Book crimes, despite the fact that most involve great sums of money, breaking and entering and transporting across state lines (making them federal crimes), are almost never taken as seriously as librarians would like. Nor, considering the irreplaceable nature of the books, are they taken as seriously as the crime itself warrants.

When Mimi Meyers was finally caught after a decade of selling off books belonging to the University of Texas she was sentenced to three years of probation, due largely to the fact of her "acceptance of responsibility."[28] In addition, she agreed to pay $381,595 in restitution and help Texas track down the remaining missing pieces of their collection. But Richard Oram, a librarian at Ransom, said that once she had cooperated with the prosecution, she wasn't required to help the library anymore and she didn't. The library had to work directly with the auction houses in hopes of tracing some of the books that had disappeared overseas.[29] Whether a person with as many financial predicaments as Meyer can pay such a hefty fine is an altogether different story.

West Texas justice, too, didn't live up to that state's harsh reputation for treatment of criminals. Dwain Edgar Manske, a University of Arkansas professor, was caught with a trunkload of pictures, letters, and court documents stolen from the Marfa Public Library, Presidio County Courthouse, and other libraries and courthouses in the area.[30] Library director, Ester Sanchez, had let Manske look at a scrapbook full of pictures from the late 1800s because he was a university professor claiming to do research for a book. She quickly became suspicious when he requested a table out of her line of sight; she wisely had a colleague watch him instead. Both women saw him appear to cut things out of the book and put them in his jacket.[31]

Despite the well over 100 documents he had in his car and the fact that he had stuffed most of those documents into his pockets, pants, and socks to get them out of the libraries and courthouses, Manski was only fined $4,813 and not sentenced to any jail time in Presidio county. In a plea for leniency, he claimed that the shame of the arrest was enough punishment: "I have never been so humiliated in my life," said the 63-year-old tenured professor.[32] Despite the fact that he had systematically stolen items from at least four other Texas counties, his humiliation extended to neither his quitting the rare book and documents business—he continued to run South by Southwest Books in Fayetteville—nor quitting his job as a professor. He retired from the Department of English at the University of Arkansas right on time, at age 66, in December 1999.

Joseph Anastasio was a security guard at the University of Bridgeport when he started routinely stealing rare materials from the library's special collections. He, as did almost everyone who worked there, had access to the special collections room on the fifth floor of the eight-floor building.[33]

During the tumultuous time of the early 1990s when Bridgeport was in some financial troubles and many of the librarians had been on strike, Anastasio lifted several letters written and signed by Abraham Lincoln as well as other rare documents. Since the university didn't have a full staff nor had the special collections been adequately catalogued, there was no way of knowing that someone was stealing the material. It wasn't until a preservation survey was conducted in 1994 that the missing items were discovered; library director Karen Smiga quickly published a list of missing items for book dealers.

At Anastasio's sentencing hearing, a tearful plea by his wife and one by his minister had the desired effect: no jail time. He was sentenced to three years probation. Due to the nature of the collection at the time Anastasio was stealing documents, the library is still not sure how many of its items it has recovered.[34]

When a staff member at the Iowa State Historical Society noticed one day that some plastic preservation sleeves that had contained photographs—and had recently been taken out by longtime patron Corey Phelps—were empty, the staff decided to take a closer look at the man on his next visit. Since item-level cataloging is not done on, for instance, each photograph in an old album, it is relatively easy to lose those sorts of things a bit at a time.[35] But when Phelps made his next visit the staff took particular note of everything present in the items he was looking at. In that way they discovered exactly how, over the course of several years, he stole more than 8,000 of their items.[36] One-of-a-kind letters, diaries, photos, maps—all taken a piece at a time and smuggled out in spiral notebooks and the like.

The 58-year-old man pleaded guilty in October 2004 to the crimes claiming that he had no interest in profit, he just liked to have them around his house. This defense seemed to work. Before his November sentencing, he faced a possible sentence of ten years in prison; what he actually received was two years probation and a suspended sentence. And he was told to stay away from libraries.

Mark Doiron had a novel approach to theft: he would check out, under his own name, various first edition books, remove the bar code, reattach it to a less valuable (usually trade paperback) version of the book and give it back to the library. Stealing books from libraries throughout middle Tennessee, Doiron took sixty-three books from the Linebaugh Library in Murfreesboro alone.[37] The thief eventually turned himself in to the police once a book shelver noticed the discrepancy; in lieu of jail time Doiron made restitution for the value of any book he could not return.[38]

David Breithaupt's interesting defense was that Kenyon had voluntarily abandoned the materials and that their loss was due to the school's own negligence and inattention. Breithaupt's defense came in a civil rather than a criminal proceeding: Kenyon sued—and won judgment from—the thief to the tune of $1.3 million. This turn of events was largely due to the fact that any criminal prosecution of Breithaupt and his girlfriend Hupp didn't appear to be in the offing. After 9/11, many federal criminal prosecutions dealing with nonterrorist related subjects met a similar fate. Breithaupt, it should be noted, countersued Kenyon for $10.5 million for, amongst other things, material damages done to him when campus security went to his apartment looking for the stolen books. That suit was dismissed.

In May 2005, five years after it was discovered that Breithaupt and Hupp had taken Kenyon's materials, and through the continued dogged effort of Kenyon librarians, the monumentally unhelpful Breithaupt was sentenced to one year in prison. He was sent to a minimum security facility south of Youngstown, Ohio.

Twenty-two year-old Timothy Naus waited less than a week after he had gotten out of jail before heading to the Bloomsburg University library to help himself to some difficult-to-acquire art books. Just starting his parole after having served a year long sentence for theft of antiquities, Naus would tear off the security tags and call numbers from the books he wanted and leave them scattered on the floor and shelves. This made it fairly simple for Bloomsburg to know what exactly had been stolen; the Head of Special Collections, Robert Dunkelberger, saw Naus "browsing" and contacted his parole officer. The officer later found twenty-seven books in Naus's apartment. In March 2005, he was sentenced to another year in jail, largely due to parole violation.[39]

Jake Oelerich received what was termed "an exceptionally long jail sentence," for his theft. Guilty of taking more than $100,000 worth of material, he pleaded to a crime defined by state law as stealing more than $1,500 worth of property. The "exceptionally long" sentence amounted to six months in a jail.[40] But at least that was jail time: James Gilreath, who stole from the Library of Congress, was given a year of home detention and a $20,000 fine.

Since Ohio State's Anthony Melnikas never actually stole anything in the United States, his sentence was based on importing and transporting stolen goods. Using his status as a respected scholar he was able to gain access to some extremely rare materials and eventually pleaded guilty to transporting seven different documents, each more than 600 years old. He could have spent up to thirty years in jail and been fined $1 million; instead he was sentenced to fourteen months "in a minimum security prison or prison camp."[41]

What is most interesting about this sentence is that there was actual jail time given. Part of that is due to the fact that in federal crimes there is little discretion once a person has pleaded guilty; unless extraordinary circumstances apply, a man who pleads to a certain level of crime will get a certain sentence regardless of his university affiliation and advanced age. But part of the sentence must be credited to an effort by librarians nationwide to make clear how damaging this sort of crime was to the culture. Roger Stoddard, in his capacity as the president of the Bibliographical Society of America, wrote to the court in a plea for a serious sentence. "All [scholarship] depends completely on the maintenance and security of library collections:

destroy, mutilate, steal, or hide the books and manuscripts and you frustrate the development of knowledge and the free interchange of scholarship and teaching."[42] Another important person in the rare book community, Susan M. Allen, sent a letter to a professional listserv encouraging her peers to write to the court and stress how damaging such thefts are. Particularly, "the institutional and personal costs associated with such crimes, and restrictions to access that have come into being because of such crimes."[43]

On August 19, 1996—a few months before his sentencing—the Columbus Dispatch echoed the views of the Book Community and asked the sentencing judge to impose a properly severe sentence. Noting that Melnikas admitted to stealing the documents to help finance his retirement, the editorial asked that the judge consider that he "probably erected a hurdle for researchers doing the sort of work he did with priceless artifacts."[44] When Judge Susan Dlott sentenced Melnikas, she specifically mentioned that he had hurt all those people who study such works and that the letters she'd received from art and documents experts had swayed her away from giving the most lenient sentence possible.[45] Though, of course, the most lenient sentence that could have been given was only two months more lenient than the one he got. Still, the Melnikas sentence in many ways presages the Spiegelman sentence that would follow. It served as a sort of rehearsal for the argument that would come years later in a much more serious crime.

What the pattern of punishment for rare book criminals seems to be is one where first offenses, no matter how egregious or large in scope, are treated with remarkable lenience. This is particularly true where the "first offense" in question is a prolonged and systematic theft of books over the course of many years. No youthful, spur-of-the-moment crimes these, most of these thefts have been well thought out and richly considered plans that not only involve large sums of money but also actually do damage to the community as a whole, the one entity criminal law is supposed to protect. Car theft and armed robbery, for example are certainly serious crimes that deserve serious punishment, but individual instances of property crime involving individuals, at worst, affect the community as a whole in tenuous way. (We're sorry when someone's Land Rover gets stolen—and certainly feel that the perpetrator should be punished—but we're not harmed by that crime in any direct way.) But the theft of books from libraries has an impact on the commonweal. It is, quite literally, a theft from everyone in the community.

The most notorious sentence—the one that really stuck in the craw of librarians nationwide—was that of serial book destruction artist Stephen Blumberg. The truth is that no sentence would have been enough, considering the sheer level of destruction wrought by Blumberg. But this differs from other light sentences in the sense that it wasn't really light at all—he was sentenced to seventy-two months in jail and eventually spent about four and a half years behind bars. But the sheer scope of harm done by him warranted triple that time, not to mention the fact that the more time he spent in jail the less time he'd have to steal when he was released. Sure enough, when he was paroled he quickly resumed his crimes and was reapprehended several times before the harm of his earlier spree had been close to undone.

Blumberg was a remarkable thief and was the sort of person least likely to be caught. He was not an insider—in fact, as an itinerant he was so constantly on the move that catching up with him was almost impossible. Nor was he captured with the aid of the Book Community or through a slip up while trying to sell his items. Blumberg was the most feared of all rare book thieves: the personal collector. He stole simply to possess the books, and that made him almost uncatchable. (The story of Stephen Blumberg is well covered in many articles and books and will not be rehashed here. For people interested in the full, sordid tale, see any of a number of good accounts, including the *Harper's* article "The Book Thief" by Philip Weiss or the book *A Gentle Madness* by Nicholas Basbanes, both of which give good and complete accounts of the story.)

In the end it was the dogged efforts of a few librarians and one notable campus police officer named J. Stephen Huntsberry that brought the thief of more than 30,000 rare items—a total of more than $20 million—to justice.

But that justice was incomplete. Blumberg started his sentence in August 1991 and by December 1995 he was out. And by all accounts—this was another great fear of librarians—he was at it again. One of Blumberg's compulsions for theft on top of old books was antiques. Victrolas, stained glass windows, artwork, doorknobs—all had been found in his Ottumwa, Iowa, house upon his arrest. He was a person who longed for the past and nothing quite fulfilled his fantasies as much as surrounding himself with old things.

In December 1997, just two years after his release, a caretaker of an old building in downtown Des Moines noticed that someone had broken in and stolen antique radiators, doorknobs, locks, window pulls, door bells, and towel racks. Instead of calling the police, the man staked out the building the next night in the hopes of catching the thief in the act. Sure enough, Blumberg and an accomplice showed up and began taking apart old pipes and wood work. They were quickly apprehended, taken into custody, and, at a later trial, Blumberg was found guilty of third-degree burglary. He was sentenced to another five years in prison.[46]

In July 2003, Blumberg, out of prison again, was arrested, this time for being "in possession of doorknobs." He and another confederate had broken in to another abandoned house, this one owned by a bank, and attempted to steal some of the antique furnishings. When Blumberg pled guilty to the crime this time, he did not return to jail. He got five years of probation.[47] The man who is the worst rare book criminal of the twentieth century, whose admitted compulsion for theft will not end, who had a well-financed lifestyle (through rich parents) that allowed him to drive around looking for places to rob, and who had been convicted of or pled guilty to more than ten separate crimes, is still on the prowl.

There appear to be two types of people who steal rare books. There are the collectors, like Blumberg and James Gilreath, who love the books themselves, as objects, and steal for the sake of possession. Then there are the people who steal books simply as a commodity. These people understand on some level that there is value in rare books and, possessing a particular avenue to get to the valuable object, they take advantage of the opportunity.

It is the former of these categories that is the scariest. Not in terms of numbers—people who steal books for profit are far more prolific—but simply because they are hardest to catch. These book lovers don't rush out to sell their stolen loot right away, if ever. They simply enjoy having the stuff around. So until they are caught in the act or they slip up and try to sell something or they die (and their unknowing family tries to unload the items), the books are essentially lost to the community. And the truth is, even when these people are caught, harsh prison sentences are not a deterrent. Like many criminal illnesses, no amount of jail time could cure a bibliophile of his compulsion. (Though this is not an argument for less jail time for bibliophilic thieves.)

But serious jail time might discourage the other type of thief. A person who steals for the sake of money and who finds that (i) the money is not easy to collect and (ii) the penalty for the theft is all out of proportion to possible payoff, will quickly retire from the book stealing business. A person who knows that rare book theft is taken quite seriously by the criminal justice system and is treated with stiff penalties will be less likely to risk serious jail time for the opportunity of a small payoff. And even if that's not true and there is some compulsion to steal books by even those people who sell them, the longer they're out of circulation the better.

The methodology for decreasing crime of opportunity requires two efforts. The library community itself needs to continue to make the crime both difficult and unprofitable. If librarians continue to be cognizant of who it is that is taking interest in their rare books, itinerant thieves and in-house thieves alike will be less likely to steal the things. The Book Community has done a yeoman's job on the second effort: making the selling of the books very difficult. Watchful eyes at book sales and highly publicized lists of missing materials continue to be the best ways of tracking down books thieves.

But the criminal justice system needs to hold up its end of the bargain. In most cases book thieves have not been treated with the swift and sure justice they deserve based on the nature of the materials they have endangered and sometimes destroyed. But here, too, Spiegelman's case was to be unique. It could well be a template for the way judges treat such criminals. What happened to Spiegelman could set the stage for a new turn in the way the federal criminal system would treat crimes of this sort, and spill his name, like ink on a Shakespeare quarto, all over the federal sentencing system.

NOTES

1. G.M.E., "Texas Rare Book Thief Gets Probation," *American Libraries*, April 2004, 14.

2. Press Release: Perpetrator of Rare Book Theft at Harry Ransom Center Sentenced, February 2, 2004. http://www.hrc.utexas.edu/news/press/2004/theft.html.

3. News Fronts, "Kenyon Employee Pleads Guilty to Rare-Books Theft," *American Libraries*, February 2004, 17.

4. Robbie Ketcham, "Kenyon Wins Suit," *The Kenyon Collegian*, February 27, 2003, 1.

5. Ibid.

6. Andrew Albanese, "Student Steals Mags," *Library Journal*, July 15, 2004, 24.

7. Henry Yaple interview with author, March 28, 2005.

8. "Walla Walla Student Charged with Selling Library's Periodicals on Ebay," *American Libraries Online*, May 21, 2004. available at http://www.ala.org/al_onlineTemplate.cfm?Section=may2004ab&Template=/ContentManagement/ContentDisplay.cfm&ContentID=66425.

9. Natalie Missakian, "Thefts of Rare Books Less Than Rare," *Register Citizen*, December 3, 2001, 1.

10. Bill Miller, "Former Library of Congress Curator Sentenced in Theft of Rare Books," *Washington Post*, July 8, 1998, D 11.

11. Skip Thurman, "Safeguarding Library Treasures from Theft," *Christian Science Monitor*, December 5, 1997, 3.

12. "Thefts of Rare Books Less. . . . "

13. Ibid.

14. Philip Weiss, "The Book Thief: A True Tale of Bibliomania," *Harper's*, January 1994.

15. Consuelo Dutschke interview with the author, March 4, 2005.

16. Lisa Speer interview with author, March 24, 2005.

17. Ebay listing for item #729965525.

18. Josh Flory, "Wrong Turn," *Columbia Daily Tribune*, October 5, 2003, 1.

19. Stephen Deere, "Faulkner letter thief sentenced to 7 years," *Arkansas-Democrat Gazetter*, 1.

20. Deborah Fitts, "National Archives Employee Charged with Theft of Civil War Documents," *The Civil War News*, April 2002, available at http://www.civilwarnews.com/archive/articles/document_theft.htm.

21. "Ex-Archivist Sentenced for Document Theft," *American Libraries Online*, August 12, 2002, available at http://www.ala.org/al_onlineTemplate.cfm?Section=august2002&Template=/ContentManagement/ContentDisplay.cfm&ContentID=10328.

22. Murray Evans, "Ky. Suspects Arrested in Rare-Book Theft," AP, February 12, 2004.

23. Sarah Vos, "A Brazen Plot Doomed to Fail," *Lexington Herald Leader*, February 20, 2005, A1.

24. Valerie Honeycutt, "Centre Art Theft Brings Indictment," *Lexington Herald Leader*, December 9, 2000, C4.

25. Louise Taylor, "Alleged Book Thief Undergoing Psychiatric Testing," *Lexington Herald Leader*, February 24, 2001, C3.

26. Bob Dyer, "Worn Pages Tell a Tale," *Akron Beacon Journal*, December 11, 2005, A1.

27. "Books Overdue, Fine $250K," *Daily Record*, December 22, 2004.

28. United States v. Meyer, Case# 03-CR-284-ALL, January 30, 2004.

29. G.M.E. "Texas Rare Book Thief Gets Probation," *American Libraries*, April 2004, 14.

30. "Records Thief Pleads Guilty," *Big Bend Sentinel*, January 16, 1997.

31. Ester Sanchez interview with author, May 3, 2005.

32. Ross McSwain, "Document Debacle Casts Long Shadow," *Standard-Times*, February 10, 1997.

33. Hartford Courant, October 17, 1996.

34. Karen Smiga interview with author, March 25, 2005.

35. Shaner Magalhaes interview with author, May 20, 2005.

36. "Man Admits Theft from Iowa Historical Society," *American Libraries Online*, October 15, 2004, available at http://www.ala.org/al_onlineTemplate.cfm?Section=october2004ab&Template=/ContentManagement/ContentDisplay.cfm&ContentID=77757.

37. Andy Humbles, "Man Surrenders, is Charged in Library Book Theft," *Tennessean*, September 19, 2002.

38. Laurel Best interview with author, March 29, 2005.

39. Robert Dunkelberger interview with author, May 5, 2005.

40. Terry McConn, "Man Pleads Guilty to Magazine Theft from Whitman," *Walla-Walla Union Bulletin*, July 14, 2004.

41. Robert Ruth, "Document Thief Gets 14 Months," *Columbus Dispatch*, November 16, 1996, 1A.

42. Christopher Reed, "Biblio Klept," *Harvard Magazine*, March, 1997.

43. Susan M. Allen letter to exlibris@library.berkeley.edu, October 28, 1996, available at http://palimpsest.stanford.edu/byform/mailing-lists/exlibris/1996/10/msg00288.html.

44. Editorial, "Retired Professor Deserves a Stern Sentence," *Columbus Dispatch*, August 19, 1996, 6A.

45. "Document Thief Gets..."

46. *Iowa v. Blumberg*, Nos 1999–178, 9–402, December 27, 1999.

47. Cindy Iutzy, "Master Book Thief Found in Keokuk," *Daily Gate City*, July 12, 2003.

CHAPTER 3

Whoever Is Interested in This Old Letter ... I Have the Originals

This is what Ashton knew. There had been a theft and it had happened quite recently. Since the longest any of them had been away from the place had been the just-finished 4th of July weekend, it seemed right to assume that the thefts could have been only hours instead of days old. In truth they were several months old, but so singular and well hidden was this crime that all logical assumptions, no matter how sound, would end up being wrong. There was no way to guess what had happened nor know what might happen next. Certainly no one at the time could imagine the scope of the crime.

Still, the thought was that with any luck, quick action might salvage a potential disaster. Ashton sent the senior staff and curators back to the stacks with card catalogs in hand. They were going to do a thorough shelf read and figure out exactly what was and what was not missing. Then she went to the Columbia University libraries administrative office to alert the university librarian of their developing situation.[1]

Like most major research libraries, Columbia had had some experience with theft from their libraries in the past. But while the two minor thefts that had taken place at other Columbia libraries in the previous few years carved a protocol path for the reporting of such crimes, they were nowhere near the scale that the RBML was about to experience. As Ashton walked over to the university librarian's place that Tuesday, she had not yet imagined the scope of what she was going to be facing.

Ashton's main fear—after she got over the initial shock of the theft itself— was that Columbia might rather sweep the theft under the rug than report it.[2]

While this sounds like a ridiculous course for an institution of Columbia's stature to take, it is actually quite common practice and, in truth, not bad policy. The publication of such crimes often has two effects, both bad. First, it alerts the criminal to the fact that his crime has been discovered. That would lessen the likelihood that the thief would sell the items out in the open. Second, such publicity has the result of drying up donations. Though the RBML wasn't any less secure than most other major academic rare book libraries, it would have the blemish of insecurity in the press. In truth, the reaction to the book crime at RBML would guarantee that it, of all places, was even more secure. Nevertheless, the fewer the donors who knew of the thefts, the better the chances that donations would continue uninterrupted. But that was Columbia's position, not the position of Ashton or anyone at the RBML. They wanted to get these items back, and the best thing for that was publicity.

The day after Consuelo Dutchske discovered the thefts the FBI was at Columbia. A quick cataloguing effort had demonstrated that at least fourteen of the medieval manuscripts were missing.[3] (It is interesting to note that, though the range of items stolen would touch almost every era in the collection, from medieval to Renaissance to early colonial to late nineteenth century, the FBI would tag the crime "Medieval Manuscripts Theft" throughout the investigation.) This was an incredible loss and the idea that any of the investigation could be done in-house or even by Columbia's own police force was right out the window. Within twenty-four hours the monetary value alone of the stolen items made this a top priority item; the fact that these sorts of things would probably not be resold right in Manhattan—and therefore had to cross state lines—made the issue a federal one.

Catherine Begley was the FBI agent with much of the expertise on these sorts of cultural crimes and so she was called in right away. She knew it was important to get the interviews of the staff done as soon as possible; some people who steal art like to take it and bury it for five years because they think the statute of limitations on the crime runs out. Also, some countries have laws that say that if a person has possession of an item for a certain amount of time, no matter the provenance, it belongs to them. For that reason it was important to get on the trail quickly.[4]

The FBI started in with people who had keys and worked out in concentric circles from that group. This was the first and most obvious place to start. Many of the items that had been taken were housed in the vault. It made sense that people with keys to the vault would be under the greatest suspicion. Ashton had those keys, of course, and so did several other people. These people were the first to be questioned and fingerprinted.[5]

Ashton, Ellenbogen, and Dutschke were at the top of the list and all three were very forthcoming since none of them had anything to hide. Ellenbogen, in particular, almost enjoyed the interview. A teacher at heart, he liked describing to the agents exactly the importance and value of the materials.

Not only did this serve the simple education purpose of the RBML but he also wanted to impress on the agents how important many of these items were to the world.[6]

At times, the library staff had given the keys out to students for the sake of short-term projects or to have them grab something quickly from the vault. This was the next line of inquiry.[7] It was not yet seriously considered that someone had gotten into the vault other than through the locked door.

While it would be unlikely that anyone—such as a student—who had the keys for only a short time, and under the direction of a librarian, could have made off with that many manuscripts, anyone with access to a key could have had a copy made. But students were unlikely to have had much free time with the keys. In a place where even the cleaning staff was supervised, no one who wasn't explicitly allowed to do so hung out for very long in the vault or had the keys for very long.[8] While that didn't acquit outsiders or student workers, it tended to focus the investigation on the few people who had permanent possession of the keys and ready access to the vault.

This was a very unpleasant process for the staff. Since everyone was a potential suspect, no one could be trusted. Security procedures that were already tight got more so. Locks were changed, keys were confiscated, and no staff members were allowed in the stacks alone. This highly stressful period wouldn't last for very long simply because the normal routine of a working library wouldn't let it, but while it lasted it was quite awful for the staff.[9] A sense of depression would last quite a bit longer. The inherent distrust of one another soon evolved into a general malaise when it became clear that none of them were complicit in the thefts. Staff members were simply upset that the thefts had taken place at all. Certainly no one at the RBML was individually responsible for the thefts, but many of them felt responsible in the abstract since it was part of their job to keep the collection safe.[10]

While the FBI was interviewing people, the effort of the RBML staff to get a better grasp on the scope of the crime continued apace. By the end of the week, the thought was that about twenty western and oriental manuscripts had been stolen. A list and description of these missing items was sent to H.P. Kraus, the noted rare book dealer in Manhattan. A quick appraisal by Kraus suggested that the value of the missing items, without actually looking at the items themselves, was between $350,000 and $600,000.[11]

By the end of the month a further inventory had revealed more thefts. Ashton and her staff's cataloguing efforts had revealed a total of twenty-four missing manuscripts. The earliest missing item was a Papal Bull of Innocent III from February 1202. The missing item that was of the most recent vintage was a Koran from 1887.[12] The rest of the missing items were dotted throughout the 685 years between and had points of origin spanning three continents. The inconceivable was becoming reality.

This inventorying of the RBML collection did not stop for another three years. That might seem like an overlong time considering the pressing nature

of the situation but it's important to note that there are approximately half
a million separately catalogued pieces in the collection. While a cursory
inspection could reveal a lot, a complete accounting had to be done. That
job would entail checking every preservation box in the place for the right
book and every book in the boxes to make sure that nothing had been
taken or cut out. So wide ranging was Spiegelman's access that nothing
could be taken for granted. Even if a preservation box felt full, the actual
book that was supposed to have been in there must be confirmed to be in
there.[13] In the later calculus of the damage Spiegelman had done to the
Columbia materials, the person hours that went into this effort would not
factor in nor would the slight but still present damage to each of the books
that took place simply by their having been gone through. The bulk of this
cataloguing effort—the fruit of which was a list of missing materials—fell
on the shoulders of Ellenbogen and Dutschke.[14]

Besides kicking off the cataloguing effort, Ashton had another immediate
job. Even if Columbia wasn't going to make the thefts public, and the FBI
was investigating, she knew that she could quietly make a contribution. She
contacted the International Foundation for Art Research and the Antiquarian Booksellers' Association of America. She sent lists of the items that she
knew were missing. This had the benefit of a press release—getting the right
people the right knowledge—without all of the negative publicity. These organizations, in turn, sent these lists to their members.[15] At the very least, if
anyone tried to sell any of the items to legit members of the rare bookselling
community there might be a positive reaction. But for the most part the
news would be kept discrete.

The FBI had the same idea. Begley made sure letters and a list of the missing
items got sent to several national booksellers who might be in the market
for such things. The Argosy Bookstore—a Manhattan store specializing in
rare maps and autographs—was contacted. So was the Kenneth W. Rendell
gallery—a rare document and map market that emphasized the items for
sale more as individual works of art than as books. On the west coast,
they sent a letter to Heritage Bookshop, another high-end concern that dealt
with book repair and the sort of clientele that would be in the market for the
types of things Spiegelman had in his possession.[16] Around the same time,
Interpol put a similar request and list of missing items out to what they call
the Cultural Property Distribution List.[17]

While this quick blanketing of the rare book dealer world would not pay
immediate dividends it would eventually prove very valuable in apprehend-
ing Spiegelman.

A month after the crime the FBI had no solid leads. The small leads they
thought they had turned out to be all wrong. One of the initial thoughts
was that the theft was related to an earlier theft at Yale. The FBI in
New York contacted several people at Yale—from librarians to the Yale

police department—and compared notes. The thefts appeared to be different enough in nature that it was unlikely to have been the same thief. In the end the FBI simply gave a list of the stolen items to the Yale police and library and told them to contact the New Haven FBI if they became aware of anything.[18]

In early September, the RBML provided the FBI with a list of twenty-five student workers who had been working there in 1993 and 1994, when the thefts were thought to have taken place. This was so the investigation could include people who had worked there at the time but were not there when the thefts were discovered. The list also included readers who had used the manuscripts in 1993.[19] None of these people was found to have known anything.

In October an anonymous man contacted the New York FBI to report that a man who was currently a fellow at the Freedom Media Studies program at Columbia had been investigated by the FBI for thefts from the Library of Congress. The caller said that the man in question had access to all of the libraries on campus. An investigation was done and nothing came of it.[20]

Around that same time Fred Schreiber, a rare book dealer in the area, contacted Columbia to say that a person had offered him a scroll of some kind that sounded similar to an item on their list of missing items. She had called him from France on the advice of a Manhattan intermediary.[21] The police interviewed Schreiber several times and the FBI tracked the woman's travels between New York and France but that investigation was eventually dropped.[22]

By November 1994 the search for the missing items was not going well. The FBI had expanded their list of interviewees to all of the people who had worked at RBML between 1990 and 1994. While this group of people seemed to be the most promising, the list would eventually turn out not to be helpful at all.[23]

Spiegelman, as it happens, was actually in New York for part of that fall. He had been traveling a lot in that year. In the previous six months he had flown to San Francisco, Honolulu, Washington, D.C., and London. All of these destinations had trips in and out of New York between them; that's where he still kept the bulk of the items he had stolen. In November he flew to Europe again; after a short stay in New York he flew to Los Angeles. In the first three months of 1995 he would fly to Chicago, Detroit, and Orlando. In March 1995 he would leave out of Newark again bound for Europe.[24] Though he didn't know it, he would be gone from New York for almost two years.

By the early part of 1995 the main thing the FBI's investigation had shown was that there didn't appear to be any connection between anyone at RBML and the crime. No local dealers appeared to have any of the stolen materials and none had surfaced anywhere in the United States or abroad. But that was about it. In truth, there was not any proof that a federal crime had been committed at all; the twenty-sixth precinct in Morningside Heights was brought up to speed on the investigation. On February 13th of 1995 the FBI shut their investigation down.[25]

The case wasn't forgotten, it was just put on hold. If it was going to be reopened it would have to wait for the thief being brought out in the open or some other development that no one could anticipate. Columbia as an institution continued to be less than helpful with the whole thing (though, in truth, there was little for their lawyers to do) so Jean Ashton maintained direct contact with law enforcement.

In early March 1995 there was a break. There were rumors that a New Jersey book dealer was selling some Arabic materials that might belong to Columbia. A woman had offered a dealer in New York eight manuscripts that appeared identical to those from the Columbia stash. She had faxed a list of the books to the dealer who had in turn forwarded it on to the FBI.[26] This seemed to be exactly what the FBI was looking for. They knew that eventually the thief had to come out into the open to sell the material and it appeared as if she'd done it, right across the river.

Still, with just the list and no pictures or actual on-site confirmation there was no way to know if the stuff offered for sale was actually part of the Columbia loot. They couldn't act without confirmation and they didn't want to scare away this small lead—and potential link to the rest of the stolen material—without getting their ducks in a row. The FBI wanted someone from Ashton's department to work with them in confirming that these items on the list were, in fact, some of the Columbia documents. This person would have to view the documents in person. Since no one in the RBML spoke or read Arabic fluently enough to recognize the materials when they saw them, Ashton asked a Columbia professor of Arabic studies if he would work with the FBI. He was going to have to act as a buyer to get a look at the items.[27]

The dealer with the documents was put under surveillance by the FBI and her conversations with the New York dealer monitored and taped. A background investigation showed the she had no criminal history and her general demeanor with the sale didn't suggest criminal intent, but there was no way to be sure.[28] She could merely be a link to the person who actually stole the stuff.

In the middle of March the FBI set up a sting. The plan was for the buyer—the Columbia professor—to go into the office of the manuscript dealer, examine the documents, and then report back to the FBI if they were the right ones. But one day before the professor was to check out the materials the FBI called the operation off. There was some trepidation on the part of the feds to cross into New Jersey without knowing for sure whether it was, in fact, the Columbia documents involved. Ashton never got the full story but it was determined by the FBI that these were most likely not Columbia documents; without more definite proof it wasn't a good idea to roust the seller with a fake buyer. So the FBI continued to monitor the dealer through the end of March and into the first part of April.[29] They would watch for anything that suggested a further link to the Columbia thefts.

Like the other leads, nothing related to the crime ever came of it.

One useful and fortunate circumstance for the ultimate resolution of the Spiegelman saga did come from the sting, though. Throughout the process of setting up the buy and surveillance of the New Jersey dealer there was a lot of interaction between the FBI and the Office of the United States Attorney. This marked the first time that Assistant United States Attorney Katherine Choo came to be attached to the case.[30] It would be on and off her desk for the next six years.

While the FBI was focusing on New Jersey, Spiegelman was driving around northern Europe. He was going by several different names. He had two American passports, one with his real name and one with the alias Craig Wesley Hesseltine. Though he had the ability to forge passports, both were actually issued by the Passport Office; the documentation underlying one of them, of course, was fraudulent. Spiegelman also carried an Arizona driver's license with a different name altogether. He carried an ID from the Tenri School of Japanese Language, an NYU student ID for Spring 1995, a Columbia ID for Spring 1994, a driver's license from St. Kitts and Nevis, a driver's license from the Cayman Islands, a driver's license from the Bahamas, an AT&T calling card, and, finally, a card attesting to his membership in the National Rifle Association.[31] Each of these cards had a different name on it.

He also had in his possession hundreds of pictures of the items he had taken. He would usually take the pictures to prospective buyers and ask them if they were interested. If they were he would negotiate price and then specify a date of delivery.[32] In this manner, by the fall of 1994, he had already unloaded several items in Germany that Columbia didn't even know had been stolen. In Stuttgart he had sold a Nuremberg Chronicle and—in another German spot—he had sold several of the maps he had cut from the Blaeu atlas.[33] In Paris he'd been to several "flea market" type shows where he unloaded many of the items to anonymous collectors.[34] At these places he would distribute flyers to groups of dealers. With a photocopy of a letter (or sometimes the page of a manuscript) he'd write on the bottom "Who ever is interested in this old letter ... I have the originals." Then he'd write a phone number and one of his aliases on the bottom.[35]

Near the end of May 1995, he started a blitz of cold-call selling. He contacted several dealers in Switzerland, France, Germany, and the Netherlands and always demanded the same thing: cash only in exchange for some very valuable manuscripts.[36] His manner and his wares sent up red flags all over the northern European book dealer community and it was just a matter of time before he was caught. In retrospect this behavior was more reckless than he could have hoped to get away with and is probably why he did it all within the span of a few days. If he got in and out quickly he could be gone before anyone figured out he was selling stolen items. It was why he was wary of meeting with dealers more than once.

But his behavior—and the shoddy story he told, about how he had inherited the items and wanted to get rid of them quickly—was so transparent that he had to count on the complicity of the people he was selling to in order to get away with it. For a while, at least, that worked. There were more than a few dealers, particularly in Germany, who were willing to turn the other way if they could get extremely valuable materials for substantially discounted prices. But the odds were against Spiegelman; sooner or later he was going to run into someone who knew exactly what he was selling and who would be more than happy to turn him in.

In late May Spiegelman was in Hamburg, Germany. He was representing himself as a British man who lived on the Isle of Guernsey. He was going by the name William Taylor and he was beginning to attract attention.[37] By this time his movements had been noticed by reputable dealers: there had already been several calls to local police departments in Germany and Switzerland from several book dealers who said they'd been propositioned by a man who appeared to be offering books off of the Columbia list.[38] Some of these dealers even called Ashton; in fact, getting calls from dealers in four different countries was the first good news she had had in a long while. It seemed like the beginning of the end of a long process.[39] At the same time it was frustrating; local authorities knew of Spiegelman but many were reluctant to act before they knew more. They were concerned that he might destroy some of the material if he got wind that he was about to be caught.[40]

In mid-May Spiegelman called Dutch rare book dealer Sebastian Hesselink to see if he might be interested in some manuscripts, for cash only. Spiegelman, who claimed to be calling from America, described what he had over the phone. Hesselink said he might be interested in some of them, depending upon condition. Spiegelman told Hesselink that he would call him back in mid-June to set up an appointment.[41]

Spiegelman called back in early June to tell Hesselink he was in Europe and was ready to meet. Hesselink was immediately suspicious of Spiegelman and of what he said he had to offer. Along with the manuscripts, Spiegelman claimed to have presidential letters by Washington and Jefferson. While an international dealer like Hesselink would certainly be interested in such items, it was unlikely that a man would travel from New York to the Netherlands to sell them; in New York alone there were hundreds of reputable places where he could have sold such valuable items. Still, Hesselink did not have Ashton's list and so he had no way of knowing if these items were stolen or not. He agreed to meet with Spiegelman.[42]

Hesselink was a dealer who specialized in atlases and printed books of the sort that Spiegelman had in spades, of course, but Spiegelman had offered him several items that were outside of his area. It's possible that if Spiegelman had simply done a bit more research and found out what sorts of items Hesselink actually dealt in, the history of the Columbia thefts would have had a completely different outcome. As it was, Hesselink called his friend and sometime business partner Sandra Hindman.

Hindman was—and remains—an expert in the sort of manuscripts that Spiegelman was offering. An emeritus professor of Art History at Northwestern University and the author of several books dealing with the subject (for instance, *Pen to Press: Illustrated Manuscripts and Printed Books in the First Century of Printing*), she was the right person for Hesselink to call. She particularly knew about the Roman de la Rose that Spiegelman had offered Hesselink and that Hesselink had in turn offered her. The Dutch dealer did not know this, but there were only 357 of these manuscripts in the world and most of them were in museums and libraries. Very few ever came up for sale to private collectors. The fact that Hesselink was being offered one of these rare items by a guy he didn't know didn't sit right with Hindman. She remembered the list of stolen items that Ashton had sent around the previous year and did a little investigating. What she found was that the description that Hesselink had given her (that Spiegelman had given him) matched exactly the paragraph description on the list of missing Columbia items. She called Hesselink back and told him.[43]

The pieces offered by Spiegelman were on the list of items stolen from Columbia and now Hesselink knew it. He asked Hindman to fax him a copy of the list, which she later did; in fact, as the fax was coming through in Hesselink's front office, Spiegelman was sitting in his back office talking to the dealer. It was the afternoon of Monday, June 5th. If the Roman de La Rose description and the faxed list of missing Columbia items weren't yet enough, the very nature of what Spiegelman was offering confirmed Hesselink's suspicions. Claiming that he had gotten this stuff from his father, the range of materials was what Hesselink referred to as bric a brac—so unrelated by date or common theme as to almost surely not have come from a small, personal collection.

Spiegelman's claim that he needed to make some quick cash in order to impress the father of his Japanese fiancé merely sealed the deal. But the demand for cash allowed Hesselink an opportunity to catch the thief. It was 4 p.m. by the time they had settled on price for two of the items so Hesselink said that unless Spiegelman wanted to take a check, they'd have to meet the next day. Spiegelman insisted on cash.[44] So they set it up for twenty-four hours later, in the lobby of the hotel across from the rail station at Utrecht Center: The Holiday Inn.

Spiegelman was to bring two documents to the meet: the Plimpton MS 284 and the Benjamin MS 5. The Plimpton manuscript was the Roman de la

Rose, verses 104–936. The pages of this manuscript were once 2–7 of a more complete work and had belonged to Antoine Moriau. The Benjamin MS 5 was a Book of Hours on parchment from the low countries. It included ten full page miniature portraits of the infancy cycle of Jesus and other portraits of the Passio. Spiegelman had offered them to Hesselink for 70,000 Dutch Guilders (approximately $40,000) but Hesselink had talked him down to 60,000 Guilders in cash.[45] (This was a substantial discount—a little over half of what they could have fetched on the legitimate market.)

That left Hesselink with very little time to get ahold of the proper authorities. The proper authorities, he knew, would not be the Utrecht police. He knew they wouldn't believe him or be very helpful if they did. So he called Jean Ashton. He thought she might have more luck with the authorities in the United States.[46]

Ashton immediately called Catherine Begley, the FBI agent who was in charge of the investigation. A few hours later the FBI in Brussels contacted Columbia; they wanted to get a positive ID on any of the stolen items that Spiegelman might have in his possession before they went forward. [47]

The next morning an FBI agent in Brussels phoned Hesselink to get the story. Hesselink told him the situation and stressed that the FBI might need to be pushy with the Utrecht police in order for anything to get done. By 2 p.m. Hesselink still hadn't heard anything from local law enforcement.

At a little after 2 p.m., less than two hours before the meet time, the Utrecht police phoned and asked if Hesselink could come down to their station and explain the situation. Hesselink immediately drove the seventeen kilometers to town. When he got to the police station he explained the situation to an officer. That officer, after listening politely, explained that it was his day off and promptly handed Hesselink to a different officer. That officer listened politely and then explained to the dealer that an operation of this nature would be handled by the "arrest team." It was their day off, too.

Hesselink was getting agitated; this was just the sort of thing he wanted to avoid by calling the FBI. The meet time with Spiegelman was approaching and it seemed clear that the thief was going to get away not through any cunning or caution but by the inertia of the Utrecht police. Finally, Hesselink convinced the officer of the importance of the situation. The officer rounded up seven more men, all of whom strapped on bullet-proof vests and piled into the back of Hesselink's small van. They told Hesselink to drive around the Utrecht Center until he spotted Spiegelman and then they'd get out and arrest him.

Hesselink knew from the beginning that this was folly. It was like fishing without bait, hoping the fish would swim by and hook itself. Spiegelman wasn't going to wait in the open for Hesselink; Hesselink had to wait in the open for Spiegelman. Still, they drove around the area a few times before Hesselink spoke up. He told the police that he'd drop them off behind the hotel and he'd wait around front. When he brought Spiegelman back to the van to get the "money," the police could arrest him then.

Fortunately for all involved—Hesselink most of all, since he wasn't wearing a vest—Spiegelman was unarmed and not expecting to be pounced on by eight of Utrecht's finest. It was an extraordinarily hot day, to boot, so the square was almost empty.[48] Despite all of the nervousness and handwringing by Hesselink, everything turned out fine. Spiegelman, astoundingly, didn't expect a thing and seemed genuinely surprised when he was surrounded by the police. Just after 4 p.m. in front of the Utrecht Holiday Inn, the first two books of Columbia's missing collection were reacquired by the authorities.

There was not much else of real value in Spiegelman's car, but in case the dealer suddenly changed his mind and wanted to do some other business, Spiegelman had brought several pictures of other items he thought Hesselink might be interested in.[49] Even if he trusted Hesselink, he couldn't have brought everything he had. He had offered some of the manuscripts to other dealers and had an appointment the next day back in Hamburg to unload five items.[50] Fortunately for Spiegelman, from Utrecht back to Hamburg was just a little over three hours drive time.

The Utrecht Regional Police took Spiegelman into custody and seized his car. The pictures in the trunk would go a long way to informing the RBML as to the full extent of the thefts.[51] A year after the discovery of the crime, there were still a few shocks waiting for the staff.

Some of the police got back into Hesselink's van. Some took Spiegelman's car. Spiegelman was loaded into a police vehicle that had showed up so he could be hustled back to the local station house. On the way to the station he made what appeared to be a quick and feeble suicide attempt but may yet have been the first in what would be a long string of incidents designed to irritate and frustrate the authorities. Whatever the nature of the attempt, it was unsuccessful.[52]

Once at the police station he was immediately interviewed. There he admitted that he was not, in fact, William Taylor from the Isle of Guernsey but rather Daniel Kikabidze, born in Tblisi, Georgia, and currently residing in Yonkers, New York.[53] He had the documents in his car to prove it.

As soon as the Spiegelman was taken into custody the FBI investigation machine that lay dormant for several months kicked into high gear. In the span of two days all that was known about Spiegelman was passed along an information triangle that included Brussells, Savannah, and New York. Several hundred sheets of paper—all answering the query "any info available"—were pulled off of fax machines by FBI agents separated by five time zones who wanted to know who this guy with all the documents in the Netherlands actually was.

Spiegelman was trailing several identities including aliases with different spellings of his last name. Had he not been caught with the fake IDs and passports attesting to all his different personages it is likely that much of his record would have escaped him. His fingerprints helped confirm some of his various identities as his own but that searching was helped along because the FBI knew where to look. As it was, he had left quite a trail. The FBI knew, for one thing, that he was a convicted felon. Charged with forgery ten years before he stole the stuff from Columbia, Spiegelman pleaded guilty to several counts and eventually spent less than a year in federal prison. Around the same time—though across the country—he also was arrested for assaulting a federal officer.[54] By Spiegelman's telling it was a very small incident that amounted to nothing. But this small incident would plague him throughout all of his future court dealings and be a recurring point for his attorneys to argue.

In Utrecht in June 1995 and to the authorities in the United States, the assault arrest meant one important thing to his classification as a fugitive: he was to be considered armed and dangerous.[55]

In November 1983, Spiegelman was attempting to cross back into the United States from Mexico. He was south of San Diego and on foot when he was spotted by a line officer—essentially, a federal border patrol agent employed by the Immigration and Naturalization Service. At about noon the officer approached and stopped Spiegelman. For a reason that is not entirely clear but probably related to Spiegelman's general inability to interact nicely with people—he had no reason to resist as he was not found to be carrying any contraband—there was a scuffle. The officer got the worst part of the physical altercation—he had small scratches and cuts and was treated at a local hospital. Spiegelman was unharmed but was quickly arrested, arraigned, and he spent the night in jail.[56]

The federal courts on the border run a little differently than those in the rest of the country. Due to the large volume of federal violations that border areas see, the trial and sentencing process is greatly accelerated. Spiegelman came before a federal magistrate the day after the incident. Charged with ordinary assault as well as assault on a federal officer, he pleaded guilty and was fined and released.[57] At the time the end result seemed like little more than a traffic ticket; fifteen years later the small scuffle would take on a life of its own, occupying a ridiculously large amount of his attorneys' time.

Spiegelman was interviewed by the Dutch authorities, of course, in Dutch. This was not a problem for Spiegelman. It was also not a problem for the FBI's offices in Belgium who could easily send an agent to Utrecht to speak with Spiegelman (in either Dutch or English). But the Dutch Public Prosecutor refused to allow Spiegelman to be interviewed by the Americans in Utrecht or in Brussels.[58]

Ordinarily this wouldn't have been a problem, either; Spiegelman could be held by the Dutch authorities while the Americans mounted enough evidence to try and get him extradited. But the Dutch authorities had made it clear that they were not planning on holding Spiegelman. The Utrecht Regional Police told the FBI that they could release Spiegelman as soon as Friday,

June 16—ten days after his initial capture.[59] If he was released, the FBI knew, there would be no way at all to catch him again. He was completely comfortable in Europe, he appeared to have plenty of money and he still had a stash of valuable documents at his disposal. The legal attaché in Brussels immediately sent out an urgent request to have Spiegelman's Dutch interview translated—this was the only link the Americans were given to Spiegelman while he was being held.[60] The Americans needed to get an extradition proceeding started right away if they wanted to hang on to Spiegelman.

The attaché eventually convinced the Dutch authorities to hold him for a bit longer so that they could get their ducks in a row. By June 21, the FBI had the translation of the statement.[61] With the information to make a more formal claim, the FBI immediately filed a request for provisional arrest and started the process of extradition. Fortunately, the quick work of the attaché paid off. Spiegelman was not released.[62]

While in custody in Utrecht Spiegelman's first and continued impulse was to lie. He initially told the authorities that the books in his possession were purchased legitimately from another man who said that he'd gotten them through inheritance.[63] This was quickly dispelled as the standard excuse of a person caught with rare materials who can't account for their provenance.

Spiegelman's next tactic was to bargain. He'd been in federal prison in the United States before and he would do anything possible to avoid returning there. With that in mind he began negotiating with the Dutch authorities. He told them that he had access to the actual books in the pictures they had found in his car. If they let him go he would give them all of the books. But the Dutch legal system does not allow plea bargaining like the United States.[64] Besides, by offering them access to the books he wasn't really offering them anything at all; none of those books belonged to anyone in the Netherlands.

After the Dutch made this point clear to him and after the United States made it equally clear that they wanted him back, Spiegelman decided he was bargaining with the wrong people. On June 30, Spiegelman's Dutch attorneys, Louwerse & van der Velde Advocaten, contacted the legal attaché in Brussels to make a similar offer: if Spiegelman was let go in Holland and the charges dropped, he would return all of the items he stole.[65] This oral offer was followed up by a letter asking the same:

> Referring to our telephone conversation today I want to present you the following proposition on behalf of my client, Daniel Spiegelman.
>
> My client will arrange for the return of all the missing documents. In return my client wants first of all that you will drop the charges against him and second that you drop the extradition procedure and set [my] client free in Holland.
>
> I would be obliged if you let me know w[h]ether or not this proposition is acceptable. If this proposition is not acceptable for you, I

would like to know which kind of proposition could be acceptable for you.[66]

The Brussels legal attaché requested an immediate response from FBI in New York, which first had to consult with the office of the United States Attorney in New York. Their answer, which came a couple of days later, was "No."

Search warrants were soon obtained for several of Spiegelman's addresses in New York. First of all, his apartment was searched. While this didn't yield any of the Columbia books there was other contraband there that would weigh in his extradition and prosecution. In truth, had his apartment never been searched the process of getting him back to the United States would have been greatly accelerated.

Spiegelman had bought several guns from dealers in Arizona in mid-September 1994. He then packaged and shipped the guns back to New York using Federal Express and UPS. Among the weaponry in his apartment were three 9mm handguns, a .45 caliber handgun, and a Tokarev handgun most closely associated with Eastern Bloc countries. As a convicted felon he was certainly not allowed to possess these firearms. On top of that, he had purchased them using a different identity. Then he had them shipped across state lines.[67] All of that added up to a serious federal weapons charge.

By late August, the FBI had interviewed Spiegelman in the Netherlands. At that time he gave up the fact that he had several safe deposit boxes in Manhattan.[68] This was important for Columbia because it allowed the FBI to execute searches on three storage facilities leased by Spiegelman—using different names, of course—in New York. As the authorities would soon discover, this was a treasure trove. A very great number of the items stolen by Spiegelman were located in these facilities.[69]

Each box was opened in the exact same way, typified by the way it worked on the first one:

Safe deposit box #362 located at the Sterling National Bank on Madison Avenue was registered to Spiegelman as Craig Wesley Hesseltine. He had paid $181.86 to get the thing on June 16, 1994.[70] On August 28, 1995, the FBI got a search warrant—good for ten days—to look in the locker for "books, manuscripts, letter, receipts, notes, ledgers, contracts, computer disks, documents or other records relating to: Benjamin MS2, Western MS29, a manuscript known as a 'psalter,' an illuminated Koran, an Arabic book, patent papers of Thomas Edison, and letters or manuscripts of George Washington." Also, if that wasn't enough, "any other means and instrumentalities constituting evidence of the crimes of interstate or foreign transportation of stolen property."[71]

On August 30th, a representative of the bank, a technician from the Mosler Lock Company, four FBI agents, one NYPD detective, and a bank guard arrived at the vault at 11:15 a.m. At 11:21 they confirmed the box number. Two minutes later they took pictures of it. Three minutes after that the locksmith began opening the safe. It took him a minute. Two minutes later an agent pulled out a box. Two minutes after that (giving time for pictures) they opened the box. At 11:35 they discovered the first Columbia item: "a leather book." Then they found a George Washington letter. Then a John Quincy Adams letter. By 11:55 they had meticulously pulled all of the items from the box. By 12:10 they had completed their inventory. At 1:36, having secured all of the items for removal, they put the box back in the safe.[72]

What they found at that location were several George Washington letters, several John Adams letters, and one signed image of James Monroe. They also found the "psalter" (a book containing Psalms), a Koran, two Illuminated texts and what they described as other "miscellaneous documents." Most disturbingly, they found one empty manila envelope.[73] Still, it was quite a haul for one location.

Two days later at the Bank of New York on Parkway Road they found three more items: another psalter and two Latin manuscripts.[74] Three weeks later at the Sofia Brothers Storage on Amsterdam Avenue they found plenty more: twenty manuscripts on vellum, seven presidential letters, numerous maps that had been cut from the Blaeu atlas, an Arabic document, another psalter and several Thomas Edison documents.[75]

For the first time in more than a year, the staff at the RBML could exhale. There was still a tough row to hoe, but a lot of their materials looked like they were going to be retrieved. Within a year, the Benjamin MS5 and Plimpton MS284 that Spiegelman had attempted to sell to Hesselink would be back in New York as well, along with the Benjamin MS1 that had also been found in his possession.[76]

Spiegelman, on the other hand, would still be in Europe.

The United States and the Netherlands had a fairly standard extradition treaty. Originally negotiated and signed in The Hague in June 1980, the U.S. Senate gave advice and consent for ratification in December 1981. On September 15th of 1983, the treaty went into effect.[77]

> The contracting parties agree to extradite to each other, subject to the provision described in this treaty, persons found in the territory of one of the Contracting Parties who have been charged with an offense, found guilty of committing an offense, or are wanted for the enforcement of a judicially pronounced penalty involving a deprivation of liberty or detention order.[78]

Included in the treaty was a list of extraditable offenses. Generally the offenses simply needed to be punishable by prison time exceeding one year for the country to be willing to extradite.[79] But there was also a list of crimes for which persons could be extradited. Both "burglary or robbery" and "receiving, possessing or transporting anything of value knowing it to have been unlawfully obtained" were specifically enumerated.[80]

Spiegelman really did not want to go back to the United States. He had spent time in federal prison in the 1980s and he did not want to return for another stint there. On the other hand, Dutch prisons are known to be fairly nice institutions, as prisons go. This item, about what new prisoners can expect in Dutch prisons, is from a *British Journal of Criminology* article published a few years before Spiegelman arrived in the Netherlands:

> The conclusion is that in Dutch prisons there is a fairly sophisticated and detailed initiation process which, apart from rare excesses, is generally quite gentle in comparison to the often violent initiation rites reported mainly by US researchers in the prisons they have investigated. One possible explanation for this phenomena is that newcomers [in the Dutch system] are at first placed in a section of the prison especially designated for them. Although they are able to come in contact with the rest of the prison, this section constitutes a protected place in which inmates can become familiar with their new environment. A second, and perhaps more important, explanation can be found in the penitentiary system in the Netherlands. One of the most important instruments in controlling prisons is frequent and direct personal contact between prison officers and prisoners. This makes it possible for prison officers to exercise a service function besides their traditional role of guard. They stand between the prisoners, and in addition to observing and reporting, also help when necessary and prevent conflict when necessary.[81]

It was clear why the slightly built and quiet Spiegelman would much rather stay in the Netherlands. But his early dealings with the Dutch authorities had not gone well. There was no deal to be made with either the Dutch or the Americans involving the swapping of the stolen items for excuse from extradition. So his next step was to ratchet up his defense. He got rid of his attorney at Louwerse & van der Velde and hired the person who was probably the best known Dutch defense attorneys, Abraham Moszkowicz. This attorney—known as the F. Lee Bailey of the Netherlands—simply by his presence made the case high profile.[82] On top of his mere presence, his tactics would quite soon get Spiegelman on the front page of all major Dutch newspapers. By doing so Moszkowicz—famous for dealings with the press—would aid Spiegelman in his quest to stay in the Netherlands. But he would also turn Spiegelman into a man whose name will never be put to rest as complicit in one of the worst terrorist acts in history.

The extradition process is ordinarily quite cumbersome. Criminals who want to fight extradition back to the United States from the Netherlands have a number of appeals in their host country. So part of the tactic by Moszkowicz at first was simply to clog up the process with paperwork and hearings. The idea was to eventually make the effort more than the payoff for the people in the United States. It was during one of these hearings that Cathy Begley caught her first sight of the man. Short, thin, and very soft spoken, he seemed timid and afraid.[83] She could tell why he didn't want to return to an American prison. His attorney, on the other hand, was anything but timid. He was in his environment and was aiming to muck up the extradition for as long as possible.

This was, as predicted, a successful ploy for a period of about five months. But by December 1995 all of the normal courses of contesting extradition had dried up and the Netherlands had decided to grant the U.S. request for extradition back to New York.[84] Spiegelman's worst fears were going to be realized. Unless there was some drastic, eleventh hour development to keep him from being sent back he was looking at a long stretch in another American prison. Fortunately for him, drastic developments were a Moszkowicz specialty.

On the last business day of the year the RBML received a call from an Oklahoma television station. The reporter wanted a comment on the news of a link between Spiegelman and the men who were responsible for the Oklahoma City bombing of the previous April.[85] The reporter said that the day before that call Dutch papers began reporting that Spiegelman had supplied weapons to the men who had carried out the bombing of the Murrah Federal Buliding in Oklahoma City, killing 168 people.[86] At the time that Timothy McVeigh and Terry Nichols were conspiring to blow up that federal building, of course, Spiegelman was already in Europe selling his wares.

Hesselink, who had managed to keep his name out of the coverage of the already-high-profile Spiegelman case during the whole affair, found a CNN and an Oklahoma NBC affiliate, and two other television concerns camped in his front yard on New Year's Day. When he wouldn't talk they interviewed his neighbors. It very quickly became the major news story in the country.[87]

The story had hit the Dutch newspapers because Moszkowicz had claimed that an American embassy official had told him that the FBI was investigating a possible link between Spiegelman and the bombing.[88] From there, the nature of sensationalism took over. The idea that Spiegelman was involved in the bombing may have seemed perfectly plausible to the people in the Netherlands. An American was arrested in their country a couple of months after the bombing, ostensibly on the charges of stealing rare books and manuscripts, but was being hounded by the United States and being sought for extradition on a federal weapons charge. Add to that the image of Spiegelman—identified as "suspected terrorist"—in front of pictures of the familiar smoking ruins of the Murrah Building, and the idea of his involvement was not difficult to believe.[89]

But the idea that it would at all benefit Spiegelman to let something like that slip would seem to be counterintuitive. Effectively taking his rather petty book crime out of the realm of serious but not dire crimes and launching it into the atmosphere of crimes against the United States would not seem at first blush to be a smart move. Unless Spiegelman's only aim was to remain in Holland.

If all Spiegelman and his lawyer cared about was keeping him in the hands of the Dutch authorities the move was actually quite savvy. Abraham Moszkowicz was certainly intimately familiar with the extradition treaty governing his battles to keep Spiegelman in the Netherlands. And he would have known one of the trump cards contained therein. Article Seven, entitled "Capital Punishment and Special Circumstances:"

> When the offense for which extradition is requested is punishable by death under the laws of the Requesting State and the laws of the Requested State do not permit such punishment for that offense, extradition may be refused unless the Requesting State furnished such assurances as the Requested State consider sufficient that the death penalty shall not be imposed, or, if imposed, shall not be executed.[90]

As predicted, soon after the idea that Spiegelman was somehow apart of the Oklahoma City bombing hit the Dutch newspapers, the grant of extradition was revoked. The Dutch were not going to extradite anyone who might face the death penalty.

Here is what the development meant to Spiegelman: At the very least the United States would have to convince the Dutch that he would not be put to death for his complicity in the Oklahoma City bombing. That would take some time. And even if he were to be eventually extradited to the United States it wasn't likely that he would be charged with anything relating to the Oklahoma City bombing since there was no proof that he had had anything at all to do with it.

So he would stay in a Dutch jail a lot longer and then, even if he were sent the United States, he would not be charged with the heinous crime. In the eyes of the public and regular people, pretending to be a financier of the Oklahoma City bombing was a savage thing to do; in the eyes of a lawyer fighting extradition, it had very little downside.

The Department of Justice, of course, immediately attempted to quash the story.

"That story is false," Justice Department spokesman Carl Stern said. "There is absolutely no known connection between Mr. Spiegelman and the Oklahoma City bombing."[91]

But what lent credence to the claim in the Dutch newspapers, at least, was that one of the charges in the extradition papers filed by the Department of Justice was that weapons charge. In that search of Spiegelman's New York apartment the FBI had found those guns.[92] On top of that, a researcher on the McVeigh defense team visited Spiegelman's attorney and claimed that Spiegelman resembled "John Doe No. 2" whose sketch had been circulated by the FBI.[93]

Being a part of the worst act of domestic terrorism against the United States, of course, brought immediate attention to Spiegelman. But while that may have helped him avoid extradition it was still not likely to get him released from captivity in the Netherlands. In fact, it might get him sent to a more secure prison. So shortly after the news made him instantly infamous, he began to deny the story. By the middle of January he was vehemently claiming that he was not involved in the plot.

"I was involved in it as much as I was involved with the assassination of John F. Kennedy," he said on a Dutch current affairs program.[94] His attorney, however, continued to insist that he was a suspect.

This was a delicate balance. All this was doing was wasting time. But he also didn't want the Dutch authorities to treat him as if he had actually been involved with the bombing. Spiegelman suspected the endgame: he was going to be extradited. But later was better than sooner. He thought that if he could delay extradition the time he spent in prison in the Netherlands might count toward his time in the United States. As planned, the attention he got in the press made it certain that he was not going back to the United States any time soon.

The Department of Justice was not amused. A person involved with the Oklahoma City bombing was going to be treated very seriously. A person pretending to be involved with the bombing in order to escape extradition was going to get a special kind of attention. The legal attaché in Belgium became the pivot point for what was turning into a circus. Somehow the Americans had to convince the Dutch that Spiegelman was a serious enough criminal to warrant extradition but not serious enough to deserve capital punishment.

The fact that Spiegelman had made an abortive attempt to escape from his holding jail didn't help matters. He was quickly moved to a high security facility, a development that further fueled the flames of the controversy.[95]

Though he was still in Europe, Spiegelman was indicted in New York on numerous charges. The complaint against him alleged violations of 18 USC § 2314 (Transport of Stolen Goods), 18 USC § 2315 (Sale or Receipt of Stolen Goods), 18 USC § 1542 (False Statement in Application of Passport), and 18 USC § 922 (Transport of Firearms by Felon).[96] Back in New York he would eventually plead guilty to all but the Sale or Receipt charge, though not until more than a year after the charges were brought.

A similar thief today would have another charge added to that list: Theft of Major Artwork. Sandwiched in between Theft of Livestock (18 USC § 667) and Theft in Connection with Healthcare (18 USC § 669) is a statute that makes it a crime to steal an object of cultural heritage from a museum. Such an object is defined as anything at least 100 years old and worth in excess of $5,000 or any object worth at least $100,000. A 'museum' is defined as a permanent institution in the United States that is organized essentially for educational or aesthetic purpose, has a professional staff and owns, utilizes, or cares for tangible objects that are exhibited to the public on a regular schedule.

United States Attorneys who prosecute rare book crimes these days routinely do so under this criminal law that didn't exist when Spiegelman was stealing from Columbia. Still, the laws that did exist would more than do the trick.

It took about a year, but the United States finally convinced the Dutch that Spiegelman was not going to be charged with a capital crime. Aside from the idea leaked to newspapers that Spiegelman resembled "John Doe No. 2" there was not a shred of evidence that tied him to McVeigh or Nichols. Still, the attention on him in the Netherlands never really went away.

When Spiegelman was finally taken from his jail in the Netherlands to the runway from where his plane would take off for the United States he had a highly secure escort. When he was back in the United States he had another extremely well-armed escort to usher him to his cell in Manhattan. Not only had he attempted an escape but he was still thought, in the minds of some, to be involved with the Oklahoma City bombing. The FBI was not going to take any chances.

Dark trucks with police escorts and men in body armor with machine guns; the sort of escort usually reserved for heads of state and criminals of the Hannibal Lecter sort was given to Spiegelman. In the end, he arrived in lower Manhattan with nary a scratch.[97]

If history is any judge, the sort of hardcore protection afforded him would have been far more appropriate for the items he had stolen from Columbia while Spiegelman, on the other hand, could well have been transported in the trunk of a car.

NOTES

1. Jean Ashton, "Picking up the Pieces," in *To Preserve and Protect* (Washington: Library of Congress, 2002), 109–110.
2. Jean Ashton interview with the author, March 4, 2005.
3. FBI Transcription, July 8, 1994.
4. Catherine Begley interview with author, February 10, 2006.
5. FBI Transcription, Ashton interview, July 14, 1994.
6. Rudolph Ellenbogen interview with author, April 7, 2006.
7. FBI Transcription, Ashton interview, July 14, 1994.
8. FBI Transcription, Ellenbogen interview, July 14, 1994.

9. *Picking up the Pieces*, 111–113.

10. Ellenbogen interview.

11. Letter from HP Kraus to RBML, July 15, 1994.

12. Letter (with list of items) from Ashton to FBI, July 29, 1994.

13. Ashton interview.

14. Ellenbogen and Dutschke interviews.

15. William Honan, "Manuscript Mystery," *New York Times*, October 8, 1994, 1.

16. Letters to three bookshops from William Gavin, July 15, 1994.

17. Interpol letter, July 19, 1994.

18. AIRTEL from New Haven SAC to New York ADIC, August 5, 1994.

19. List of Names from RBML, September 6, 1994.

20. Memorandum, Special Agent, September 17, 1994.

21. Fred Schreiber interview with author, April 10, 2006.

22. Unclas Teletype, October 13, 1994.

23. Letter from Columbia to FBI, October 18, 1994.

24. Investigative Information Request Form, FBI, Savannah Information Technology Center, June 9, 1995.

25. Memorandum, Theft of Medieval Manuscripts, February 13, 1995.

26. Synopsis of Investigation, 87B-NY.

27. Ashton interview.

28. Synopsis; numerous surveillance sheets.

29. Memorandum, Consensual Monitoring Overhear Indexing, March 31, 1995; Letter from ADIC with enclosed audio tape, March 24, 1995.

30. Grand Jury Subpoena offered by Katherine Choo, March 3, 1995.

31. Letter to Regional Liaison Officers, 5220:BL788.160, June 9, 1995, 6–10.

32. Ibid., 5.

33. *United States v. Spiegelman*, Plea Hearing, April 17, 1997, 14.

34. Ashton interview.

35. Copy of Spiegelman flyer, sent October 19, 1994.

36. *United States v. Spiegelman*, Complaint, June 14, 1995.

37. Letter from NYPD to Interpol, Request for Assistance, June 1, 1995.

38. Letter from Legat to URP, July 24, 1995, 2.

39. *Picking up the Pieces*, 112–113.

40. Unclas Telex fr. Legat London, June 8, 1995.

41. Letter from ADIC, NY to Bonn Legat, 3540:3613, 3.

42. Sebastian Hesselink interview with author, April 28, 2006.

43. Sandra Hindman interview with author, April 24, 2006.

44. Hesselink interview.

45. Telex from Legat Brussels to Field Offices, June 9, 1995, 3–5. Quoting description of items put out by RBML.

46. Hesselink interview.

47. Spiegelman, Complaint.

48. Hesselink interview.

49. Telex from Legat Brussels to Field Offices, June 6, 1995, 3–5.

50. Telex from Legat Bonn to FBINY, 5300:BON473.164, June 6, 1995, 2.

51. Ibid.

52. Ashton, *Picking up the Pieces*, 114–115.

53. Spiegelman, Complaint.

54. Telex from Legat Brussels to various FBI offices, June 9, 1995.

55. Telex from Legat Brussels to New York, June 21, 1995.

56. INS Report of Assault on Service Employee, November 22, 1983.

57. US Magistrate, Felony Case Information Sheet, November 22, 1983.

58. Letter to New York FBI from Brussels Legat, 5220:BL818.167, June 16, 1995, 3.

59. Ibid., 2.

60. Letter from Legal Attaché to FBIHQ, June 19, 1995.

61. Letter from Legal Attaché to ADIC, NY June 21, 1995.

62. Letter from Legal Attaché to Belgian Gendarmerie, July 24, 1995.

63. Letter from Legat Brussels to Director FBI, June 16, 1995.

64. Ibid.

65. Telex from Brussels to FBIHQ, 5220:Bl860.184, July 3, 1995.

66. Letter from van der Velde to Brussels Legat, June 30, 1995.

67. United States v. Spiegelman, 97 Cr 309, Plea Agreement Hearing, April 17, 1997, 16.

68. Lelystad Interrogation, Waiver of Rights, August 25, 1995.

69. Spiegelman, Complaint, Begley Statement.

70. Receipt, Sterling National Bank, for $181.86.

71. Search Warrant on Written Affadavit, 95 Mag. 1750, August 28, 1995.

72. Search Warrant Log, August 30, 1995.

73. FBI Receipt for Property Received, August 30, 1995.

74. Valuable Evidence inventory, November 27, 1996.

75. Valuable Evidence inventory, October 24, 1995.

76. Valuable Evidence inventory, November 27, 1996.

77. Presidential Proclamation, October 11, 1983.

78. Extradition Treaty Between the United States of America and the Kingdom of the Netherlands, TIAS 10733.

79. Ibid., at Article 2.

80. Ibid., at Appendix, Schedule of Offenses.

81. M. Grapendaal, "The Inmate Subculture in Dutch Prisons," *British Journal of Criminology*, 1990, 30:341–357, 350.

82. Ashton interview; Hesselink interview.

83. Begley interview.

84. Telex from Legat Brussels to New York, December 20, 1995.

85. *Picking up the Pieces*, 115.

86. AP, "Dutch Suspect Reportedly Tied to McVeigh, Nichols," *Buffalo News*, December 30, 1995, A2.

87. Hesselink interview.

88. AP, "Dutch Suspect Reportedly...."

89. *Picking up the Pieces*, 115.

90. Extradition Treaty, Article 7.

91. AP, "Dutch Suspect Reportedly...."

92. Ibid.

93. AP, "Man Held in Netherlands Described as Resembling 'John Doe No. 2'," *Buffalo News*, January 7, 1996, A8.

94. AP, "US Man in Netherlands Denies Role in Bombing," *Buffalo News*, January 12, 1996, A4.

95. *Picking up the Pieces*, 114.

96. *Spiegelman*, Complaint.

97. Begley interview.

CHAPTER 4

No Mere Procedural Formality

Ralph Blakely, by all accounts, was a difficult man to live with. When his wife, Yolanda, decided that she had had enough and finally filed for divorce, he did not take it well. He begged her to reconsider; she wouldn't. So he kidnapped her at knifepoint, duct-taped her into a box in the back of his pickup truck, and drove her from eastern Washington to Montana. He was not overly concerned with anyone seeing him do this and, in fact, the couple's 13-year-old son, Ralphy, witnessed the whole thing. Making things worse, little Ralphy was ordered by his shotgun-wielding dad to follow him in another vehicle. The boy did as ordered until the whole dysfunctional caravan stopped to fuel up at a gas station along the way. Ralphy took this opportunity to escape and phone the police. Blakely and his boxed and bound wife continued on; they made it as far as a friend's house in Montana before the friend turned him in.[1]

It was the type of crime that gets people talking locally, but this was nothing like the sort of thing that would ordinarily make national headlines. No pretty bride or blonde teenager disappeared, no one died, there was no long standoff or a bullet-riddled ending. Blakely was captured and, by most accounts, the whole episode ended up pretty well. A violent and unstable man was off the streets and his wife and child could get back to their lives. But soon enough, for reasons that Blakely could only dimly understand, his name would be on the lips of law professors, judges, and United States Attorneys all over the country. Along with two or three other people, his would be a name around which lights were draped in the federal criminal system—a name that would quite literally halt the sentences of federal criminal convicts in their tracks. He would forever be associated with the dismantling of a federal sentencing system that would not only change the way justice is doled out in the United States, but also add a new wrinkle to the legacy of the Daniel Spiegelman case for librarians.

By the mid-1970s, criminal sentencing in federal courts was a mess. There was widespread disparity between the sentence a person might get for a similar crime from one part of the country to next, from one socioeconomic class to the next, and from one race to the next. But even people who looked at data that told them so could not agree on whether the problem was that some judges were too harsh or that some were too lenient.

Racial bias in sentencing seemed obvious. Convicted black criminals tended to get far lengthier sentences than similarly convicted whites. (The notable exception to this was in murder where whites typically got longer sentences than blacks.)[2]

But there was also more than a racial component to sentencing disparity—there were very significant swings in the sentencing for crimes committed from one area of the country to the other. In Nevada the average liquor law sentence was two months, in northern Alabama it was twenty-five.[3] While different applications of penalties on state crimes could be excused, disparity on federal crimes from place to place is intolerable: federal crimes are supposed to be crimes against the United States and so should be punished similarly regardless of where the person is sentenced. But that was not the case.

Take the example of men avoiding the draft, a crime clearly national in scope. At the same time that more than half of convicted Selective Service violators in Oregon were put on probation, none in Texas were given that light sentence. Where in Oregon not a single of the thirty-three men convicted of dodging the draft was given a sentence of over three years in prison, in southern Mississippi every defendant was convicted and given the maximum of five years. Clearly, the same laws were being treated with different levels of seriousness in different parts of the country.[4]

The more difficult question of whether this was because judges were too harsh in some places or too lenient in others could easily remain unanswered if everyone simply agreed that all federal judges had too much latitude. That is, the answer to the question of whether judges were too harsh or too lenient was: *both*. In truth, "too much latitude" understated the power of federal judges in sentencing. Not only were they given essentially carte blanche in sentencing, they were given little guidance at all beyond their own experience and statutory minimums and maximums. And aside from the occasional reduced sentence by an appeals court, there was nothing keeping in check the sentencing performance of federal judges. They could pretty much sentence how they pleased and know that little could be done about it.

This disparity indicated that judges were not acting as the unbiased, neutral arbiters they were supposed to be. Senator Joe Biden made this unpopular point on the floor of the Senate chamber when discussing the need for sentencing reform: "If we believed what the judges said we would not be here on the floor. If we had confidence in the judges being able to do this thing, there is no reason for us to be here. But the reason we are here with sentencing is we do not like the way the judges are doing it ... We find out judges are not color blind and judges do not leave their baggage at home. Judges do not leave their prejudices at home."[5]

But all blame could not be laid at the feet of the judges; lack of structure in sentencing was as much the fault of Congress as it was the Judiciary. "It is the legislature, not the judiciary, that must bear the blame," wrote Ted Kennedy after he had introduced the bill that would eventually remake federal criminal sentencing.[6] What Kennedy meant, of course, was that Congress would take the blame only in the sense of that word that actually conferred no actual blame at all nor was accompanied with any of the normal consequences of failure. In fact, what Kennedy meant to do was shift not blame but the responsibility so that sentencing was removed from the realm of the judiciary, which couldn't be trusted, and dropped squarely in the lap of Congress which, presumably, could.

Unfortunately for Kennedy—and the federal sentencing structure—no simple solution presented itself. There were plenty of ideas as to how to reform the system but even those remedies that seemed simple proved not to be. Not only would most of the implemented ideas prove quickly unpopular but also surprisingly ineffective.

One of these failed fixes was adopted by a few states and endorsed by the American Bar Association as early as 1968: judicial review of sentences. Under this scheme, sentences given by a single judge were later reviewed by a panel of similarly situated judges. This review panel looked to the reasons given for the sentence and compared it with other, similar cases. The idea was to come up with coherent and practical guidelines formed by the heavy industry of practical experience: numerous jurists looking at the same case (and same types of cases). This, in the end, was supposed to reduce disparity a case at a time as well as set some standard for judges beyond the often extremely punitive minimum and maximum limits. The judicial review system's requirement that sentencing judges set out in print their reasons for the sentence was thought not only to make them more circumspect in their reasoning but also to put the reviewing judges on notice as to why a certain sentence might appear to be radically out of step with the norm and yet still be justified.[7] This natural pause in the sentencing process was thought to allow for second thoughts on sentences that might be either too lenient or too harsh.

In theory, it sounded great. That the judicial review trend barely made a blip on the radar screen of American sentencing after the early 1980s, however, was due to two different yet equally inconvenient facts. First, judges were not excited about the prospect of an already crowded schedule being loaded with new responsibility. Not only on the sentencing end, where judges would spend a lot more time on written justification of their sentence than they had before, knowing that the sentence would be gone over with a fine tooth comb. But also on the review side where the new responsibility of having to consider the sentences of other judges as part of a panel was not only slightly awkward but also very time-consuming. Second, there was little indication early on that judicial review lessened in any significant way the original problem of disparity. Not only did the review of sentences fail to yield any body of principles that could be uniformly applied, but it did not seem to lessen the geographical differences in sentencing: panels in one part of the country were more lenient or more harsh—just as their component sentencing judges were—than in other parts.[8]

Another possible solution lay in the use of "sentencing councils." This theory rested on the idea that sentencing suffered from lack of communication between judges rather than any inherent biases (or, to the extent that biases did exist, that they could be tempered through the inclusion of several judges). The first sentencing council began in Detroit in 1960 and for the next couple of decades numerous jurisdictions experimented with the process. The basic scheme was for judges to memorialize in procedure what had often been done in practice. Chief Judge Joseph Zavatt of the U.S. District Court for Brooklyn put it this way: "All that our system asks of the sentencing judge is that he put his tentative sentence on the line, listen to the expressed opinion of two colleagues, and, not until then, make up his mind as to what the sentence will be."[9]

But there were significant drawbacks to the system. Not only did it, like the judicial review scheme, ask more of judges, but also didn't necessarily fix any of the problems. A particular judge was not bound by the recommendations of his colleagues and so could disregard their advice. And while the system certainly lessened intra-district discrepancy, there was no way to control for disparity of sentence across geography. Ultimately, the interpretation of existing data on the courts employing the councils was that they could do as much harm as good. At least one commentator thought they functioned like loaded guns: "Whether a loaded gun is an instrument that preserves human life through hunting or an instrument that destroys human life through murder greatly depends on whose finger pulls the trigger. Whether a council decreases or increases disparity seems to depend heavily on which council is considering what types of sentencing decision."[10]

But the lack of a clear and easy solution didn't lessen the problem. Sole discretion in the hands of sentencing judges was not working and the expensive proposition of judicial review was a federal nonstarter. At the same time as proponents of a judicial review system and sentencing councils were starting to be heard, a much more vocal and public group of cheerleaders were presenting their plan of sentencing guidelines to a much more receptive and well-heeled audience—an audience that had not only money and voice, but the sort of connections that would tend to magnify both.

The most well known of their converts, Massachusetts Senator Ted Kennedy, was on the cusp of a run for the presidency. Just then, in 1975, he proposed in the Senate a comprehensive overhaul to the federal sentencing system. This legislation, in turn, was due largely to the ideas and efforts of a single Columbia University professor.

In 1972 Marvin Frankel's book *Criminal Sentences* was published. It was a collection of his thoughts on sentencing as formed in the years he spent as a federal judge after having taught for many years at the Columbia law school. Frankel's book was intended to galvanize the opinion of the literate and caring—though not necessarily law-affiliated—American public.[11] While there was not what could be called a groundswell of support for a sentencing guidelines system (or, indeed, much reform at all) after the publication of the book, the ideas eventually seeped into the American consciousness like Marx, not by being much read by a wide range of people, but by becoming the book most often cited by reformers as their own inspiration.

Criminal Sentences was well written, well reasoned, and easy for the lay reader to understand. Better still, it was easy to quote: "[T]he great majority (ranging in some jurisdictions to around 90 percent) of those formally charged with crimes plead guilty. So it is ... tragically incongruous, that we weave the most elaborate procedures to safeguard the rights of those who stand trial, but then treat as a casual anticlimax the perfunctory process of deciding whether, and for how long, the defendant will be locked away."[12]

Frankel thought that what he saw as arbitrary sentences meted out by imperfect judges were not only not fair to individuals but also made a mockery of the constitutional protections so particularly afforded Americans earlier in the criminal process. In his final chapter titled "Proposals for the Lawmakers" he forwarded a number of what he deemed discussion points for people to consider in the coming years so that reasonable people could come to a consensus both on the purposes and mechanisms of punishment.

His first points for discussion were those that dealt with the theory behind punishment. Was it for retribution? Deterrence? Rehabilitation? Though Frankel certainly had his opinion—as does almost every law professor or judge who is given to think about the matter much—there had yet to be anything like a consensus on the theory behind why we punish criminals. (And there still isn't. Every year in Criminal Law classes in law schools nationwide, this discussion is joined but not answered by a group of future lawyers. Like a sprig of garnish, the subject seems to be included in every such book dealing with incarceration or punishment without really adding anything to the final resolution.)

It was Frankel's next discussion point that was far more concrete and, as it turns out, permanent in the discussion of criminal sentencing. Late in this last chapter of the book he suggested—almost timidly, as if he were just writing down thoughts off of the top of his head—a kind of checklist or systematic guideline that would help a judge mechanically weigh the offense for which the criminal had been convicted in combination with other factors. While he stated that this might seem too overly technical, unromantic, or mechanical, he thought a chart that sentencing judges could use to prescribe sentences, that lawyers could inform their clients exist, and that appeals judges could look to in determining the fairness of the sentencing judge could only be helpful. Since judges quite often face sentencing a criminal for violation of a statute that allows for a huge range of prison time—he used the example of armed robbery of a federally insured bank where a convicted person could get anything from probation to twenty-five years in prison—Frankel thought that a grid would lessen not only the disparity in sentencing but also some of the unease that federal judges felt about the process.

An understated point in that last chapter, but one that seemed to be implied, was that the judges themselves were never entirely sure what appropriate sentences were; they were doing a tough and complicated job to the best of their ability. Sentence disparity, so often ascribed to personal prejudice, could then be better explained by ignorance. Either way, a strict guideline would be helpful.

Frankel suggested that one slope of the grid be concerned with the gravity of the particular offense, a system numbered one through five into which all crimes could fit and be given an objective numerical moniker. (In a later incarnation of his suggested grid—the Guideline itself—this five level approach was adopted by what would become the other slope, Criminal History.) So concerned was Frankel with objectivity in the sentencing process, in fact, that he recommended the use of computers as disinterested number crunchers as much as possible. But unlike many of his ideas in this chapter, there is little evidence that the use of computers in sentencing was much considered. Federal judges, it seems, were only willing to give up so much power.

As his last suggestion Frankel proposed a commission—a sin he almost immediately apologized for. Fresh from the 1960s and early 1970s with their commissions to study everything, Frankel was worried that this suggestion might simply be considered another of those meaningless bodies that, after they are named and celebrated and fed, get around to the task of either restating the obvious or doing nothing much at all. So what he hurried to explain was that his proposed commission would actually *do* something. What it would do—what it, in fact, would end up doing—would be to study the problems with sentencing and then create the aforementioned grid that might aid in solving those problems. Occupying that hazy land of administrative law that is quasi-legislative and quasi-judicial, his proposed commission would study sentencing patterns, make recommendations for changing the system, and then, most importantly, design the envisioned grid. This end product would then have the heft of law behind it. At the time a relatively radical suggestion (as Frankel noted, Congress does not give up its legislating power lightly), this proposed commission was to become the most important suggestion in the book, the idea without which the Guidelines would most likely not have come into being.[13]

In the many critiques of the then current criminal sentencing system there had been criticism not only of judges but also of the legislatures, both state and federal. And consistent with the standard remark that people hate Congress but love their Congressman, the criticism of the legislatures was not only similarly virulent to that of the judiciary but also similarly abstract: there ought to be a law.

It was that faith in the power of Congress—and not a little lobbying from academic and intellectual constituents—that first propelled Kennedy to forward Senate Bill 2699, "A Bill to Amend title 18, United States Code, so as to establish certain guidelines for sentencing, establish a United States Commission on Sentencing." The original bill required federal judges to consider four major things when sentencing: (i) the nature and circumstances of the offense and the history and characteristics of the defendant; (ii) the need for the sentence imposed to reflect the seriousness of the offense and the providing of adequate deterrence to criminal conduct; (iii) whether other less restrictive sanctions have been applied to the defendant frequently or recently; (iv) whether any sentencing guidelines were established by the Commission under this Act.[14]

That last item, an idea that had been recommended by Marvin Frankel and was included in that first bill, became what Kennedy said was "finally, most importantly," the establishment of a Commission on Sentencing.[15] It was also the one part of the bill that would survive all the defeats that proponent to an overhaul of sentencing would suffer over the years and be included in the one bill that was eventually signed into law—ten years and two Presidents later—in what came to be known by some as "Mr. Reagan's Bill."[16] This Commission was about the only concrete idea from that original bill that escaped unscathed.

Barely two months after Kennedy had introduced that first bill in the Senate, Congressman Peter Rodino introduced identical legislation in the House.[17] But in a book published shortly after these bills were defeated—and for which Senator Kennedy wrote the foreword—the two bills came in for some criticism. While the spirit of the bills was certainly in keeping with many law professors' desire to see sweeping changes with the federal sentencing arena, there were a few missing elements:

> The Kennedy-Rodino bill omits a number of provisions that we believe are essential. Our basic presumption against incarceration is missing.

The bill fails to define its sentencing goals clearly and lacks specific instruction for sentencing judges, such as our lockstep progression to carry out those objectives. The bill also does not require a statement of reasons for fines and probation; reasons are required only for sentences of imprisonment. While the bill adopts our suggestion for a sentencing commission, it maintains the present indeterminate sentencing structure, including parole and "good time."

The Kennedy-Rodino bill contemplates more limited appellate review of sentences than permitted by our proposal. The defendant has no right to appellate review, but must file a petition for review with the Court of Appeals. The Court of Appeals may refuse to consider the petition. Such a limited system would encourage the appellate courts to review only egregious sentences and not the full range of sentence imposed by trial courts.[18]

But the law professors and activists who were the greatest proponents of the system had made a crucial mistake: they thought that a scheme that was both complicated and expensive, and therefore mirrored much successful legislation, would easily pass through Congress. Kennedy knew differently. He knew that his bill as it was introduced probably had little chance of being signed into law. But a bill that included all that the liberal reformers wanted—without any concessions to conservatives—might not even make it out of committee. A bloated and confusing sweeping change to the criminal sentencing system would quickly be labeled as social science nonsense by most members of Congress, particularly if it contained the words "presumption against incarceration." If there was to be any comprehensive change in federal sentencing, the proposed bills would have to become less, not more, like the ideal that the law professors envisioned. With that in mind, the next attempts—in 1978 and 1980—still failed to move past the earlier criticisms.

In 1981 the Senate changed hands. The Republicans were suddenly in the majority. Kennedy had had success in the Senate with his earlier reform bills but had been rebuffed in the House of Representatives. Now he faced the daunting proposition of having trouble in his own house. By 1982 he had settled on what was to be the most important philosophical change in sentencing reform in terms of making new law: the new commission and guidelines were to evolve from a left-of-center, progressive reform to a right-of-center, tough-on-crime structure. Instead of a Senate Judiciary Committee chaired by Kennedy, the post was now held by Strom Thurmond; it was onto a bill cosponsored by Thurmond and Joe Biden that the sentencing reform measures were attached.

The 1982 bill was called the "Violent Crime and Drug Enforcement Improvements Act of 1982" and was mostly a reflection of the new tough-on-crime stance that followed the election of President Reagan and a new

Republican Senate. Though the bill, and Kennedy's reforms, passed the Senate with only one dissenting vote, it was once again stalled in the House. Representative John Conyers refused to accept what he thought of as the Senate's radical tinkering with the criminal sentencing system in the United States.

It was this strange bedfellows approach to the reform of the system that made the ultimate passage so compelling. On both sides of the aisle came vehement support and loud denunciations of the overhaul of federal sentencing. That the Reagan administration was finally credited with passing the ultimate bill—attached as it was to an omnibus spending act—despite the fact that it contained much of what Ted Kennedy, not a Reagan acolyte, had included ten years earlier, was a perfect synopsis to the whole long episode.[19]

The Act created the United States Sentencing Commission, a body similar to that originally forwarded by Frankel and included in Kennedy's original bill. By 1985, the Commission was up, running and on its way to creating a new system of guidelines for federal judges to use in sentencing. The Commission would work on the design and implementation of these new guidelines from November of 1985 until completion a year and a half later in April of 1987. The Commission had two main objectives for the grid. First, it wanted to get rid of the sentencing disparities that had so plagued criminal sentencing for years. Second, it wanted truth in sentencing—that is, when a person is sentenced to ten years in prison he gets ten years in prison. By November of 1987 the Guidelines fit that bill and were ready to be implemented. Federal judges began using them at the beginning of that month, though not without a little trepidation.

They were—and remained until their demise—the same basic grid pattern envisioned early on. On one side of the grid was the offense, broken down into numerical level based on severity of the crime. On the perpendicular plane is the criminal history background of the convict based on previously committed crimes. The point at which those two traits intersect on the grid would give the sentencing judge a range of months from which he could choose the sentence.

This point on the grid became known as the 'heartland,' the meaty part of the curve where a sentence should fall. The concept of the heartland was a small, informal concession to the sentencing power of the judges. Since the grid allowed for some play within the heartland of, depending on the crime, up to several years time, the judge was given some discretion even if he followed the Guidelines assiduously. For instance, a crime of level 18 and a criminal history category of III allows the judge to sentence anywhere from thirty-three to forty-one months. The high end of that example is almost a 33 percent increase over the low end. For a sentence of less than three years that is a fairly broad piece of latitude.

On top of that, judges had some say in which numerical category of crime the thing would fall in the first place. On top of the standard range for a particular crime—which is identified for each crime in the Guidelines—each crime has "specific offense characteristics" that allow the judge to add to the base level slightly if certain factors were present in the crime.

All of these steps were to add up to a sentence that was both appropriate— in league with what an ordinary sentence for a crime of this nature was before the Guidelines—and standard. On top of all of these steps, the Commission added in another step that allowed sentencing judges to retain at least the veneer of independence in sentencing. These were known as "departures."

The idea behind departures was to allow sentencing judges to fill in those spaces in sentencing that the Commission hadn't thought of. If a crime was committed that didn't fit well within the descriptions allowed for in the Guidelines or if a person acted in a way—either positively or negatively— that wasn't otherwise taken into consideration by the Commission, he could be given a departure.

The Federal Sentencing Guidelines were thought to be a unique combination of both worlds: Rigid for consistency's sake and yet flexible to take into account the myriad stories of American criminals. And like most sweeping changes that have been well thought out and generously financed, the whole thing worked just fine—for a while.

The reason the Guidelines worked so well for a while was mostly because early on federal judges mostly minded their sentencing manners. The Guidelines were a clear and unabashed rebuke of judges' abilities to be impartial and fair in sentencing. Even a cursory look at the system by an outsider would show that it was designed to take the guesswork out of sentencing; or, not to put to fine a point on it, take sentencing out of the hands of judges. While the Guidelines may well have been an attempt at righting what was clearly a ship adrift, they could very easily be seen as simply a power grab. And with all the talk that activist federal judges were making new law not interpreting it, the attempt by Congress to encroach on a role that was squarely in the judiciary couldn't help but seem an overreach.

Some judges' reaction was to rebel against the Guidelines. There was one of two ways to do this. The first was straightforward: publicly criticize the system either in articles, interviews, or opinions. While this had little to no effect—Congress was used to being criticized and would have expected nothing less from federal judges—the second was an exercise of real power. The second had more teeth. Since it is "emphatically the province and duty" of federal courts to say what the law is, they could certainly have a say on a piece of legislation they felt was contrary to the Constitution.

Federal judges, essentially, could find the Guidelines unconstitutional. The nature of the federal circuit court of appeals system is such that, depending upon who rules the law unconstitutional, a law could essentially go unenforced for years while lower courts are waiting for clarification from above (with the *Blakely* episode some years later, this same scenario would be played out). In the case of the Guidelines, it wasn't until 1989 when the Supreme Court—in *Mistretta v. United States*—affirmed the constitutionality of the Commission and the Guidelines that the experiment could begin in earnest.

The final, more passive/aggressive way that judges could show their displeasure for the Guidelines, wouldn't be fully realized until Congress noticed a steady increase in the amount of downward departures given out by federal judges. Fifteen years after the beginning of their use, the Guidelines got some major attention from the legislature. What this attention seemed to show was that judges could work within the bounds of the system set up by the Commission and still subvert the Guidelines all the same. They simply had to use departures, the one small bit of wiggle room in the grid that the Commission had given the courts.

It would be a mistake to think of the Federal Sentencing Guidelines as some sort of appliance into which a bunch of disparate ingredients is fed and out of which a palatable sentence is dispensed. While the fairly mechanical looking façade—and ten year delay—of the Guidelines might suggest that all the kinks were worked out in advance, that was not the truth. The Guidelines were a work in progress; there was at least as much thought about the functioning of the Guidelines after their inception as there was before.

In that way they were like any sort of device—car, weapon, electronic equipment—that is introduced to the public and is occasionally improved as the designers see the flaws and shortcomings highlighted with steady use. But the Guidelines were not supposed to be like a new model car—better than the one before but necessarily in need of some fine tuning. They were supposed to be like Major League Baseball umpires—perfect at the beginning of the season and improving from there. It didn't help that the people who would judge the Guidelines were not only actual judges, but judges whose discretion had been replaced by lines on a page.

Part of the reason that the Guidelines were routinely tinkered with was that a comprehensive sentencing effort of that sort had never been tried on such a scale. Part of it was that the Guidelines were such a radical change from the previous system that it was shocking. And part of it was because, though federal judges had their latitude significantly curbed, they steadily worked their way into having much more of an impact than the Guidelines conceived.

But the Guidelines were unique in American laws for another reason altogether that helps to explain a bit the antagonism that the federal courts might have felt. In the American system it is the job of the federal courts to interpret the laws handed down by Congress. Usually the way this works is Congress passes a law and then someone who objects to that law because it is vague or unconstitutional (or any of a hundred reasons) brings their complaint in the federal court system. A judge or panel of judges makes a ruling and then the law is either upheld or overturned. But in almost all of those cases, the underlying law has no direct effect on the court one way or another; they are merely arbiters who are supposed to be neutral on the law's intent. But with the Guidelines Congress was directly legislating against the powers of the courts—and then the courts were directly sitting in judgment of that legislation.

In that way it would be like a brother not liking the behavior of his sister and making rules limiting her right to go places. But the sister, in turn, gets to interpret those rules as a neutral arbiter. If she really wants to go somewhere, and is given the final say on what her brother's rules mean, she can interpret her right to go to that place into his rules.

By 2003, Congress had had enough. Congress knew that federal judges were slipping the surly bonds of the Guidelines and sentencing with almost unlimited zeal in ways contrary to the specific aims of the Guidelines, and almost entirely in one direction: leniency. While upward departures from the Guidelines held fast at roughly the same, moderate rate throughout the course of the fifteen years, downward departures seemed to be growing annually. Even a cursory look at the numbers bore this out. With the passage of the PROTECT Act in 2003, Congress ordered the Commission to study the intent of downward departures and the justification for them and appropriate amendments to the Guidelines "to ensure that the incidence of downward departures are substantially reduced."[20]

What the report did was to confirm that downward departures—more lenient sentences than the Guidelines called for—had been steadily increasing every year since their implementation. Downward departures in 1991 were used in 5.8 percent of cases; by 2001 they were used in 18.1 percent. Upward departures, on the other, fell steadily, though their numbers were much smaller to begin with and there was little room for them to get much lower: In 1991 they were 1.7 percent and by 2001 they had fallen to 0.6 percent.[21]

Of course, 18.1 percent was simply the national average—throughout the United States the departure rates differed greatly. In 2001 the Eastern District of Kentucky had a downward rate of only 1.4 percent while Arizona in the same year had an eye-popping rate of 62.6 percent. With Arizona, Washington, California, New York, and Massachusetts leading the way in downward departures and the south and Midwestern states comprising the large hinterland of low departure rates between these areas, it was looking like fifteen years after the implementation of the Guidelines to settle geographical disparity, the disparity had crept right back in. Two of the purposes of the Guidelines—to end geographical disparity and truth in sentencing—appeared at the time of the report to be close to failure.[22]

What is most interesting to note is that the departures tracked so well with pre-Guidelines geographical degrees of punishment. That is, judges in most parts of the South and Midwest departed downward no more after a decade of using the Guidelines than they did at the beginning; it was only in those places where lenient sentences had been given before the advent of the Guidelines that the downward departure rate shot up.

While Congress did not take particular note of these geographical differences, there was a desire to know from the Commission what was causing this increase in downward departures. One idea that was forwarded was that one particular case—*United States v. Koon*—had changed the appeals dynamic, giving more power to trial courts. The idea was that if a sentencing judge knew that an appeals court would only strike down his sentence if (i) the government appealed it and, (ii) the appeals court found that there was no reasonable way for the sentencing judge to have come to that conclusion, the sentencing judge was more inclined to rely more heavily on his conscience rather than the grid.[23]

Another thought as to why the rate had increased so dramatically in those states sharing a border with Mexico was that federal immigration violations were a whole different animal from ordinary federal crimes. In border states, government officials in conjunction with the courts had set up what is known as the "fast track" system. Due to the almost overwhelming immigration violation caseload, the courts were forced to take on a sentencing system that only resembles the rest of the country's federal sentencing system in nomenclature. But while this explained the departure rate in Arizona, it did little to show why New York, Massachusetts, and Washington were such prolific downward-departing states.

The fact of increasing departures was not new to the Commission, which had taken periodic steps to curb their use. In 1999, the Commission promulgated a rule that prohibited departures based on a person's postconviction rehabilitative efforts. More pointedly, the Commission clarified a rule on the use of "aberrant behavior" as a reason for departure ("aberrant behavior" being some crime that seemed outside the normal course of a person's normal behavior). Many circuits had been granting a departure on behavior that the Commission considered less than aberrant. So they came up with a definition of such an offense. It had to have been committed without significant planning, be of limited duration and represent a marked deviation from an otherwise law-abiding life.[24]

This was just the sort of specificity that Congress had in mind. And the PROTECT Act compelled the Commission to take more of these sorts of steps to shore up the crumbling walls of the Guidelines. Deemed an Emergency Amendment, these new requirements for departures had a familiar ring to them: one requirement was for the departing judge to state with specificity his reasons for going outside the Guidelines. The new rules also prohibited several reasons for departure, restricted certain existing departures to specific incidents, and limited departures available for certain offenders. In essence, the Commission tried to bring the fear of departure back in judges that had slowly leaked out over fifteen years. This Emergency Amendment became effective on October 27, 2003.

Eight months later, the Supreme Court brought the whole system to a full stop.

Ralph Blakely eventually pleaded guilty to second degree kidnapping involving domestic violence and use of a firearm. The ordinary sentence range for such a crime is between forty-nine and fifty-three months. But the sentencing judge, upon hearing the testimony of the kidnapped woman, departed upward with a sentence of ninety months—thirty-seven months beyond the standard minimum. The Supreme Court struck this sentence down emphasizing that a "statutory maximum" is the "maximum sentence a judge may impose solely on the basis of the facts reflected in the jury verdict or admitted by the defendant."[25] That is, the sentencing judge's discretion does not include adding factors to a sentence based on crimes he thinks the convicted person committed but which weren't proven beyond a reasonable doubt or confessed.

This was big. It severely curtailed the ability of judges to depart upward. It said that a judge, as a part of governmental machinery, could not be trusted with the power reserved by the Framers of the Constitution for the jury. Here is the language of the majority opinion, written by Justice Scalia, but joined by four other justices:

> [The right of a jury trial] is no mere procedural formality, but a fundamental reservation of power in our constitutional structure. Just as suffrage ensures the people's ultimate control in the legislative and executive branches, jury trial is meant to ensure their control in the judiciary . . .
>
> [Blakely's] 90-month sentence exceeded the 53-month standard maximum by almost 70%; the Washington Supreme Court in other cases has upheld exceptional sentences 15 times the standard maximum. Did the court go *too far* in any of these cases? There is no answer that legal analysis can provide. With *too far* as the yardstick, it is always possible to disagree with such judgments and never to refute them.
>
> Whether the Sixth Amendment incorporates this manipulable standard rather than [a] bright-line rule depends on the plausibility of the claim that the Framers would have left definition of the scope of jury power up to judges' intuitive sense of how far is *too far*. We think that claim not plausible at all, because the very reason the Framers put a jury-trial guarantee in the Constitution is that they were unwilling to trust government to mark out the role of the jury.[26]

The opinion was clear: these sentencing guidelines were unconstitutional. A judge could not unilaterally increase the sentence of a convicted felon beyond the statutory maximum by relying on crimes not proven to a jury. Unfortunately, far from clearing up the situation with federal sentencing, the ruling merely muddied the waters. The sentencing guidelines in question in *Blakely* were not those of the federal system, but rather the similar acting criminal sentence scheme in the State of Washington. The Federal Sentencing Guidelines were not directly addressed at all.

In a vacuum, of course, that would be true. But in the real world the Washington guidelines were so similar to the federal Guidelines that both were called into question. If *Blakely* didn't actually mean anything to the federal system it at least put the country on notice as to how at least five justices felt about the matter. Certainly the allusions to the Framers and the right of trial by jury so important to Justice Scalia's opinion also pertained to the federal as well as state system. It was only a matter of time before the federal Guidelines were challenged.

Since the opinion didn't actually reach the federal system, there was no formal change in the way the Guidelines functioned. But since prosecutors, judges, and defense attorneys all suddenly knew something about the way the Court felt, and that sooner or later a similar question involving the actual Guidelines would surface, many people began acting as if the Court's ruling actually did involve the Federal Sentencing Guidelines.

Between June 24, 2004 and January 12, 2005, the federal criminal justice system was in limbo. Some judges continued to act as if *Blakely* had nothing at all to do with them (which, in truth, it didn't), some judges acted just the opposite—that *Blakely* was the specific intent of the Court with respect to the Guidelines—and some judges simply refused to sentence at all until the Court clarified their stance. Two cases—*United States v. Booker* and *United States v. Fanfan*—were heard by the Court in October of 2004 and were supposed to clear up the whole mess.

Still, speculation—as to when the cases would be decided, what they would say, and what it would mean to the system—became a cottage industry. One law professor in particular became the epicenter of the sentencing world after the *Blakely* decision, and the one-stop shop for all things Guidelines.

Douglas Berman was a criminal law professor at the Moritz College of Law at Ohio State, editor of the *Federal Sentencing Reporter* and coauthor of a textbook on sentencing. In the fall of 2003 he started a blog as a way of making himself keep up with the goings on in the sentencing realm and helping his academic peers keep up along with him. Right from the beginning the blog was successful amongst his target audience: academics and some judges and attorneys who worked in the field.

But then came *Blakely*. Almost immediately his site became the place to look for speculation on exactly what the decision meant and links to the opinions of federal judges who had used the decision in their own reasoning. In the middle of July Berman's face was on the front page of the Marketplace section of the Wall Street Journal with the title "Law Professor's Weblog is a Jurists' Must Read." The story mentioned that a week earlier the blog had been cited in testimony before the Senate Judiciary Committee. In October, he made the front page of that section again and was quoted in no fewer than five WSJ stories on the Guidelines by the end of the year.

It was not strange that a law professor was a clearinghouse of information for a single subtopic in a larger legal field; what was strange was that this subtopic was supposed to be governed by laws. And yet it was to Doug Berman (a graduate of Princeton and Harvard, but not Columbia), a private citizen, to whom judges, prosecutors, and other professors often turned for their answers.

In January of 2005 the Court finally cleared the whole thing up and said what many people had predicted: the Guidelines were unconstitutional. That would appear to mean that federal sentencing was right back to the place it was before Frankel and Kennedy came on the scene. But that's only partly true.

In the absence of any other official system, federal judges still rely on the Guidelines in their sentencing. Partly this is due to habit, partly it is due to an absence of another formal system, and partly it is because, despite the Supreme Court's ruling, many judges still consider the Guidelines perfectly constitutional.

On January 4, 2005, a supplement to the textbook Berman authored with three professors, was released. It began this way:

> June 24, 2004, witnessed a revolution in the law of sentencing. The name of the revolution was Blakely v. Washington. Whether that revolution will topple old sentencing regimes, restructure them, or simply change daily life under them remains to be seen.[27]

But all of these developments were in Spiegelman's future. They would have no impact at all on his situation in 1996, when he was finally returned to Manhattan.

When Spiegelman came back to New York in late 1996, he was feeling very good about himself. He wasn't excited about the prospect of going back to prison but he knew that there was a better than average chance of that not happening, considering his time in jail already and the fact that he was being sentenced for a nonviolent crime in the Southern District of New York. In the decade since the Guidelines had come into use, it was the downward type of departure that had consistently gotten the most use and, in 1997, he was to be sentenced right before Congress started taking a closer look.

If Spiegelman had been in Kentucky or Mississippi, where the downward departures rates were notoriously low, he might have been worried. But in New York, the downward departure rate was amongst the very highest; the commission later set up by Congress to study the departure system produced data suggesting that from 31 percent to 40 percent of all sentences in New York got downward departures. Neighboring Connecticut—a future Spiegelman haunt—had similarly generous rates.[28]

In fact, in 1997, when Spiegelman was originally due to be sentenced in the Southern District of New York, the downward departure rate was 34.6 percent or, in raw numbers, 430 of the 1,242 people sentenced in that district received a downward departure on their sentence. Eight hundred and one people were sentenced within the heartland of the Guidelines while only eleven people, comprising less than 1 percent of all those sentenced, were given upward departures.[29] In practical terms, that meant that someone who pleaded guilty to a federal crime could do much worse than to be sentenced in the Southern District of New York. Less than one in every hundred people sentenced there got more jail time than what was recommended by the Guidelines. More than one out of every three, on the other hand, got less time.

This was all good news for Daniel Spiegleman. He had committed a nonviolent crime and had pleaded guilty. Part of the plea agreement was a stipulation that the government would not seek an upward departure. Yet despite the generous sentencing numbers in the Southern District of New York, the favorable plea recommendation from the U.S. Attorneys and the nonviolent nature of his crime, Spiegelman was about to fall within that less than 1 percent. That was due almost entirely to a strange confluence of events punctuated by a librarian who had never heard of the Federal Sentencing Guidelines before Daniel Spiegelman started stealing her books.

NOTES

1. *Blakely v. Washington*, 542 US 296 (2004).
2. Willard Gaylin, *Partial Justice* (New York: Knopf, 1974), 29–33.
3. Ibid., 6–8.
4. Ibid.
5. 130 Cong. Rec. 839, January 30, 1984.
6. Ted Kennedy in foreward to Pierce O'Donnell, Michael J. Churgin, Dennis E. Curtis, *Toward a Just and Effective Sentencing System: Agenda for Legislative Reform* (New York: Praeger, 1977), at viii.
7. Peter A. Ozanne, "Judicial Review: A Case for Sentencing Guidelines and Just Deserts," in *Sentencing Reform: Experiments in Reducing Disparity* (Beverly Hills: Sage, 1982), 177–187.
8. Ibid., 178–181.
9. Charles David Phillips, *Sentencing Councils in the Federal Courts* (Lexington: Lexington Books, 1980), 12–20.
10. Ibid., 99–102.

11. Marvin E. Frankel, *Criminal Sentences: Law Without Order* (New York: Hill and Wang, 1974), at vii.

12. Ibid.

13. Ibid.

14. S. 2699, 94th Cong. 1st sess. November 20, 1975.

15. Cong. Rec. 122, November 20, 1975, S. 20514.

16. Stuart Taylor, "New Crime Act a Vast Change, Officials Assert," *New York Times*, October 15, 1984, A1.

17. H.R. 1165 94th Cong. 1st sess. February 5, 1976.

18. *Toward a Just* at 89.

19. *New Crime Act.*

20. PROTECT Act of 2003, Pub. Law 21, 108th Congress, 1st sess. April 30, 2003, Sec. 401(M).

21. United States Sentencing Commission, Report to Congress, *Downwar Departures from the Federal Sentencing Guidelines*, October 2003, 31.

22. Ibid.

23. Ibid.

24. Ibid.

25. *Blakely*, 296–300.

26. Ibid., 306–308.

27. Douglas Berman, Nora Demleitner, Marc Miller, and Ronald Wright, *Sentencing Law and Policy: 2005 Interim Supplement: The Blakely/Booker Revolution* (New York: Aspen, 2005), 1.

28. United States Sentencing Commission, *1997 Sourcebook of Federal Sentencing Statistics* (Washington: GPO, 1997), 33–35.

29. Ibid., 53.

WITHDRAWN FROM STOCK

CHAPTER 5

The Wrath of Columbia

By April 1997 Spiegelman assumed it was all figured out. He had finally succumbed to extradition and had been sitting in a New York jail waiting for the next stages of the process. He wasn't happy about going to federal prison, of course, but he knew that, with a little luck, his time served in the Netherlands would work in his favor. And with a little more luck his attorney could get him some leniency.

On top of all of that, his time spent waiting for the final disposition of his case was definitely working in his favor. Whatever his final sentence, his time at a holding cell in Manhattan and the Federal Correctional Institution (FCI) in Otisville, New York, was much more appealing than time in a higher-security prison, the place where a man convicted of multiple felonies and with at least one escape attempt (though that was in the Netherlands) was likely to land. About seventy miles away from New York City, FCI, Otisville, is a medium-security facility with a minimum security affiliated "camp."[1] He would spend a lot of time at Otisville.[2]

He had come back from Holland and was arraigned on November 22, 1996. This was the first appearance by his new attorney, Irving Cohen.[3] Four days later a detention hearing was held in which it was determined that Spiegelman was a flight risk and so would be kept in jail while he waited for his sentence.[4] At that same time he asked for a continuance of twenty days before he had to plea. During that time Cohen met with U.S. Attorney Choo to start the process of plea bargaining.

On December 20 Spiegelman and Cohen were back in court, this time to ask for an additional thirty days of continuance. The idea was that the further extension of time would give Spiegelman and Cohen a chance to come to an agreement with Choo. The continuance was granted until January 21.[5]

On January 21 Cohen asked for another continuance. It was granted.[6] On February 20 he asked for another. It was granted.[7] On March 24 he asked for another. It was granted.[8] Finally, on April 3, 1997, he appeared in court to enter his plea. The negotiations with Choo had not gone to Spiegelman's liking, so he entered a plea of not guilty.[9]

Two weeks later Spiegelman was back in court to change his plea to guilty. The parties had finally come to an agreement: Spiegelman would cop to three of the four charges.[10] By then Spiegelman had spent five months in an American jail. Including his time in the Netherlands he had been incarcerated for roughly twenty-two months.

Spiegelman and his attorney had agreed with Choo to a guilty plea. In exchange for the plea, Choo would agree not to seek an upward departure and both parties would agree to a sentencing recommendation. If the judge was amenable to the agreement, that would amount to a sentence of between thirty and thirty-seven months for Spiegelman. There was no reason for either party to anticipate a problem with this scenario, one similar to so many that each had taken part in before.

Part of the deal was that Spiegelman would sit with Choo and Cathy Begley and tell them about how he had committed the crime. He lived up to his end of this bargain, but only grudgingly—and only halfway. Begley got the impression that he wasn't completely forthcoming. He said what he had to say in order to get a lesser sentence but he wasn't being cooperative. He gave off the impression of someone who was holding things in reserve, as if he didn't want to give up all his secrets because they might still benefit him.[11] In short, he was thinking ahead.

But he had at least gone through the motions. So at 9 a.m. on April 17, 1997, Spiegelman sat before his sentencing judge and answered a series of "yes" and "no" questions.[12] These questions were designed to see if Spiegelman both understood his rights—which had been explained to him by his attorney—and understood the ramifications of a guilty plea, which he was about to enter. Judge Lewis Kaplan also explained a little about the sentencing process.

"The sentence in your case is required to be imposed in accordance with the United States Sentencing Guidelines," Judge Kaplan said. "They require that the Court take into account the actual conduct in which you engaged, which may be more extensive than what is charged in the information; consider the victims, if there were any; the role you played in the offense; whether you have engaged in any obstruction of justice; whether you have accepted responsibility for your actions; and criminal history, if you have one."

The judge had been talking in this manner for about ten minutes and elicited nothing but monosyllabic answers from the naturally taciturn Spiegelman. So quiet was the thief, in fact, that several times the judge had to ask him to repeat his answers. This was important, because Spiegelman was admitting guilt on several charges. Among the charges he pleaded guilty to were interstate transportation of stolen goods, interstate transportation of firearms after having been convicted of a felony, and falsely applying for a passport.

"The Guidelines provide for a range of a minimum and maximum number of years of imprisonment and you must be sentenced within that range unless the Court chooses to depart upwards or downwards which the Court elects to do in some circumstances," Judge Kaplan said. "The probation office will prepare a written report setting forth the results of the investigation it will conduct into your background and the offenses to which you are pleading guilty. It is only after it does that investigation that it sets forth its view of the applicable Guideline range. For that and other reasons, it is impossible to say with any certainty right now what your Guideline range will be."[13]

The judge then went on to explain that the plea agreement into which Spiegelman had entered with the U.S. Attorney was not binding on the court and that he had a perfect right to disregard both the agreement and even the sentencing recommendations of the probation office.

"If anyone had tried to predict to you what the Guideline range would be," Judge Kaplan said, "that prediction could be wrong for all the reasons I have alluded to and it is important that you understand that you will not be able to withdraw your guilty plea on the ground that any prediction as to the Guideline range, if you heard one, turns out to be wrong or if the court imposes a sentence beyond the Guideline range."[14]

To everyone sitting in the court that morning, this was boilerplate. The judge was expected to explain to the person in front of him exactly what the ramifications of a guilty plea were. Not only did this prevent the possibility of a defendant later claiming to have been duped—and the consequent small but still existent chance of a sentence overturned on appeal—but it was also only fair to the guilty party who was about to commit, at the very least, his immediate future to the man on the bench in front of him. But in 99 cases out of 100, the upward departure talk was just hot air.

As part of the process of admitting guilt, Spiegelman admitted to the judge what he had done. He said he had stolen and transported the Columbia items, he had gotten a passport in Manhattan using a false name, and he had bought a number of firearms in Arizona and had them shipped back to New York. That part of the half-hour-long hearing took less than three minutes and seemed almost perfunctory. To anyone sitting in the courtroom at that point it seemed like the whole matter of Spiegelman was about to come to a tidy end.

Spiegelman's attorney Cohen was, in fact, so confident that Judge Kaplan was going to lean toward sentencing on the lower end of the Guidelines' possible spectrum that he decided to make a special request.

"Your honor," Cohen said. "May I be heard on sentence date?"

"Yes," Judge Kaplan said. "Go ahead."

"I've spoken to your deputy before and he indicated the normal sentence date would be sometime around the end of July," Cohen said. "Your honor, the stipulated Guideline range, I assume your Honor accepts that, is 30 to 37 months. If, in fact, your Honor does impose the 30 months—and of course we don't know what your Honor would be imposing—my analysis of the time that Mr. Spiegelman has already spent in custody and speaking to the Bureau of Prisons, with respect to the time, it is conceivable if your Honor did sentence him to the 30 months that he would not be released until after he—his time is actually over. The sentence date, in other words, would be past the time that he could conceivably be released. In other words, pursuant to my conversation with the Bureau of Prisons, the earliest possible—"

"How long has he been in custody?" Judge Kaplan said.

"Almost two years now because he was in the Netherlands being held there," Cohen said.

"And that counts?"

"That counts," Cohen said. "In fact, I spoke to Mr. Reams from the Bureau of Prisons and he assured me that he would get credit for the time he was in the Netherlands. Based upon that, the earliest release date, if your Honor sentenced him to 30 months, would be August 14, 1997. Mr. Reams told me it takes about two months after the sentence to calculate the release date."

Judge Kaplan contorted his face in disbelief. Whether it was because of the audacity of Cohen asking for such leniency immediately after his client had just admitted to interstate transport of not only stolen goods but also firearms—all a few years after being sentenced for a different felony—or due to the fact that it took the Bureau of Prisons two months to calculate a release date, is unclear. But Cohen took it as the latter.

"I understand, your Honor. I also made a face as well," Cohen said. "I don't want a situation where in fact if your Honor does sentence him to 30 months he ends up doing more time than your Honor intended. I'm asking your Honor if you could sentence him at the end of July or the—excuse me, the middle of June, just in case that occurs."

Judge Kaplan considered this.

"The only problem is whether I am going to have the presentence report," Judge Kaplan said. "That is the problem."

"I understand that, your Honor," Cohen said. "But I think that can be—probably be expedited and I'll do whatever I can to get an early interview date and speak with Mr. Spiegelman. If they're not ready, they're not ready and we'll have to take that chance."

"I am willing to do whatever I can to expedite the process," Judge Kaplan said. "But you have to recognize that the probation department will do whatever it does and expediting the process might not ultimately be it."

"We can only try," Cohen said. "I'm asking for a date in about the middle of June, your Honor."

The clerk looked at the calendar.

"Wednesday, June 18th," he said. "4:30."

So, contingent upon the expedited processing of the presentence report (PSR) and a low-end sentence by Judge Kaplan, Cohen was confident that Spiegelman would be out of jail by the end of 1997.

But Judge Kaplan had a final thought for Spiegelman.

"You will be interviewed by the probation officer who prepares the report," Judge Kaplan said. "It is, of course, important that you be truthful and accurate with the probation officer. That is in your interest. The report will be important in the decision as to what sentence to impose."

The judge asked Spiegelman if he understood.

"Yes," Spiegelman said. "I do."[15]

But whether he actually understood is another matter. He certainly did not tell the full truth to the probation officer in his interview nor was he very helpful. As he had been at every other opportunity given him, he was withdrawn, duplicitous, and unpleasant. He felt he was in a good position and that the rest of the procedures were simply a few more hoops through which he had to jump. And since being hard to get along with hadn't hindered him at all thus far, he didn't see any point in changing his tune then.

But the justice system had grown tired of Daniel Spiegelman and to prove this it had set down Judge Kaplan in his way. Though the judge didn't know it yet on that April morning, he was about to get to know Spiegelman and his crimes much more intimately. And what he found he didn't like.

Lewis Kaplan graduated from Harvard Law School in 1969 and, after clerking for a federal judge for a year, was a lawyer at a large New York law firm until 1994. In that year he was appointed to the Southern District of New York by President Clinton.[16] Like most federal trial court judges he came to the bench with a good resume and lots of legal experience. So his first major case—later appealed to and affirmed by the 2nd Circuit—in 1996 was high profile but by no means too big for him.

Pulitzer Prize winning author John McPhee had written a book called *The Ransom of Russian Art*, detailing the work of Norton Dodge, a wealthy university professor. Dodge had spent the 1950s through the 1970s traveling the Soviet Union and collecting art. Forced into many clandestine meetings with artists and their couriers over the course of his travels, the case before Kaplan involved the suggestion by McPhee that a man named Ilya Levin may have had something to do with the death of one of Dodge's major art contacts.

Levin's complaint was that this was defamation of his character; essentially, he claimed that McPhee had accused him of cowardice, complicity with the KGB, and involvement in the murder of the artist. He promptly sued both Farrar, Straus, and Giroux, the publisher of the book, and the *New Yorker*, where part of the story had run. Kaplan ultimately concluded that the laws of New York didn't allow liability of McPhee (or his codefendants) in the case.[17]

From that time on his cases weren't out of the pages of major newspapers for very long. Partly that is due to working in the Southern District of New York where a lot of high-profile cases are adjudicated and partly that is due to Kaplan's very sharp mind. As recently as April 2006, the *Wall Street Journal* lauded him in an editorial. Not his final ruling on a case but rather his ruling on single motion in that case. The editorial staff praised not only his legal logic but also his ability to quickly come up with a sharp and correct answer at the spur of the moment.[18] This skill would come in handy again and again during the Spiegelman case.

Kaplan came to the Spiegelman case not only well respected by the press and colleagues but by most of the attorneys who had come before him. One said: "His legal ability is outstanding. He is very smart. He is known for being very creative. If you have an interesting argument he will listen to it. He is one of the best judges in the country."[19] By just about every account Kaplan was a very sharp judge with a great memory; he also made good on-the-spot observations and was able to interact with the attorneys before him as if their banter were scripted.

Most importantly of all, he had an open mind about hazy areas of the law. And that made all the difference.

Susan Galligan knew nothing about rare books. But before attending law school she had clerked for a judge who did sentencing work and so had information of the sort that changed everything. She knew that judges often gave great value to the probation officers' opinions highlighted in their presenting reports.[20] Particularly, any letters or testimonials accompanying the PSR were considered by the judge who, prior to the sentencing, did not usually have a whole lot of contact with the case. If a case hadn't gone to trial, the judge had no real way, aside from the PSR, of knowing much about the parties involved. The great majority of the contact that a defendant would have had with the government would have been with the prosecutor.

Galligan was relatively new to the Columbia legal staff—in fact, she was not even on staff when Spiegelman was stealing their books. She liked New York and knew that there were a lot of benefits to working at an Ivy League school, particularly one on Manhattan. At the point in her career when she began talking to Jean Ashton, she was very much enjoying her job. A rare book theft—a combination of a criminal matter with the interesting subject of antiquities—piqued her interest even more. Ashton, who knew of the tendency of major universities to sweep rare book crimes under the rug, had gotten very little help from Columbia counsel in the years immediately after the thefts. Galligan, who knew of no such policy, was only too happy to help.

But both Galligan and Ashton knew that the role of the Columbia attorneys was quite small. The investigation of the crime had been conducted by the police and the FBI; any criminal prosecution would be done by the United States Attorney's office. So in the absence of a civil suit, Galligan didn't really have any formal role. Still, she could advise Ashton about the process and answer any questions she might have. It was during one of these discussions about the likely sentencing process that Spiegelman might face that the subject of the PSR came up. Spiegelman's probation officer had phoned Ashton to make an appointment during which Spiegelman was to meet with the librarian and explain how he had stolen so much stuff. Also, he was to provide any information he could about the still missing items.

But what Galligan explained to Ashton was that this probation officer would also be putting together the PSR. Any information she could provide that would be helpful might be worth the effort. On top of that, a letter intending to explain to the judge exactly how much damage Spiegelman had caused the RBML might also be a good idea. Most likely the letter would have little impact, but it would, at the very least, be a way for Ashton to express her opinion.

Ashton was only too happy to do it. The librarians at Columbia had been left pretty much in the dark for three years, picking up bits of information here and there from the police and FBI, but never being in the loop. They were always glad to help—as when they almost had a role in the New Jersey sting—but they were almost never called upon. Once it was known that none of them had stolen the books or helped with the effort, their contact with the investigation had dwindled. Ashton jumped at the chance to contribute; she liked the idea of explaining how valuable and singular many of the things Spiegelman stole actually were. In bringing Galligan up to speed, Ashton began to understand that there was little hope of a judge taking the crime seriously if he didn't know the impact of what had been done.

Galligan came to the same conclusion. If it had taken her a little while to learn about the value of the material stolen, it might take the judge the same. She knew that Spiegelman would have a good attorney arguing for leniency and that the U.S. Attorney, somewhat hamstrung by the plea bargain, would probably not push for even the maximum sentence allowed for by the Guidelines. So the only one representing Columbia's stake in the matter would be Ashton and whatever justification she could muster.

And one thing stuck with Galligan above all else. "If you razor out a map from a book," she had learned, "it can't just be glued back."[21] Simply returning many of the pieces—even if they could be found—would not be adequate if those pieces had suffered damage. This was a permanent crime; a crime that was irreversible absent the ability to travel back in time to collect the pieces anew. Spiegelman should face the consequences for such a crime; it might not help much in this case, but it could send a message to other thieves that the destruction of rare material was far different than the destruction of ordinary property—and the federal judiciary took such crimes seriously.

It started as simply as that—a conversation between Galligan and Ashton about the true value of the rare books and manuscripts. But in order for the message to get across—and actually back to Spiegelman—there would have to be a unique confluence of events. A judge who read Ashton's letter and sympathized with her theory, a U.S. Attorney who, acting within the bounds of her agreements, helped the cause where she was able, and a defense attorney not prepared for any of it.

On May 28, Jean Ashton sent a letter to Jineen Forbes, Spiegelman's probation officer who was in charge of creating the PSR. By this time Forbes had already compiled the bulk of the PSR and was planning on sending it to Kaplan. When the letter from Ashton to Forbes came the probation officer had already completed her report. In order to include the information that Ashton had sent Forbes would either have to rewrite the report or simply attach it to end of the PSR she sent to Judge Kaplan. There was nothing wrong with doing the latter so that's what she did.

The opening paragraph of that Ashton letter to Forbes was but a few sentences but it set the ball rolling on what would be an extraordinary turn in Guidelines history:

> The purpose of this letter is to provide both you and Judge Kaplan with additional information that Columbia University believes is relevant in determining the sentence to be imposed on Daniel Spiegelman, who pled guilty on April 17, 1997, to stealing hundreds of rare and valuable manuscripts and documents from Columbia University's Rare Book and Manuscript Library. As the Director of that library, I am fully aware of the devastating effect that this crime has on its victims, which include not only Columbia University, but also the worldwide academic community and future generations of teachers and students.[22]

The letter went on to detail the elements of the crime, showing that Spiegelman was far from a random thief who simply stumbled upon a target of opportunity. Rather, he was a very cagey thief who spent numerous days casing the library before starting his months-long thievery spree. He had been to the library so often, in fact, that some librarians had been able to identify him by photograph as a regular patron.

She noted how he had concealed his thefts by destroying certain books and only taking the most valuable parts. She gave an inventory of the wide range of materials that had been stolen—many of which were still not recovered. In essence, she tried to personalize the crime so that Judge Kaplan might feel about it the same way that the people who worked at RBML and those who relied on its materials felt about it. And she forwarded the most radical idea that rare materials are worth far more than their sum at auction:

> Although the stolen documents had a high financial value and were in demand by collectors throughout the world, there is a far more devastating effect of rare book theft and destruction. The very existence of rare books and manuscripts provided the basis for new discovery and interpretation in almost every area of study, and can continue to do so only for as long as these treasures remain preserved and protected. As Roger Stoddard, curator of rare books in the Harvard College Library, aptly stated with respect to a situation similar to the one presently before the court, "We need all the evidence that we can get to understand history—scarce as it is, and we depend on the continuing accessibility of old books and manuscripts, so we can test the accuracy of new interpretations ... All depends completely on the maintenance and security of library collections: destroy, mutilate, steal, or hide the books and manuscripts and you frustrate the development of knowledge and the free interchange of scholarship and teaching."
>
> Mr. Spiegelman's mutilation of certain documents is a prime example of how the destructive acts of one person can cause a piece of history to be lost to all future generations.[23]

The day after Ashton sent her letter to Forbes, Irving Cohen sent one of his own that also made its way to Judge Kaplan. Where Ashton's letter painted a dim picture of the thief, Cohen had a rather high opinion of his client. He told of how cooperative Spiegelman had been both with authorities and with the Columbia librarians despite that not being part of the plea agreement. And he preemptively brought up a subject that would pop up with surprising regularity in the future—the arrest of Spiegelman for assault against a federal officer in San Diego.

"Since there was never any prosecution and, according to Mr. Spiegelman, he committed no crime," Cohen wrote, the mention of the arrest in the PSR should be excised.[24] Spiegelman didn't want such a charge following him to prison.

Included in the PSR compiled by probation officer Jineen Forbes, as usual, were several factual determinations, including Spiegelman's criminal history. His prior conviction for forgery was noted (as it had been in his original plea) but there was also that 1983 arrest by Border Patrol agents in San Diego. The PSR also ratcheted up the monetary worth of the items stolen by Spiegelman to a level greater than had been in the plea agreement— an amount that would increase his level on the Guidelines by one. And then there were some question as to whether or not he was a citizen.[25]

Cohen, who was still confident after reading the PSR but less upbeat about his client's prospects than he had been during the original hearing, sent a second letter to Judge Kaplan before the sentencing hearing to address the report. Since there was some question as to what Spiegelman's actual citizenship situation was—he had more than one passport proclaiming a false identity—Cohen assured the judge that he was a citizen despite having emigrated from the Soviet Union. Then Cohen got quickly back to the subject of the arrest for assault in San Diego.

"Since no charges were filed," Cohen wrote, "this should be removed from the record. The mere mention of this purported arrest, despite the fact that no charges were ever filed nor any prosecution taken, could affect the Bureau of Prisons in the manner they treat Mr. Spiegelman."[26]

Cohen mentioned a couple of other factual disputes with the PSR, which would be discussed at the sentencing hearing two days later, and again noted how cooperative Spiegelman had been despite, of course, not having been required by the plea agreement to help. Then Cohen got personal:

Mr. Spiegelman's arrest and prosecution has had stressful consequences on his mother. They are very close; she is his only family. This separation, coupled with the abandonment by his wife, is a factor which we hope Your Honor will consider and to which you will be sympathetic. Family means very much to Mr. Spiegelman, but, unfortunately, he has been continuously disappointed. His mother emigrated with him from the Soviet Union when the situation there was still difficult. His mother then remarried but, again, divorced.

Lastly, Mr. Spiegelman has learned a lot in the last several years about his reaction to authority and his heritage. While trying not to be an amateur psychiatrist, it is obvious that Mr. Spiegelman's childhood experience in the Soviet Union, and then his family life were significant factors contributing to his conduct. This is not to justify his actions but simply an attempt at an explanation.[27]

Cohen then noted that while sentencing Spiegelman on the high end of the proposed thirty- to thirty-seven-month range would not be critical to society's need to show its distaste with his criminal acts, the thirty-month minimum would "demonstrate to Mr. Spiegelman that someone in authority is willing to put some faith in him and give him a more positive outlook and spur him to do well on his three years of supervised release."[28]

On the afternoon of Wednesday, June 18, 1997, the crowd that had been in that very courtroom two months earlier started a bit before the scheduled 4:30 p.m. time. This expedited sentencing hearing had been requested by Irving Cohen so that Spiegelman wouldn't have to serve even a day longer in confinement than was to be called for by the anticipated sentence. But the high level of confidence with which Cohen had asked for this earlier-than-usual sentencing hearing had begun to wane, starting almost as soon as he got the PSR. The sentencing range that had been agreed upon between the defense and the government was thirty to thirty-seven months. Cohen had expected to come to court and simply listen to the judge assign the Guideline minimum thirty months to his client. Instead, after reading the PSR, he had come to the conclusion that the judge might sentence in the middle or high end of that range. That would be bad but not awful. It would mean a few more months of jail time but Spiegelman had already jobbed the system somewhat by spending so much time in the Netherlands. A couple more months wasn't the end of the world.

What Cohen didn't know was that he was about to be on the defensive, struggling to ensure that his client get no more than the range *maximum* of thirty-seven months. This was due largely to a small factual dispute—the PSR had estimated the worth of the goods Spiegelman stole as higher than the agreed upon sum in the plea.

"Before we go any further," Judge Kaplan said, to open the proceeding, "let me make clear right at the outset that I am inclined to the view that the offense level computation to which the parties stipulated and which is in the presentence report is erroneous, essentially because I believe that the determination of the amount of loss as being the amount net of the property recovered, as distinguished from being the total amount taken, a difference between $1.8 million and $2.9 million, is incorrect. I believe as a matter of law it's the amount taken without regard to the property recovered."[29]

This was not a departure from the Guidelines. Whereas a departure is time added too or taken from the sentence simply for reasons outside the scope of what the Commission took into consideration, what Judge Kaplan was suggesting was simply that the initial computation (the "offense level") had been wrongly figured. The offense level that both parties had agreed to was based on a loss of $1.3 million in property. Judge Kaplan was claiming, based on what was in the PSR, that the actual loss was much higher.

"Your Honor," Cohen said, "may I quickly respond?"

After saying a few more things, Judge Kaplan let Cohen do just that.

"Well, your Honor," Cohen said, "this case has been going on for quite some time, and the government and I have had lengthy discussions about the eventual disposition of this case. We have come to rely over the last several years—and I am not new at this and neither is Ms. Choo—we have come to rely upon plea agreements which try to eliminate those issues which would normally be the subject of a hearing and other litigation. This is a very complicated matter, obviously. These items, your Honor, are very difficult to ascertain as to their value. Ms. Choo and I came to a final conclusion as to what the reasonable value was of these items, and I believe Ms. Choo is prepared to tell you that she believes ... our view is correct, your Honor.

The evaluation is reasonable and it was agreed to in order to avoid the necessity of protracted litigation to cover all of the issues in the case. It's an extremely difficult situation, your Honor, when you enter into a plea agreement such as this, which we do all the time with the understanding that neither side can ask for a downward departure or upward departure, and then find that what we believe was reasonable under the circumstances is not the final conclusion of the situation."

"I guess if that were the view," Judge Kaplan said, "we could dispense with judges doing the sentencing and just have the defendant and the government negotiate the sentence."

There was a pause, then the judge acquiesced on that point. After fifteen more minutes of discussion in which Choo—who was bound by the plea agreement—supported Cohen's estimation of $1.3 million, the judge decided to stick with the previously agreed upon sum.[30]

"Inasmuch as the government seems to have no problem with the defendant's position as to the amount of the loss," Judge Kaplan said, "and inasmuch as, accepting the figure or figures that are in paragraph 38 of the presentence report, by my analysis ultimately makes only a one level difference in the base offense level calculation, inasmuch as I am considering an upward departure anyway on the ground that the dollar loss figure, no matter what it is, understates the gravity of the offense, I don't see any reason to off and have a *Fatico* hearing in which there is no adverse party."[31]

There is no record of the looks on the faces of either Spiegelman or Cohen when the judge made this seemingly offhanded remark about the upward departure, but a healthy mix of surprise and indignation would have probably been most appropriate. The judge never paused to consider any looks, he simply continued talking as if he had said nothing at all out of the ordinary.

"Are there any other objections to the presentence report?" Judge Kaplan said.

That Cohen was able to quickly recover from such a potential major blow to his cause and immediately continue on, forcing himself to not immediately address the surprising new issue of the upward departure but rather get back into his planned objections to the PSR, showed his skills as a courtroom attorney. Again, up until just before that hearing there seemed to be an outside shot at a *downward* departure. The most normal reaction would have been for him to immediately address—if only to make sure he'd heard the judge right—the talk of upward departure. But instead he went back to the Issue That Wouldn't Go Away.

"Your Honor," Cohen said, "I raised this as well in my letter to you. There appears to be an arrest in San Diego, California, many years ago. There was no prosecution, there was no arrest. Apparently he was stopped at the border and fingerprinted and then released. And so I am concerned not because it raises any offense level in this case, but I am concerned because that notation remains in the presentence report, the Bureau of Prisons must consider that in this way. So I ask that it be removed because it can only prejudice Mr. Spiegelman's type of confinement perhaps, and the conditions under which he is held when there is actually no basis for it here."

"What is the government's position on that?" Judge Kaplan said.

"Your Honor," Choo said, "the government would take no position on that."

"Mr. Cohen," Judge Kaplan said, "I understand your point, but where I come in, when the Border Patrol or whoever stops somebody and fingerprints them, that is an arrest. Certainly, if they had interrogated him and he had made inculpatory statements without giving him a Miranda warning, it would be your position it was an arrest too, right?"

"I am not saying it wasn't an arrest or maybe a term of art," Cohen said. "I am saying that no charges were ever filed against him, no prosecution, so it seems to me that it shouldn't follow him forever to the Bureaus of Prisons. If there was really a charge, if there was any substance to the charge that is contained in there, then he wouldn't have been just summarily released and left to go on his way, and I think that the nature of the charge there that troubles me, because that is something that the Bureau of Prisons might say, well, assaulting an officer or something like that, we better be careful with him some way or another, and that is clearly not the case. That is what I'm concerned about."

"Does the government agree that no charges were brought," Judge Kaplan said.

"Your Honor," Choo said, "we have no dispute with what the Probation Department reports."

"Your Honor," Cohen said, "I brought this matter to the attention of the Probation Department in my letter to them, and the answer we got back was we have no further information which would be more than what they had in the original report."[32]

Cohen then paused to look at something in his files and Judge Kaplan asked Choo about Spiegelman's citizenship. The topic of the arrest in San Diego never came up again in that hearing and Judge Kaplan never made a ruling on it one way or another.

For ten more minutes they discussed whether or not Spiegelman was a citizen, all the time avoiding the gigantic elephant in the room: the upward departure.

Finally, after all the undercard issues had been discussed, the hearing moved toward the main event. On the subject of an upward departure, Judge Kaplan wanted to hear from the attorneys.

"Your Honor," US Attorney Katherine Choo said, "the government is bound by the agreement in not seeking an upward departure, but your Honor obviously has upward discretion, and you are not bound by the parties' agreement."

Prior to that point Choo had been—and acted—hamstrung by the plea agreement. She hadn't betrayed the slightest sense that she was interested in increasing Spiegelman's penalties at all beyond what was agreed to by the parties earlier. Judge Kaplan, as the neutral arbiter, could also not really argue Columbia's side of the issue though the PSR gave him some standing to do so. But Choo, with that comment, had at least left open the door to "assisting" the judge in any deliberations he might have.

"All right," Judge Kaplan said. "Mr. Cohen?"

"May I have a moment with Mr. Spiegelman," Cohen said.

"Let me also make clear, Mr. Cohen," Judge Kaplan said, "that if you would like a continuance in order to address that, I would be happy to accommodate that because you didn't have any before today, but I am not sure what is likely to change in the intervening period, so it's up to you. If you want to go ahead, we will go ahead. If you want a little more time, I will give it to you."

So, despite the fact that this meeting had been expressly asked for by Cohen in order to expedite the sentencing process, the judge was willing to postpone the ultimate sentencing date in order to give Cohen a chance to marshal his defenses.

"I know the case as well as I am ever going to know it, your Honor," Cohen said, "and obviously we are, I guess I used the word dismayed before, and I guess I can use it again, and I am very concerned here. Obviously, we strenuously oppose your Honor upwardly departing in this case. I don't think this is a case that comes—it wasn't contemplated by the Sentencing Commission and sentencing Guidelines. The loss figure certainly doesn't, and there is nothing terribly unusual about the situation."

"Well, there is something unusual," Judge Kaplan said, "and you may as well know what's on my mind so you can address it. This is not a case in which the defendant stole money or fungible commodities in which the loss table necessarily and fairly encompasses the gravity of the crime. The crime in a case involving money or fungible commodities is more or less serious than another crime in direct proportion to the amount of dollars involved, and the loss table does perfectly well in dealing with that. But the loss table can't even begin to approach, even assuming accuracy, as to valuation of materials such as these, which you have made quite clear, and Ms. Choo has made quite clear is extremely hard to achieve. It's the fact that we are dealing here with unique historical and scholarly resources which your client has in part destroyed and in part made disappear, and by doing that he has done something here which is far more serious and hurts not only the victim, Columbia, but hurts the society at large in a way that the theft of money or fungible commodities simply does not hurt the victim or society. Someone who is the victim of a bank robbery can be made whole by the payment of money equal to that which was taken. There is no way that the payment of money can make either Columbia, the scholarly community, or the rest of the world that benefits from the product of the scholarly community whole for the loss that occurred here; and to sentence your client purely on the basis of somebody's estimate of what those manuscripts would have brought at Sotheby's, it seems to me, is to ignore a serious part of the damage he has done. That is what is on my mind, and that it seems to me is what you ought to address."

"Judge," Cohen said, "in making those comments, if I may ask, your Honor, I don't believe I have seen any cases that are similar to this, and perhaps your Honor has. In that case I might need some time to review that, but I haven't seen any cases which have indicated that items such as these are so different that it takes it out of the traditional loss table calculation."

"You know," Judge Kaplan said, "I can't cite you a case either. All I have done is read the Guidelines."

"That is what I have done, too, your Honor," Cohen said, "and I have done some research on it, but I haven't found such a case."

"It does make clear—the Guidelines—5k2.5 says departure is appropriate where the offense cause loss not taken into account within the Guidelines," Judge Kaplan said. "What the Guidelines take into account, they only take into account what the dollar value of the property is, because that is all the loss table speaks to; and so it seems to me an inescapable inference that the Guidelines did not take into account the unique character of the property and the unique importance of the property, and the irreplaceable nature of the property to society at large quite beyond even the academic community and the institution that was victimized."[33]

What Kaplan was talking about was §5, Part K of the Guidelines. That section deals specifically with departures. Both of the attorneys as well as the judge had the Guidelines in front of them so they were able to consult the actual language. §5K2.5 states:

> If the offense caused property damage or loss not taken into account within the guidelines, the court may increase the sentence above the authorized guideline range. The extent of the increase ordinarily should depend on the extent to which the harm was intended or knowingly risked and on the extent to which the harm to property is more serious than other harm caused or risked by the conduct relevant to the offense of conviction.[34]

"I don't know, your Honor," Cohen said, "if I can agree with that. It seems to me that the Guidelines Commission, in deciding what types of property would be the subject of these lawsuits, would necessarily consider property that in some ways is irreplaceable, and in deciding therefore that we can only put a dollar amount on such items to come up with a Guideline figure. It's inconceivable to me that in developing this vast framework, especially in crimes of theft, that the Commission didn't consider the types of items that are subject to be stolen and transported; and by not referring to that specifically it seems to me that they made a decision that we can only evaluate the Guidelines based upon a reasonable dollar figure. I would suggest that this cannot be the first case in which similar items have been stolen and there has been prosecution. I would imagine there would be some cases that would have dealt with this issue, and because—I can't say that I have exhausted everything possible, but it would seem to me that if there were any cases of these types of items which would indicate that the last figure is not a fair way of dealing with it, then we should know that. I just think it seems like something the Commission must have considered in determining how to compute the loss figure even of items such as these."

"I must say I saw nothing in the application notes, either the 2B1.1 or its analog, 2F1.1, that suggests that the Commission did take it into account, first of all," Judge Kaplan said. "Secondly, 5K2.5 speaks of an offense causing damage or loss not taken into account within the Guidelines. Now, certainly, that language would apply to a circumstance where the Guideline that was being applied was for an offense that didn't ordinarily involve a property for an offense that didn't ordinarily involve a property loss, but in the peculiar circumstances of the given case involved a loss of that character, and therefore, in that kind of case, for example, a crime against a person where there was some property loss, you would be ordinarily determining the Guideline without reference to the amount of the loss, so 5K2.5 would apply. On the other hand, it also reads in my view on this situation rather well, and that more or less suggests that if the Commission thought about it at all, they thought that a situation like this was one in which a departure was appropriate, but I have not found a case."

"I haven't either, your Honor," Cohen said.

"Ms. Choo, you were jumping up?" Judge Kaplan said.

"The only thing I'd like to bring to the court's attention which may interest the court in its analysis," Choo said, "is under §2F1.1 in the Guidelines. The application notes, paragraph 10, talks about how an upward departure may be warranted, and again I inform the court I am not seeking one, I am merely bringing this application note to the court's attention."

What the note said was this: "In cases in which the loss determined . . . does not fully capture the harmfulness and seriousness of the conduct, an upward departure may be warranted."

"Thank you," Judge Kaplan said. "I see what you are referring to. Right on the money, right on the money."[35]

It became clear to all concerned that the judge felt he was justified and was prepared to depart upward right at that moment. Cohen conferred with Spiegelman for a few seconds and then decided to ask the judge for some time to prepare against such an action by the court.

"Your honor," Cohen said, "my client is very anxious and very nervous. He wants to get this over with, but deferring to my view as to whether we should postpone the sentence, and it is my view, your Honor, that I would like some more time."

"All right," Judge Kaplan said.

"I don't know whether it's going to change things," Cohen said. "Maybe there is something that any one of us overlooked, perhaps, including myself. He was anxious to get it over with today, big strain on him and his family, his mother in particular. She couldn't even come here today because she was so upset. But if I am going to be the one that makes the decision, I would prefer to ask that it be adjourned."

"How much time do you want?" Judge Kaplan said.

"Your Honor, while I don't think the amount of time that I take will affect anything as far as this eventual sentence, Mr. Spiegelman's ultimate release, I would prefer more time. He is extremely anxious to have this matter resolved, so I will do everything I possibly can to resolve this matter as quickly as possible. I am suggesting July 1 or July 2."

"The sentencing will be adjourned to July 1 at 9 o'clock in the morning," Judge Kaplan said, "and any written submissions are to reach me by June 26. Let me also be sure of one thing, Mr. Cohen. Attached to the presentence report I received a letter from the director of the rare book library at Columbia dated May 18. I want to make sure you and your client have seen it."

"We have not seen it," Cohen said.

So Judge Kaplan asked Choo to provide the defense with a copy of it.[36]

The Butler Library at Columbia University opened its doors in 1934 as South Hall. In 1946 it was renamed Butler Hall in honor of Nicholas Murray Butler, a former president of Columbia who had retired the previous year. The building was in the Italian Renaissance style and had all the then state-of-the-art library furnishings. The stacks were air conditioned, special lighting was made to approximate natural light, and there was, of course, an electric book lift.[37]

On the sixth floor of the Butler Library, and also open to the public, is the Rare Books and Manuscript Library, a space that houses the greatest treasures in Columbia's collection and some of the greatest in the United States. The range of the collection spans back 4,000 years to cylinder seals created in Mesopotamia.[38] The formation of the rare books collection at Columbia can be traced back to a donation made by Stephen Whitney Phoenix in 1881 but the collection can be traced back to the beginning of the University: In 1914 the personal libraries of Columbia's first and third presidents were presented to the University. The shelves housing these collections demonstrate the typical reading material of eighteenth century academics and clergymen and represent the thoughts and ideas present at the very beginnings of the upper Manhattan school. Still, it wasn't until almost fifty years after the original bequest that an actual rare books space was designated to allow for preservation and use.[39]

The materials housed in the collection—starting with the Phoenix bequest—were added in fits and starts. In 1892 the Temple Emanuel in New York donated its library of 2,500 printed and fifty manuscripts of Hebraica, the earliest of which is a tenth century piece of Genesis on vellum. In 1902 the Dewitt Clinton papers were donated. In 1906, the same man who had procured the gift from the Temple Emanuel set out on a buying trip in southern France and returned with an extensive collection of original documents and correspondence dealing with the history of the Jewish communities at Avignon and Carpentras.

The RBML's Joan of Arc collection was formed from the private collection of an alumnus donated in 1920. A Columbia professor later in the 1920s donated his collection of the history of accounting, a body that spanned five centuries including the earliest Italian editions on the subject and a ledger kept by Josiah Winslow in Plymouth Colony from 1696 to 1759. The first major effort of Columbia to acquire rare materials by selective acquisition began shortly after this. Already, it was a very impressive collection—and the school was looking to build on its momentum.

In 1929 an internationally known collection on the history of economics came on the market. Beating out bids by the Soviet Union and Japan, the University purchased the collection of thirty-five thousand volumes that covered the subject from the fifteenth century to the then present day. The library included all of the reports and works published by Alexander Hamilton as Secretary of the Treasury as well as all of Karl Marx's major writings culled from the bookshops of London, Paris, and Berlin. The purchase of this economics library significantly broadened the collecting parameters of the RBML and marked the beginning of the rapid growth of various specialized sources for the library.

The year 1930 was big for rare books at Columbia. In July of that year a funded Rare Books Department was officially established providing the library with the means for collecting, preserving, and making available to scholars and students the use of rare and unique materials housed at the university. That same summer Columbia accepted a donation of a comprehensive collection of materials, comprising one thousand books, pamphlets, and manuscripts documenting the development of standard measures in all countries, beginning with those published in the fifteenth century. Shortly thereafter, Professor David Eugene Smith, a math teacher and passionate collector of the subject, revealed his intentions to leave his entire collection to the University. When he gave it in 1931 it contained the early printed books of Euclid and Newton (including volumes from Newton's own library), medieval and Renaissance documents and letters of mathematicians, astronomical and calculating instruments, manuscript and printed Rubaiyats and a manuscript of Omar Khayyam's treatise on algebra and trigonometry from the thirteenth century.

This special Rare Books Department—particularly given the breadth of topics covered—put Columbia at the forefront of American universities in the offering of specialized, comprehensive research sources to its students and scholars. The established department also allowed benefactors the luxury of donating their materials knowing that they would be going to a worthwhile and professional cause. In the post-WWII era, its growing reputation as a world class repository—as well as an IRS concession that allowed tax deductions at retail value for some donated rare materials—led to many more donations along with the steady acquisitions, which continued apace.

By 1975 the Rare Book Department had become the current Rare Book and Manuscript Library (it had also been called the Department of Special Collections for a time). It housed one of the most impressive and comprehensive rare book collections in the United States including a great many items that continued to come from alumni, professors, and others tied to the university who donated their personal libraries to the cause. For instance, in 1976 the files of the American literary firm Curtis Brown Ltd. were received. They contained letters and documents of W.H. Auden, Elizabeth Bowen, Joyce Cary, John Cheever, Lawrence Durrell, Ian Fleming, Robert Graves, Christopher Isherwood, Ogden Nash, Mary Renault, and C.P. Snow. A treasure trove of previously unavailable materials from a laundry list of the twentieth century's great writers, simply reinforced Columbia's claim as one of the great scholars' destinations for rare material.

In 1984 the new Rare Book and Manuscript Library facility located on the sixth floor of the Butler Library was dedicated. At that point, roughly fifteen thousand rare books per year were being consulted by scholars. Among the written materials these scholars could hope to find was a letter from 1629 from Johannes Kepler in which he discusses his financial problems in attempting to print his tables of planetary configurations; a 1773 letter from Samuel Johnson to the then president of Columbia College; the drawing of a compass by Galileo from the late sixteenth century; from 1477 one of the eleven extant copies of the first printed edition of Marco Polo's account of his voyage; the diary of John Jay kept in Paris during the second half of 1782 while he was negotiating peace to end the American Revolution; a handwritten and signed copy of *Annabel Lee*, Edgar Allan Poe's final poem.[40] Any one of these items would be the centerpiece of a good collection; at Columbia they were collectively a testament to the scholarly value of a destination that was greater than the sum of its parts.

The monetary value of the collection is almost inestimable. But the less tangible value, the worth of the place to the scholarly community and to a better understanding of the shared history of civilization is, quite literally, priceless.

The question that Judge Kaplan of the United States District Court for the Southern District of New York had before him in the summer of 1997 was how to value a thin slice of priceless.

The same basic group of interested parties that had been in the courtroom at the previous two hearings was there again on July 30, 1997—the defense had asked for and been granted another extension. But the audience had one addition: Jean Ashton. Since writing the letter that made such a difference, she had been informed that the judge was thinking of departing upward. She and Susan Galligan, in consultation with Katherine Choo, had decided that it might be best for her to be around in case of any immediate need for the clarification of the Columbia perspective. Ashton didn't have anything planned but if something came up she would be more than happy to answer questions.[41]

Judge Kaplan, it was clear, was ready to sentence Spiegelman. The docketing responsibilities of a federal judge were significant enough that extraordinary hearings—accompanied as they were by a flurry of briefs and motions—quickly became a burden. But if Cohen thought that an aversion to more work would compel Judge Kaplan to side with the defendant, he was wrong. In fact, to the extent that the judge seemed increasingly irritated during that late July hearing, it was Cohen who appeared to be the source and to most fully bear the brunt.

The idea of the hearing was for Cohen to offer objections—beyond those he'd already offered—to Judge Kaplan and his inclination to depart upward. He'd specifically asked for a month and a half of extra time after the original sentencing hearing in order to be prepared to challenge the judge. But within the first minute of the latest hearing it did not appear to be going well for the defense. Cohen and the judge had a disagreement, the resolution of which critically aided Ashton's cause.

"Your Honor," Cohen said, "first I would say that it is our view, according to the plea agreement, that this is strictly a matter between the defendant and your Honor. The government has indicated that they would not ask for an upward departure, and it is our view that any comments on their part to argue against our position that an upward departure is not appropriate here would be taking a position on that."

In other words, Cohen wanted Choo to be kept silent.

"Let me just note," Judge Kaplan said in reply, "that I believe the government has a perfect right, as does a defendant who agrees not to seek a departure, to furnish information to the Court in response to an indication by the court that it is considering a course of action, without breaching an agreement not to seek a departure."

"Very well, your Honor," Cohen said.[42]

His objection to a matter perfectly within the realm of Judge Kaplan's discretion had been rebuffed so he decided to proceed on to the jurisprudence and see if he had any more luck on that front.

Not only did Cohen not think an upward departure was warranted but he also planned to demonstrate that fact by arguing that no case that anyone could find seemed to use a similar justification for departure. The most similar case was that of Stephen Blumberg in Iowa and in that case there had been no departure.

Cohen spent a quarter of an hour explaining that no loss was exactly like another but that it would be impossible to value each and every item stolen on its own scale, separate and apart from what the Commission had done. In particular, Cohen noted that in the Blumberg case, which dealt with much the same type of item, the judge did not depart. Not only did this, for Cohen, constitute federal case law precedent, but it also offered a philosophical guide to the Court: stolen rare books were to be treated exactly like any other stolen item.

"Mr. Blumberg stole . . . 20,000 books for at least apparently about a 10 to 15 year period," Cohen said, "from over 300 different institutions, from 45 states, including Canada and the District of Columbia. It was an ongoing, long-term process. Despite all of that, your Honor, despite what seems to be a case that makes Mr. Spiegelman's actions here much, much less significant, the judge did not upwardly depart."

"It seems to me, your Honor," Cohen continued, "there is no question that the *Blumberg* case squarely and clearly holds that an upward departure on these grounds is not appropriate and in fact is not permissible under the Guidelines. That is the authority that we have found. There doesn't appear to be any other cases that are even similarly on point. But this case, the *Blumberg* case, certainly was and is. *Blumberg* was, as I found out doing some work in this area, a very well known situation. In spite of all that the government's strenuous arguments in that case, the judge did not upwardly depart on the exact same basis that your Honor has suggested he might be interested in doing so."[43]

Cohen must have really believed it because he spent a great deal of time reiterating the same point. But both Katherine Choo and Judge Kaplan had also read the *Blumberg* opinion and a careful reading of it seemed to refute Cohen's main point.

Choo rose after Cohen was done.

"Your Honor," Choo said, "as Mr. Cohen has noted, we in the plea agreement have agreed not to seek an upward departure and, as your Honor is aware, we are not seeking one. I do merely wish to state the following. We have not found any cases on point where there has been an upward departure for art cases such as this. I have read the sentencing transcript form the Blumberg case and would just point the Court to page 162."

"And 163?" Judge Kaplan said.

"Yes, 163," Choo said, "and also page 166, where it does appear that the Court had facts before it that distinguished it from this one. Namely, the properties taken, the books and manuscripts and what not, were not that rare. The Court found that it did not have tremendous historical research value. The Court did say, and I quote, 'I think it is entirely possible that I could depart upward if I wanted to. I think it's borderline.' It appears to me that the Court is making a discretionary decision not to upwardly depart, does not determine that it has no discretion to do so, but finds on the circumstances of that case that it should not. To the extent your Honor finds that the circumstances here were not considered by the Sentencing Commission, your Honor obviously has the authority to make that decision."[44]

So the *Blumberg* Court had not ruled out the possibility of an upward departure—in fact, the sentencing judge had explicitly considered it—but it had ultimately concluded that it wasn't warranted in that case. One reason, according to Choo, was that many of the items stolen by Blumberg weren't of the singularly rare kind stolen by Spiegelman.

"Your Honor," Cohen said, "May I briefly comment?"

"Yes," Judge Kaplan said. But, judging by past history, commenting *briefly* was not Cohen's long suit.

"Firstly, as to Ms. Choo's last comment," Cohen said, "the Guidelines Commission did consider these types of items, your Honor. There is no question about it. Section 668 is directly related to these types of items. So they must have considered it in determining what guideline level to use and whether any enhancements were appropriate. Now, beyond that, your Honor, as far as what the judge said in this case—"

Cohen stopped. "You're looking puzzled at me," he said to the judge.

"I am," Judge Kaplan said. "You got up to respond to the government and your response does not relate to anything the government said. You simply repeated something that you have spent quite a lot of time already saying."

"I think her last comment was that the Guidelines Commission has not considered these types of things," Cohen said.

"Whatever, Mr. Cohen," Judge Kaplan said. "The point is we are getting into the realm of repetition."[45]

If there is one criticism of Judge Kaplan's censure at this point it might be that it didn't come soon enough. In each courtroom occasion before Kaplan, Cohen repeated himself quite often and on a range of different subjects. Part of that is simply trial tactics; but there is a fine line between repetition in order to emphasize a point and repetition because there is nothing else to say.

After Judge Kaplan's comment, Cohen quickly segued from the *Blumberg* case into other dangerous territory.

"As far as her reference to the transcript," Cohen said, "the judge had before him a motion made by the government on the exact same grounds. If Ms. Choo is making a factual argument, then we are going to need a hearing, because she had referred to a particular section here where the judge says that they were of limited historical research value. It is interesting that an expert was called who apparently was at least equivocal on that particular point in that case. Your Honor, as I indicated in my letter, I have attempted to obtain the services of several experts who are all well recognized in the field, they are at the top of their field."

Judge Kaplan sat there without saying anything for a few beats.

"Mr Cohen," he said, "let's not play games here. All right? I am beginning to feel that you are, frankly, toying with the Court."

"No, I am not, your Honor."

"Let me be clear as to why I think that so if I am mistaken about that, you will be able to point that out and I will be very happy to say I am mistaken," Judge Kaplan said. "I made clear on the record on June 18th that I was prepared to sentence then and there and I explained in detail precisely the basis for the proposed departure, namely, the possibility that there was a noneconomic loss here that was not reflected in the dollar valuation and therefore not adequately reflected in the sentencing guidelines. You initially urged me to go ahead and do that right then and there. Then I repeatedly prodded you, because you seemed surprised by my suggestion, to take more time to brief the issue, and you did. It was your right. Indeed, I urged you to do it. Now, at no time during that hearing in June did you for a minute suggest that there was a need to take evidence. Over a month later you submitted a letter of eight single-spaced pages in which there is no suggestion of any need to take evidence or of the existence of any issue of fact, unless I missed it."

"Let me refer your Honor to page 7," Cohen said, leafing through some papers in front of him, "starting on the third line, where I indicate, "I have spoken to several leading experts in this field who are in agreement with this and that the dollar value of such items as contained in the loss table is already reflective of the unusual nature of the items, that is, their significance for historical and cultural reasons. For professional reasons, including having worked with Columbia University in the past, each was unavailable to make a submission to this Court. However, one well-known expert, Jeff Dalton [not his real name], is prepared to do so and testify, if necessary, if deemed a 'court expert.' I submit, however, that a testimony hearing is not necessary, as the law is clear."

He closed the letter and continued talking: "If your Honor is making a decision, and the government pointed it out here, that maybe there is a factual question as to whether these particular items have historical value, which I have indicated we dispute, as far as research purposes are concerned, then it is my view, your Honor, that that is a factual dispute that would require a hearing," Cohen said. "I have spoken to Mr. Dalton, your Honor. He is well known in this field. I have spoken to several other people. Most of them had relationships with Columbia, because Columbia and two or three other institutions in this area have collections in this area. They all somehow or other have some connection to Columbia or feel uncomfortable."

"I don't know if I am going to be on senior status by the time you conclude this afternoon, Mr. Cohen, I have to tell you that," Judge Kaplan said. "Would you get to the point?" [46]

"The point is, your Honor," Cohen said, "what I am saying is that in my letter, as I got into the subject matter after our last proceeding, it seemed clear to me that these items, especially according to *Blumberg*, were not of this nature. I have spoken to experts who said—Mr. Dalton has told me, you Honor, that he believes that our position is correct, but he was reluctant to come in and testify on behalf of a defendant because he is well known in the field. But if he is made a court expert, he is prepared to come to court and testify. I would like the opportunity if your Honor is still considering upwardly departing."

"Mr. Cohen," Judge Kaplan said, "I am very much considering upwardly departing. If you say that you have witnesses you want to present, I would like to know now the names of the witnesses and what they would testify to if they appear so I can make a determination as to whether it is relevant and material to listen to them."

"Very well, your Honor," Cohen said. "Your Honor, this had been a very difficult area to research and also to get into—"

"With all due respect, Mr. Cohen," Judge Kaplan said, "you said that a minute ago. You said that at length in your letter. What I would like now is names and testimony summaries."

"Your Honor," Cohen said, "I spoke with Jeff Dalton, who is an expert. He is in the state of New Jersey, your Honor. I told him the issue. He indicated he felt that there was no basis for the conclusion that the items had such historical value for research and intellectual purposes, and that in his view the loss was already reflective of the significance. He told me that based upon his professional standing in this city, in this area, that if he was made a court expert, he would come in, but he was reluctant to come in as an expert just for the defendant because, he said, his name is known in these circles. That was the best I could do. I approached several experts, most of whom had connections to Columbia."[47]

There is no record of exactly who those "experts" were but they were most likely people like Mr. Dalton. That is, not experts at all but rather dealers in rare books. To the extent that they have expertise in valuation of books it would be exclusively in the value of books at market. In truth, Dalton, a rare book dealer in New Jersey, would have a vested interest in explaining that the *only* value of a book is what it can get on the open market. While that is a perfectly valid opinion for a rare book dealer to have, it hardly qualifies as expert in the pursuit of refuting Ashton's claims.

"Mr. Cohen," Judge Kaplan said, "it is a very simple matter. I am not the prosecution and this is not a civil law country in which it is the job of the court to bring the witnesses in. My question to you is, do you have any witnesses who are prepared to come to court at your request under subpoena by you, and if so, what is it they propose to testify to?"

"Your Honor," Cohen said, "Mr. Dalton said he would come to court but not as an expert for the defendant, only if he were made a court expert. We would be willing to pay him and he would be willing to come to court if he was deemed a court expert by your Honor."

"That is not in the cards, Mr. Cohen," Judge Kaplan said. "He is either prepared to testify or he isn't."

"Prepared to testify as an expert on behalf of the defendant?" Cohen said.

"That is correct," Judge Kaplan said.

"If we hired him to come in, he has no problem with being paid by us," Cohen said, "but he wants to be designated a court expert. That is the best I could do, judge."

"I don't give merit badges," Judge Kaplan said.

"I'm sorry," Cohen said. "I have checked with other experts, all associated with Columbia, who agreed with the position we took. But they have relations with Columbia. After I contacted one in another state, he got back to me and said he couldn't do it."

"So is the long and the short of this that you have no witnesses?" Judge Kaplan said. But it was a rhetorical question so Cohen answered by asking for more time to get witnesses. And he explained, again, exactly what they'd be testifying to.

Katherine Choo rose when Cohen then mentioned that two of the "experts" he'd spoken with had worked for Columbia. She had a Columbia employee of her own who didn't refuse to testify.

"Your Honor," Choo said. "I want to bring one other fact to the Court's attention. Ms. Ashton from Columbia University is in the courtroom today. I just wanted the Court to be aware of that and Mr. Cohen to be aware of that."

"Are you telling me that Ms. Ashton would like to be heard if I take evidence?" Judge Kaplan said.

"Your Honor," Choo said, "what I'm really saying is to the extent your Honor had any questions of Ms. Ashton, she is here and prepared to answer any questions you have."

The judge then confirmed with Ashton that she was indeed willing to testify that day. So the government, which had requested neither the departure nor any of the hearings, was prepared to go forward. The defense, on the other hand, had asked for an expedited sentencing process. When they didn't like what that sentence was going to be, they had asked for another date. Then they asked for a further extension on that date. Then, in late July, when the judge was ready to sentence Spiegelman for a third time, they were again unprepared.

"It is my view that the manner in which the defense has approached this sentencing is a tremendous imposition on the court," Judge Kaplan said. He then spoke for ten minutes about how the case had unfolded before him thus far and how it would unfold from then on. He rejected the idea that the *Blumberg* case had any influence on his decision. And then he got to his conclusion.

"[I] am being asked to adjourn the sentencing yet again so that the defense can continue the hunt that they should have undertaken the minute the notion of an upward departure was put on the table and which to some extent Mr. Cohen's letter indicates they clearly did undertake," Judge Kaplan said. "I believe I have every right to go ahead and sentence this afternoon, and I am sorely tempted to do so. Nevertheless, I am going to give the defense one last chance. I will adjourn the sentencing today. I will consider thereafter whether to conduct a *Fatico* hearing, and if so, on what issue. The defense is to submit to me, not later than August 15th, a statement listing by name each witness it proposes to call at a *Fatico* hearing and a summary of the witnesses proposed testimony and the basis for the witnesses giving that testimony."[48]

The judge said that after he'd seen all of what the defense would present at that proposed hearing he would decide whether it was needed or whether it would be another waste of time and they could, instead, just get to the actual sentencing. He also, when again prodded by Cohen, said that he would not make Dalton a "court expert." If he was to testify he would simply have to do so on behalf of the defense.

With that it appeared that the hearing was about to end for lack of forward motion. It was 5:30 p.m. on a Wednesday and there didn't seem to be much getting resolved. But Cohen had another subject to revisit at this late point in the day when Judge Kaplan's irritation was already so close to the surface.

"Your Honor," Cohen said, "there is one factual issue unrelated to this issue that I noticed when I got the minutes had not been resolved, and that was the issue of that alleged assault that is mentioned, in California."

"That is not a factual issue," Judge Kaplan said. "I have already dealt with that."

"I didn't see your ruling on that," Cohen said. "Maybe I missed it."

"I think what I made clear on the point you raised, counsel, at the last session is that the arrest is on the record," Judge Kaplan said. "The fact that there is no disposition does not persuade me to delete it from the presentence report. There is no dispute that the arrest occurred. You just don't think it belongs there because there was no prosecution, right?"

"I think my argument was that 'arrest' is a term of art," Cohen said. "Some people could say that a stop by police and you are in custody for a while and then you are released is not an arrest, and some people say it is an arrest. It seems to me that if he was stopped at the border, which apparently is what it was, and then no charges were brought and he was then released, that should no be considered an arrest and it should be removed."

"Here we go again, Mr. Cohen," Judge Kaplan said. "Are you now going to tell me that you prepared to put on evidence that there was not an arrest within the accepted legal definition of that term? That is to say, that he was never taken into custody, he was never deprived of his freedom to leave?"

"No," Cohen said. "I said the exact opposite. I said he was taken into custody and after a while he was free to leave and no criminal charges were brought."

"Right," Judge Kaplan said. "That is the end of it."

"Then we are strictly looking at the interpretation of those facts, which we agree to, and that it should not be in the report because he was not charged with any crime, and it would be unfair for that to be in the report because it will travel with him wherever he goes."

"It is staying in the report unless you can point to me some law that says that an accurate statement in a presentence report that someone has been arrested must be deleted or is improperly included if the arrest did not result in a conviction or prosecution."

"It is a little before that," Cohen said. "It is not like he was arrested, brought to court, and then charges were dismissed. He was brought into custody, questioned apparently, it was a border situation, and then let go. So I don't think that that qualifies as something that should be classified as an arrest and be in the report. It is not just that charges were dismissed. No charges were even brought."

Though no one in the courtroom—except Spiegelman—knew it, that was far from the truth. Charges had certainly been brought and Spiegelman had not simply been captured and released. He was arrested around noon on November 22 and did not come before the magistrate until the next day.

"Mr. Cohen," Judge Kaplan said, "you are irrepressible but not persuasive."

"I'm sorry, judge," Cohen said.

"I respect your advocacy on behalf of your client," Judge Kaplan said. "But what you are telling me is that you don't like the fact that probation accurately stated something that happened. That is what you are telling me."

"I don't like the characterization of it is what it is," Cohen said. "If they say he was stopped at the border and released, no charges were filed, I would prefer that."

"As I said to you last time," Judge Kaplan said, "if they stopped him and from all physical and psychological standpoints nothing happened to your client on that occasion other than what you acknowledge happened, but moments after he was in custody, to use a word you adopted, after the authorities gave no Miranda warnings, he said, 'By the way, I shot my mother,' if you are prepared to tell me that you are seriously arguing that there would have been no arrest and that that was a noncustodial statement and was admissible against him, maybe we would have something to talk about, although I have some problems with it. Quite honestly, it was an arrest for that purpose, wasn't it?"

"I don't know what purpose your Honor is saying," Cohen said. "People get stopped at the border all the time and then get released."

"What you are really doing is quarreling about a word," Judge Kaplan said, "and the word obviously is accurately used, and you would be the first to say so if the consequence of so characterizing it was suppressing a confession. Here the consequence is different but the facts are the same."

"Yes," Cohen said. "The term 'custody' is a legal term of art. I understand that."

"Right," Judge Kaplan said.

"No question about that," Cohen said. "I just think it is unfair that this is going to follow him. If they just said what the fact was, that is one thing. But they have characterized that, and that is the problem that I have. I just don't think it is—"

"They characterized it by using a term of art which we all agree was an appropriate use of the term of art," Judge Kaplan said.

"Somebody is going to read it later and say, 'oh, he was arrested, he probably beat the case' or something like that," Cohen said.

"How many people are walking around with disorderly conduct convictions for sitting-in in lunch counters at Selma, Alabama?" Judge Kaplan said. "It can be misunderstood, there is no question. It is not fair, no question."

"This is assault on an officer," Cohen said. "That is why I have a problem with it. It is not just sitting at a luncheon counter."

Judge Kaplan sat there without speaking. He had come to the end of a long procedure.

"I don't think there is anything else to be gained by further hearing that issue," Judge Kaplan said. "Anything else?"

"No, your Honor," Cohen said.

"Thank you," Judge Kaplan said, and adjourned the court.[49] There was still not a sentence and nothing had really been decided at the hearing.

On August 12 the judge got a letter from New York attorney H. Elliot Wales indicating that Spiegelman had retained him as cocounsel for Cohen.[50] On August 14 Wales sent a second letter to Judge Kaplan officially requesting the *Fatico* hearing.[51] On September 3, Spiegelman himself sent a letter to Judge Kaplan stating that he was no longer retaining Irving Cohen; the following day Cohen followed up with a letter of his own confirming the termination.[52]

The first major act of H. Elliot Wales' tenure as Spiegelman's new attorney was to send a letter to Judge Kaplan asking for another hearing. It also contained a great deal of text espousing his opinions on the case. This Wales letter claimed that the earlier letter sent to Judge Kaplan by Jean Ashton was not only not sufficient evidentiary basis on which to depart upward but was written by "a librarian, and *not* a scholar in a discipline which encompasses the relevant documents and manuscripts." Further, Wales questioned her "competence to assess the research value of her broad-based collection."[53] He wanted a chance to cross-examine her on the stand.

Of course, it is possible to be both a librarian *and* scholar, and Ashton certainly fit that description. She got her B.A. from Michigan, her M.A. from Harvard and her Ph.D., in American Literature, from Columbia. Fifteen years after getting her doctorate she went back to school to get her MLS. In 1984 she began working in the field of rare books at the New York Historical

Society; she was there for nine years before coming to Columbia.[54] She was certainly qualified to speak on the research value of her collection.

The other parts of the Wales letter indicated that the loss, while regrettable, was not devastating like Ashton suggested and did not warrant the "severe punishment" that was "sought by Columbia University, as victim." "Obviously, the victim has a deep personal interest in revenge and vindication which may color their view of events."[55] He knew so much about the case and Columbia's deep personal interest in revenge, presumably, from following the case in the newspapers; he had only officially been Spiegelman's attorney for a few days when he sent the letter.

Wales went on to note that much of what was stolen was of limited scholarly value, anyway. He claimed that to "the extent that the presidential letters and Edison papers have *any* scholarly value, reference to them already appears in existing scholarship." Which he quickly followed with the claim that in "no significant way do the medieval and Arabic (Oriental) manuscripts differ from other available medieval and Arabic (Oriental) manuscripts in any way that would aid scholarship."[56]

Also, there "are other available editions of the Nuremberg Chronicles—in fact, Columbia has two others." And the "two incunabula, while old (15th century printed book), have little scholarly value. If age alone conferred scholarly value on a printed book, then five hundred years from now we could expect all of the millions of books (trash and near trash) published since 1945 to automatically have scholarly value." This argument about the future worth of present-day printed trash would be made again.

Judge Kaplan would months later write of such Wales comments—shortly before pointing out a specific factual error in one of Wales' claims—that "the problem with these broad assertions, however, is that the competent and persuasive evidence is all to the contrary."[57] This was a charitable assessment of Wales' comments on the value of the stolen items and Ashton knew it. But it would be her burden to prove that what the defense attorney had claimed was utter nonsense. And she couldn't do it alone.

She knew that what Wales had written was not only factually wrong but also easily refuted. And if it was actual experts that the Spiegelman team wanted giving actual scholarly opinions, she knew the right people to ask. She talked with eight scholars from around the country who would be willing to testify and, in advance, give written evidence of their future testimony. This was exactly the sort of thing that Judge Kaplan had required before making a decision on the *Fatico* hearing; the defense, of course, had not yet compiled such a list. Ashton gave her list to Choo who then informed Judge Kaplan that these people were prepared to testify at the hearing.[58]

So at the end of September 1997, a flurry of a very different kind of letter than the ones that had been coming from the defense team was heading Judge Kaplan's way. He was about to hear the full scholarly side of the story.

And the sentencing of Spiegelman was about to become contentious.

> I once discovered an unpublished letter by Jean-Paul Marat, the fa-
> mous leader of the extreme Left during the French Revolution. Any
> letter by Marat is important, if only as a collector's item. But this one
> was written from Paris before the Revolution at a time when Marat's
> biographers thought he was serving a prison term for theft in England.
> When I looked into the matter, I discovered that a large literature ex-
> isted around the question of whether the first proto-socialist populist
> actually practiced what he preached—namely, that property is theft.
> In fact, Marat preached nothing of the kind; and although he was a
> radical, he never was a thief. By itself, with some exegesis added, the
> document disproved a whole line of socialist hagiography.[59]

So wrote Princeton Professor Robert Darnton to Judge Kaplan on the
value of even a single letter to the greater academic community.

Jean Ashton's lone letter had had the effect of opening Judge Kaplan's
mind as to the true value of rare books, now she wanted the help of other
scholars to make the point more fully and slam the door shut on any attempts
by Spiegelman to refute that truth. She knew that Spiegelman was preparing
for a pitched battle and that his new attorney had been hired expressly to
rid Judge Kaplan of the notions that her letter had introduced to him. She
also had heard Cohen talking about *his* expert—a rare book dealer. With
that in mind she contacted several true scholars in their respective fields. She
wouldn't mind taking the stand to represent the rare books community, but
she would like to have a little bit of backup.

Ashton asked these various scholars to write letters explaining what they
saw as the value of rare books and materials to the judge. None of the
letters were scripted by Ashton or anyone at Columbia; each person was
simply asked to give his or her impression of the value of the materials in
the RBML to their field in particular or the culture at large. Between the end
of September and the middle of October, nine such letters made their way
to Judge Kaplan's chambers.

Of all the missives written for the purpose of explaining the nonmonetary
value of rare books, letters, and manuscripts, Darnton's most ably refuted
what was—and continued to be—Spiegelman's defense: that a few missing
rare books or mundane letters weren't that big of a deal in the grand scheme
of things. Professor Darnton was able, with examples, to make the case
that Spiegelman's thefts could not at all be accurately measured in monetary
terms; that one single missing piece could be catastrophic to the academic
community, could, in fact, destroy a line of history before it began.

But beyond that, Professor Darnton explained that even those items of
which there were copies had a value that could not be ascertained merely by
looking at their content:

A second point may be far more difficult for non-specialists to grasp: printed documents are essential for reconstructing the history of literature, even though they may be readily available in reprints. We have only sketchy knowledge of crucial passages in Anthony and Cleopatra, which contain some of Shakespeare's most beautiful poetry, because no manuscript survives and the printed versions were botched in the first editions. To reconstruct the text, analytical bibliographers have devised a complex set of arguments that depend on close study of the very rare folio and quarto editions. They count chipped type, discover the pecularities of "Compositor C," and investigate patterns of signatures and running heads—esoteric business, but fundamental if you care about Shakespeare's poetry. Without the editions preserved in rare book collections, this work would be impossible; and if one page of one edition is razored out, the entire analysis would have to be abandoned.[60]

Again, the theme of Spiegelman having taken a razor to certain books made a deep impression. Professor Darnton continued with another example:

Roger Chartier, one of the best book historians in France, has examined different editions of classic works as they became adopted for a mass audience in the so-called "Biblioteheque bleue" or chapbooks of early modern Europe. The texts remained basically the same, but their meaning shifted while their format changed. From magisterial folio volumes or elegant octavos, meant for reflection and delectation among the elite, they took the form of little paperbacks meant to be read aloud or passed around among groups of semi-literate laborers. Their paper was crude, their type worn, their illustrations, when they had any, cobbled together from old woodcuts that often had little relations to the story. Sentences were shortened, paragraphs cut into bit-size units, narrative sliced into self-sustaining episodes. The physical work corresponded to the implicit readers and the readings envisioned by the publishers—that is, an experience that eliminated the analysis of character and complexities of plot in order to convey quick, striking episodes, rather as comic books do today. In short, the variations of the editions, in all their physicality, opened the way to an understanding of the nature of the audience and even of the experience of reading itself.[61]

It happens that Judge Kaplan would have a chance to contrast these passages—and what was written by the other scholars—with a letter specifically written in response to them by H. Elliot Wales. Wales was an old hand at trial work in New York and was hired for his experience. But experience

in the courtroom could not make up for him being as behind on the case as
he was in January 1998. He, too, was sent copies of the letters and, in an
attempt to refute them, he continued to send letters of his own to the judge.
The Spiegelman case in the winter of 1997–1998, then, boiled down to a
battle of letters between the competing sides, each trying to win over Judge
Kaplan's opinion.

The first of the response letters of Wales to Judge Kaplan tried to immediately counter the scholars' letters he'd received. But the hurried nature
of Wales' first letter to the judge couldn't have made a good impression.
Whereas Darnton's letter was well thought out and seemed backed up by
specific knowledge, much of what Wales wrote seemed dashed-off, igno-
rant, and oddly condescending to both judge and scholar. Here is one of the
defense attorney's passages:

> Of course, we are all saddened by the loss caused by the Spiegelman
> theft.
>
> In that regard, we need not quarrel with the thrust of the Columbia
> letters that in their research today, some scholars work with duplicates
> and photocopies in addition to originals. However, in our calculus, we
> need not equate "original" with "rare." While "original" limits each
> document number to one, "rare" conveys a value apart from its "orig-
> inal" quality. A letter from Oliver Wendell Holmes may indeed be
> "rare," one from Elliot Wales may be just one of many. The Elliot
> Wales' letter may have some significance for the moment. The argu-
> ment of a scholar 500 years from now that the Elliot Wales' letter is
> priceless and unique to scholarship, and its loss irreparable to scholar-
> ship, falls on deaf ears (especially to this writer). As such, we cannot
> have a per se approach—not every aged document deposited in a uni-
> versity library ipso facto has a value beyond measurement, so that its
> loss has a real and genuine impact upon meaningful scholarship.[62]

This section is almost incomprehensible. The first substantive sentence
("In that regard...") makes no sense. What Wales suggests as the thrust of
the "Columbia letters" (a term he uses for a very specific purpose despite
the fact that the bulk of the letters came from non-Columbia scholars) was
neither a theme nor even discussed at length. The idea that some scholars sometimes work with photocopies or duplicates—a fact that is beyond
debate—was never the subject either supported or denied in the letters.

Beyond that sentence there is nothing there that even attempts to refute
what Professor Darnton wrote. There are scare quotes around "rare" in
order to let the judge know, presumably, that much of what Spiegelman
stole is not genuinely rare but only so in the estimation of the scholars. Then
there is the strange digression about the value of a Wales letter 500 years
hence; this mirrors his earlier statement in the August letter about the value of

printed material in 500 years. The argument makes no point at all aside from the odd conclusion that his own letter would be of no value in 500 years. If Judge Kaplan's ultimate rulings are any indication, Wales estimation of the value of his own letter was perfectly right, he simply overestimated the passage of time by exactly 500 years.

Other scholars' letters furthered the Columbia cause. George Saliba, a professor of Arabic and Islamic studies at the National Humanities Center and Columbia, wrote about the negligible value of copies as compared to the originals, as well:

> As you may well know, the type of ink used to produce such manuscripts, the kind of paper, and the kind of starching used to glaze the paper, as well as the kind of binding, the color of leather dies and the like are all clues that a modern scholar could use in order to determine the kind of technologies that were used in producing such manuscripts at the time when they were produced. For history of technology, none of these issues is a trivial issue, especially when we know that none of those clues would be readily apparent in a photograph. Only a detailed study of the condition of the actual manuscript can yield such information. Similarly, the type of writing, especially in the case of Arabic script where we still do not have a well defined field of paleography, and whether the hand-written manuscripts were first lined by dull stylus or were produced by free hand would not appear in a photograph and the information they would give a paleographist would be lost forever. Think also of the unrecoverable loss of information regarding the type of paints that were used to produce the miniature painting that adorn some of those manuscripts that are also of interest to historians of art and historians of technology alike. In most instances, only a chemical analysis of the paint itself would determine the age, the school of painters, the region where it was produced, and at times the date of the actual production of the paint.[63]

Wales' response to this line of argument was particularly feeble. Concerning the loss of a letter written by George Washington:

> It is not a work of art, like a Rembrandt. It is merely a letter—a message—and the color of the ink or the thickness of the paper does not add to the message.[64]

In response to a series of scholars who claim the opposite of him, his only response was to restate his opinion. But beyond that he even admitted that some things—works of art, for instance—are worth keeping in the original form. This is a curious admission since there is little question that much of what Spiegelman stole *was* art. It was displayed simply for its artistic merit and the thief took many items—certainly the maps—simply for their value as works of art. So Wales would allow that a reprint of a *Descent from the Cross* is nothing compared with the original while a reprint of Western MS 29 is just as good. That augured poorly for the defense.

Consuelo Dutschke, the person who had discovered the crime in the first place, and whose collection had been most ravaged by Spiegelman, also contributed a letter.[65] Roger E. Stoddard, the curator of rare books at Harvard, wrote a letter in which he reminded the judge that scholars from around the world try to secure travel grants with the express purpose of coming to Columbia to do research using their rare books.[66] David Scott Kastan, a professor of English and comparative literature at Columbia, wrote that part of the tragedy of the theft was that it left in its wake a necessary limiting of access to even those things that *weren't* stolen: "The atmosphere of trust that enables genuine scholars to consult rare and valuable materials has been violated."[67]

Simon Schama, the noted author, echoed many of the same sentiments and added that not only were the thefts a loss for scholars but also for students:

> I should like to stress that the stolen and harmed objects are not only important for the scholarly historian. They are crucial teaching tools. I have used the materials in the Columbia Rare Book library any number of times for undergraduate seminars and can confirm that the imagination of the students is kindled by making contact with original works in ways that never happens when they merely see them as reproductions. They respond not just to the content, but everything about the work that conveys the texture of the past—typography or calligraphy; engravings and lithographs; autograph signatures; and even (or especially) wills and contracts which seem to yield up, almost inadvertently, the daily fabric of a distant culture. In a world of short-shelf-life values and disposable memories, such treasures are absolutely priceless—they are what connects our ancestry with our posterity. No one has the right to break that chain of memory.[68]

William Joyce, a rare books librarian at Princeton sent a letter to Judge Kaplan. So did UCLA professor and chair of the ALA's rare book and manuscript section, Susan M. Allen. Nancy Cline, from Harvard, wrote that aside from the monetary value of the materials taken from the Columbia, "The climate of fear and suspicion, the disruption of work, and the effect on the staff morale is incalculable."

Elliot Wales, of course, thought differently. And he had plenty more to say. But aside from his lack of expertise, he had a direct interest in seeing the value of the Columbia items denigrated. That was in contrast with the scholars, who had no real interest in whether Spiegelman spent one or ten years in jail, but did have a host of expert opinions as to the true value of the materials that he took. A combination of a dismissive attitude and poor reasoning didn't impress Judge Kaplan, a man Wales knew was inclined to take seriously the claims of the Columbia librarian's claims.[69]

With respect to the scholars, and the letters as a whole, Wales had this to say:

> Obviously I admire them and respect them and am moved by their passion and commitment. I would not dare to deny that true scholars place value upon original documents and manuscripts, and have done so for decades and for centuries. As such in the Western World we have considerable number of great institutions—universities, public and private libraries, museums, churches, synagogues—who have accumulated a vast amount of "rare books and manuscripts" (a generic term), of which Columbia is but one. Jean Ashton told us that Columbia has over 500,000 books and 28 million manuscript items in its rare book and manuscript collections. Multiply that huge number by the considerable number of great depositories of rare books and manuscripts in the western world, and we now realize that we are dealing with astronomical numbers of books and manuscripts which have been characterized as "rare" by our scholars and librarians.
>
> With that context, Spiegelman's theft appears like but a single star in the vast terrain of the Milky Way, discernable only to an MIT astronomer, with a Hubbell telescope.[70]

This first part appears to be Wales' attempt at making the thefts seem like not such a big deal after all, a familiar refrain. It also signifies the major difference in representation between Spiegelman attorney Cohen and Wales. Cohen was a holding-pattern attorney; a competent lawyer who was there to nursemaid his client through what all parties thought was a fait accompli. But Wales was the attorney to call when things started heading south. He was aggressive and refused to be put on the defensive, a position from which Cohen had been fighting since the middle of 1997. Wales was not going to let someone else frame the argument; he certainly was not going to be bested by a librarian.

His quotes around "rare" again were designed as a wink and a nod to the judge to let him know that the term is really just bandied about by librarians without any real meaning. Sure they're rare, he was saying, but so is almost anything if you look at it with a broad enough lens: "I note that there is a uniqueness to everybody and everything that has ever lived or existed," he later wrote.[71]

Cohen had mentioned the possibility of further proceedings in the hopes that the judge or the government would simply lose their will to continue the upward departure talk out of sheer attrition. But Wales actually wanted to get into court; he actually wanted to cross-examine those who had written the letters. He was an attorney who liked being in court—it was where he did his best work. And he knew the Southern District of New York quite well; not only had he practiced there numerous times, but his son was at the time a United States Attorney there.

But none of that mattered to the judge. He was used to seeing terrific lawyers argue in front of him. He was a federal judge in New York City—he could expect little else. He had taken seriously Jean Ashton's claims about the value of books and the continued efforts of the scholars to drive home that point had convinced him all the more. Professor Darnton's letter made clear that a single written letter—able to narrow a man to a certain time, place, or practical application of a philosophy—was enough to make immediately obsolete volumes of written work. Spiegelman's thefts, therefore, had the potential to devastate whole fields of learning. It was not the sort of thing that should be dismissed lightly.

Yet Wales continued to paddle upstream:

> In our own legal system (which has a rich history and rich scholarship), we respect and utilize duplicate copes of great treatises (Blackstone, Williston, Pound). Photocopies of significant documents and manuscripts do not cease to be valuable to scholars simply because a particular original document has been lost or displaced.[72]

But that depends on the scholar. Certainly Blackstone is important for what he wrote and there are scholars dedicated to researching exactly that. But just as many are concerned with the way the treatises were published and distributed, not to mention the marginalia in many early Blackstone copies. A combination of what was published, how it was disseminated, and what people thought of it can all be discerned from looking at an early Blackstone owned by a practicing attorney in Philadelphia; almost none of that can be learned from a reproduction.

But broad factual statements were not Wales' forte in the Spiegelman proceedings. On several occasions in the coming months Judge Kaplan would point out misstatements by Wales (that, in truth, seemed to be made more from spur-of-the-moment bluster than actual duplicity). But the pressure of the trial court environment could not excuse the errors that riddled his written work. In the letter sent to Jineen Forbes the day after the one sent to Judge Kaplan on January 19th, Wales excoriates George Saliba for such "exaggeration that it renders his statement meaningless."[73] But in the very next sentence Wales claims that Islamic societies flourished for centuries, starting in the sixth century. George Saliba, had he had the chance, might have pointed out to Wales that the word "flourished" in that context would be a bit of an exaggeration as well since Islam wasn't founded until the seventh century.

The most interesting thing about this last Wales letter to Judge Kaplan, though, is the last couple of paragraphs. He first requests what is known as a *Fatico* hearing, "to resolve the contested issue of the impact of the loss to scholarship." And then, after questioning the wisdom of the continued proceedings, this:

> If finality can be achieved at this time, I have been authorized to consent to modification of the plea agreement to the extent of an increase of one level—be it increase in value (from $1,300,000 to $2,400,00) or upward departure (from offense level 18 to level 19). Such an increase would permit the high end of the sentencing range to be increased from 37 months to 41 months.[74]

This was a major concession by the defense. Not only was this the precise ground that Cohen had gained as a victory in July, it came close on the heels of Wales' earlier admission that with works of art, at least, it is important to have the original. Taken together it was an indication that Spiegelman was warming up to the idea that forces had marshaled against him.

Wales' letter had the feel of a phoned in effort and perhaps that was because he was rapidly trying to get up to speed on the case or simply that he knew he would be in court in a couple of months doing the equivalent of a cross-examination on the letter writers. It was possible he was saving his best arguments for that hearing. But that hearing, like just about everything else since Spiegelman had gotten back to the United States, had the feel right from the beginning of bad news.

In March 1971 a couple of truckloads of fur pelts were hijacked after leaving New York's Kennedy airport. Salvatore Montello, a man who ad-mitted to being closely affiliated with a Colombo crime family, was largely responsible for that hijacking but was willing to testify that it had been at the behest of two other people he knew from organized crime: Carmine and Daniel Fatico. Montello had known the Faticos for several years from his visits to Mulberry Street "social clubs" and his presence on the New York and New Jersey illegal gambling scene. In 1976, when the matter came up with United States Attorneys at a trial for the Faticos, Montello had remembered specifically the 1971 fur hijacking due to a price dispute that had subsequently involved a "sit down" with Gambino family underboss Aniello Dellacroce in Manhattan.[75]

Montello and another person testified against the Faticos in their 1976 trial and, bolstered by the evidence proferred by an anonymous FBI agent, the United States was successful in garnering a conviction on one count and a guilty plea on another. But during the sentencing phase of the procedure the defendants objected to the characterization—most notably forwarded by the anonymous FBI agent—that they were "made" members of an organized crime family. Since that had not been proven in court, and the anonymous witness was obviously not present to be cross-examined, the defense felt that it could not be used against them in sentencing. The district court agreed but on appeal to the Second Circuit Court of Appeals, that decision was overturned:

> We must recognize that most of the information now relied upon by judges to guide them in the intelligent imposition of sentences would be unavailable if information were restricted to that given in open court by witnesses subject to cross-examination. And the modern probation report draws on information concerning every aspect of a defendant's life. The type and extent of this information make totally impractical if not impossible open court testimony with cross-examination. Such a procedure could endlessly delay criminal administration in a retrial of collateral issues.[76]

So the case was remanded back to the district court in order to work out the specifics. The district court decided that since the sentence imposed on the Faticos would be greater if it was proven that they were members of an organized crime family, the government had to prove that fact. But—per the Second Circuit—that proof didn't have to meet the ordinary criminal trial burden of beyond a reasonable doubt, but rather a lesser standard of clear and convincing evidence. A specific hearing was held so that the sentencing judge could hear evidence from both sides as to whether or not the Faticos were made men.

An excerpt from a later sentencing of Michael Milken in a different Southern District of New York case explains the *Fatico* hearing rationale perfectly:

> The hearing is not a formal trial of guilt or innocence. Instead, it is a way to educate the judge about the defendant's character, to help the judge decide where a sentence should be set within the range of penalties permitted for the crimes that the defendant has admitted. Because guilty pleas are expected to save both the defendant and the government the time and expense of a full blown trial, a Fatico hearing is not meant to be the same as a criminal trial. It is shorter than a criminal trial would be and more informal. There is no right to a jury and no requirement that the government establish facts beyond a reasonable doubt. The court simply has to be convinced that the facts the court takes into account are reliable, that the government carried its burden of establishing them by a preponderance of the evidence, preponderance being a lesser standard than beyond a reasonable doubt.[77]

So in the Spiegleman case, the defense team wanted a chance to ade-quately cross-examine and attempt to refute evidence that was to be used in sentencing, similar to what they would have done had there been a trial. That meant that Wales could cross-examine, in front of Judge Kaplan, any scholar who had written a letter since the judge was basing his sentence on their opinions. The defense could also put up their own witnesses in order to expressly counter the assertions in the letters. The defense chose only to cross-examine Ashton and Prof. George Saliba.

For testimony in their favor the defense chose to call Dr. Nancy Davenport, director of acquisitions at the Library of Congress, and Dr. David Wigdor, assistant chief of the Manuscript Division at the Library of Congress. Unlike the experts that Cohen had been interested in bringing for the defense, these two were both legitimate professionals who couldn't be said to have had an interest in the "open market" theory of valuation that rare book dealers might. Not only were they highly credentialed librarians but they worked at the Library of Congress, one of the few libraries in the nation that could be said to bring to bear as much name recognition and credibility as did Columbia. And Wales was very concerned with the institutional reputation angle.

In another letter to the judge before the hearing, Wales made it clear that it was not the United States Attorney, Katherine Choo, who was pressing for the upward departure, but rather Columbia's Susan Galligan. He even went as far as to claim that Galligan—"an alumna of Harvard Law School and the Schulte Roth law firm"—had failed to inform the court of the Association of College and Research Libraries guidelines as to rare books.[78] This was a not-too-subtle suggestion to the judge about the duty of counsel to disclose such information. It would later be confirmed that Galligan had no duty to disclose anything as irrelevant as the ACRL guidelines.

But Wales saved his best for the final paragraph to Judge Kaplan. It was a perfect synopsis of the way Wales felt and the first real indication that he—himself a Columbia grad—would pull out all the stops in trying to paint Spiegelman as some persecuted innocent and Columbia as the institutional aggressor:

> In our proceeding, Columbia is the "victim." Obviously, they have a vested interest in the proceedings—they want revenge (they call it jus-tice). It is important that we view their position cautiously. Columbia is not a dispassionate observer as is the Library of Congress. It is impor-tant that the Court recognize, but not adopt, the wrath of Columbia.[79]

This also explains best why Wales only wanted to call two people to the stand instead of many of the other scholars whose letters were far more damaging: Ashton and Saliba both worked for Columbia. Prof. Darnton, for instance, worked at Princeton and Roger Stoddard worked at Harvard, so they couldn't be as easily painted as part of the larger Columbia scheme. If anyone besides Columbia faculty had been called it surely would have been a lot more difficult to portray Columbia as a lone, aggrieved dissenter from a valuation formula followed by the neutral Library of Congress. (No mention was made of the fact that United States Attorney Choo was also a Columbia grad. That might have made the whole Columbia-as-aggressor idea crumble under the weight of a nutty, full-blown conspiracy theory.)

Judge Kaplan was against the idea of a *Fatico* hearing, given the time that the case had already spent in litigation. Also, in light of the earlier stipulations, the Judge didn't see the point. "Nevertheless, in the interests of fairness," the Court would have the *Fatico* hearing "for the purpose of affording defendant the opportunity to cross-examine Ms. Ashton and Mr. Saliba and presenting testimony of Ms. Davenport and Mr. Wigdor."[80] When it later became clear that Prof. Saliba couldn't make the hearing, Judge Kaplan agreed to excise his letter from those that might influence his decision. So now the hearing was down to three witnesses.

Since there would be no jury—and the hearing wasn't bound by the strict protections of the Federal Rules of Evidence usually in play during trials—this was to be a more informal affair. And the only person that either side had to convince was Judge Kaplan.

At 9:30 a.m. on March 20, 1998—almost a year after that original hearing in which Cohen confidently asked for a speeded up sentencing date in order to get Spiegelman out of jail by the fall—United States Marshals walked the thief into the courtroom wearing his prison garb. Wales' first request was to ask if Spiegelman could change into the more comfortable clothes that his mother had provided.

"Mr. Spiegelman feels very, very self-conscious and uncomfortable," Wales said. "I asked the United States Marshals if they would permit him to change clothing, and they said no, and I ask your Honor if you—I have the clothing, it can be inspected."[81]

The judge called one of the Marshals to a sidebar to consult with him. The Marshal explained that the clothes had not gone through the requisite safety inspection as required, a process that took some time and that the defense was well aware of. Judge Kaplan refused to allow it at that point. He was tired of delays. Spiegelman stayed in his prison outfit.

The courtroom was not packed but there was a substantial audience. The *New York Times* had been following the case fairly closely so there were some interested spectators. On top of that, a group of fans of the Southern District—usually older men—routinely watched trials and hearings for the mere enjoyment of it and many of them were in the courtroom that day.[82] Judge Kaplan was known as a smart judge whose wit and banter was fantastic; this sometimes made his courtroom proceedings interesting to spectators. Many had brought snacks.

As the proceeding got under way Paul Kurtz rose instead of Elliot Wales for the defense. Kurtz was cocounsel for Spiegelman along with Wales and had been added in January when it became clear that the sentencing process might become a protracted fight.[83] He was hired as a specialist in federal criminal sentencing matters; he was called in not during the trial phase of any court proceeding but usually after the person had been convicted or had pleaded guilty and was trying to ensure a low sentence. That is, he was there for his expertise on just the sort of procedure that the Spiegelman case had become.

As the director of the National Correctional Counseling Center in Bethesda, Maryland, he was supposed to be a ringer. He knew the ins and outs of federal sentencing and, while he wouldn't do much speaking before the judge, he would do a lot of the behind the scenes work and writing of motions and briefs. A conversation that would take place five days later with a different judge on a different case had him explaining the origin of his particular expertise.

"Mr. Kurtz," Judge Leonard Sand, another United States District Court Judge in the Southern District of New York, said, "I note that you are listed in the letter as being with the National Correctional Counseling Center."

"That is an adjunct part of my practice, your Honor," Kurtz said.

"This is the first instance in which a member of that center has appeared before me," Judge Sand said. "Would you tell me what its role is?"

"Well," Kurtz said, "actually, your Honor, it was an offshoot that we developed some years ago with the advent of the Sentencing Guidelines. We found that there were a number of people that were not becoming specialized in it, and we decided to do so. Our primary focus in the National Correctional Counseling Center, part of our practice, is to deal with sentencing matters."

"Are you privately retained by the defendant?" Judge Sand said.

"Yes, I am, your Honor," Kurtz said.[84]

But five days prior to this exchange on behalf of another defendant, Kurtz's first courtroom act for Spiegelman was a bit of a retreat. He rose to explain that one of their witnesses, the one person who the defense was to going to call to refute the claims of Jean Ashton, had reconsidered.

Nancy Davenport, director of acquisitions for the Library of Congress, was supposed to testify, among other things, about a concrete valuation of books based on their monetary price. Aside from the heft that the LOC would bring to bear, Davenport was thought by the defense to be a believer in the concrete monetary value of books. In a roundabout way, this was true. When books are damaged or destroyed by natural disaster, the opinion of the LOC as to the monetary value of books was important in getting insurance reimbursement. To Wales that would suggest a concrete monetary valuation of books. But that idea is not mutually exclusive of a valuation scheme that also places the value of books to the community beyond a concrete value. The difference is subtle, but it's still a difference. But the nuances of this point wouldn't have mattered to Wales who only wanted to get someone from the LOC to appear to be on his side.

But Davenport didn't know that was her role. In fact, Wales had not apprised her at all of what she was to talk about. She was just to come to New York and answer some valuation questions. She knew enough to be uneasy about this and she quickly consulted the LOC counsel about her ability to testify.[85]

By telefax, she explained to Wales why she wouldn't be testifying on Spiegelman's behalf. "I must decline your request to serve as an expert witness in the matter of U.S. v. Daniel Spiegelman. After careful consideration of your request, the General Counsel's office has determined that it would not be appropriate for me to attend and provide testimony at the hearing." Davenport told Kurtz on the phone that there was a particular LOC regulation stating that when the United States is party to a suit, an employee could not testify against the government since it might be a conflict of interest.[86]

In the end that was probably best for Spiegelman's case. Davenport would not have been a sympathetic defense witness. Having dealt recently with her own internal theft she was not going to side with the defense against the scholarly community. And she certainly had not been told of her role in the hearing.[87] An unprepared and contrarian witness was not going to help the defense win points with Judge Kaplan.

"So we have two witnesses," Judge Kaplan said. "We have Ms. Ashton from Columbia and another witness that you're going to present. Is that right?"

"No," Elliot Wales said, nodding to his cocounsel. "Paul Kurtz will address that."

Kurtz stood up again. "Dr. Wigdor is on sabbatical," he said. "And he is in London, sir."[88]

So within five minutes of the start, Spiegelman had learned that he couldn't wear his regular clothes and that his only two witnesses wouldn't be showing up. Then United States Attorney Katherine Choo told the court that she brought with her some of the recovered items that Spiegelman had stolen. He didn't know it yet, but he probably could have guessed that that, too, was a sour development.

At the time of the hearing a great many items still remained unrecovered despite Spiegelman's claims of having been cooperative and forthcoming and despite the amount of material that had been seized in his safe deposit boxes. Among the items still missing were several letters signed by American presidents. There was a commission signed by John Adams and Thomas

Pickering on December 4, 1798, an appointment of a Captain of Artillery signed by Thomas Jefferson, a land grant in Illinois signed by James Monroe, an appointment to Second Lieutenant in the Infantry signed by Andrew Jackson, an appointment to the Military Ordinance Department signed by Abraham Lincoln.

Also unrecovered were several Korans. One was from 1887, another from 1845 and a third from 1802. An eighteenth-century version of the famous Persian work *Shahnameh* was also missing. An 1875 United States Army map of the 1864 Atlanta campaign was missing as was a 1913 map of the Gettysburg campaign. A map of Ireland from 1690 was still gone along with an Italian map from 1750 and Moroccan map from 1834. These maps were among more than twenty that were still missing, not including the scores that had been cut from the Blaue atlases.

Among the Thomas Edison materials that were still gone was a letter written by Edison in November 1883. Also still gone was a power of attorney given to Grosvenor Lowery in 1875, a contract with Western Union in 1870, a contract with American Printing Telegraph Company in 1870, a contract with Marshall Lefferts in 1870, and another contract from that same year with the Gold and Stock Telegraph Company. Several other Edison legal documents and letters remained unrecovered.

Among the incunabula that remained missing was a book printed in Augsburg in 1489, a book printed in Nuremberg in 1493, and another printed in Paris in the same year.[89]

Wales didn't have any witnesses available to rebuff any of what was in the letters from the scholars nor what Ashton was going to say. So his only recourse was to attack her directly, on cross-examination, and hope that he could impugn her credibility. Ashton was nervous about this. She was uneasy about the whole idea of taking the stand anyway—she didn't want to slip up in some way that would give the defense some advantage—but she was particularly wary of facing Wales when it appeared he was backed into a corner. She was certainly prepared; she had been through each of the items that she was going to be discussing that day and she had been warned what to expect many times by Galligan, Begley, and Choo. But all the preparation in the world can only help so much. At some point she knew that it would be just her up there on the stand by herself.[90]

She took the stand and was sworn in. As she had suspected, she would be the focus of attention for the next three hours or so. For much of that time she would be on the defensive.

Attacking Ashton would have been a long shot even if she was ill prepared or unconvincing. But, in the event, she was exactly the opposite. Poised in the face Wales' hostility and as knowledgeable as could be about the things that had been stolen from her library, the defense attorney could do little but badger and fish around. Judge Kaplan, who was not ever in favor of the

Fatico hearing at all, was not inclined to let Wales do that. Any time the defense attorney got too far a field of the point, he would rein him in.

"In 1992, were you at the Columbia Library," Wales asked of Ashton, after the hearing began in earnest with its sole witness sworn in.

"No, I was not," Ashton said.

"What year did you come there?" Wales said.

"September, 1993," Ashton said.

"After you got there," Wales said, "did you ever hear in any way from anybody that in the prior year there was a theft from the Columbia Library with regard to the Russian writer Alexander Pushkin?"

"No." Ashton said. "I read there had been a theft of Russian newspapers from the library, but they were not in the rare book and manuscript library. There are 22 libraries at Columbia."[91]

"Let me show you what has been marked Defendant Exhibit A for identification," Wales said. "I ask you to read it to yourself. Then I want to ask if it refreshes your recollection?"

"I think they were what we referred to as the Russian newspaper case," Ashton said. "They were in the Lehman Library, which is not a library I have any responsibility for. So I had heard of a Russian newspaper theft of Russian papers theft. This, I didn't know if that is what that is; that is, this, but it was in a different part of the Columbia University system."

"Did it come to your attention sometime shortly after you arrived at Columbia?" Wales said.

"I had heard after I arrived at Columbia there had been a theft of Russian newspapers," Ashton said. "I have not heard anything to do with Alexander Pushkin. It was not in a library under my jurisdiction."

"I see," Wales said. "Thank you. Did you hear what happened in that case?"

"I heard that someone had been apprehended and prosecuted," Ashton said.

"Was he prosecuted in New York?" Wales said.

"I don't know that," Ashton said.

"Was he convicted?" Wales said.

"My understanding is that he was," Ashton said.

"Was he sentenced to prison?" Wales said.

"I don't know that—well, I think, actually, I asked that question within the last week, and I think he did receive a sentence," Ashton said. "But I don't remember what it was."

"Let me ask you to look at the last—"

"Mr. Wales, I am going to interrupt you," Judge Kaplan said. "This is a hearing that I called to afford you an opportunity to cross-examine Ms. Ashton's written statements, the general burden of which was that there was a loss to Columbia and to the community at large as a result of your client's actions that cannot adequately and accurately be measured in money. I asked you for an offer of proof of what you would do if you had the opportunity to cross-examine, and you gave me at least one. We are, with this line of inquiry, far beyond the purpose of this hearing, so I'd like you to tell me how it connects to anything we're here to do."

"Well, I want to show through this witness in this and other instances that Columbia has had theft experiences and that the value of the loss is mentioned on appraised value, not loss of scholarship," Wales said. "It has never come up in prior instances. This is the first instance it has come up either in Columbia or any other place in the United States. This is not the first time we have had theft of good material. Columbia, Library of Congress, others have had experience with it. There has never been a concept of loss of scholarship previously. This is unique, your Honor, it is unprecedented, and I don't think there is a basis for it."

"Other than the one case cited by our predecessor counsel," Judge Kaplan said, referring to *Blumberg*, "are you aware of a single instance involving Columbia or any other institution in the United States in which the issue of how a sentence should be determined under the Sentencing Reform Act and the United States Sentencing Guidelines is in a circumstance like this?"

"Yes," Wales said. "I am aware of four."

"Get to them now, please," Judge Kaplan said, "or go to another subject you properly should cover with this witness."[92]

But Wales did not get to them. Instead, he continued asking questions about other matters about the valuation of books. He had counted on getting much of his information in by asking Nancy Davenport. Since she was not there, he attempted to get her testimony in through the back door.

"I show you what has been marked Defendant's Exhibit D for identification, and I ask you to read it to yourself," Wales said, showing Ashton a paper. "I am going to ask you some questions about it."

But before he could do that the United States Attorney hurried to her feet.

"Your Honor," Choo said, "this is a document that appears to be written from Nancy Davenport to Mr. Kurtz. Unless this witness has seen this letter before, I will object to any questions pertaining to that letter as inappropriate. I ask Mr. Wales to first inquire whether she has ever seen it before."

"Yes," Judge Kaplan said, addressing Wales, "why don't you start that way, anyway."

"Okay," Wales said. "Remember, I haven't offered it for evidence, your Honor."

"Well, I understand that," Judge Kaplan said, "and I haven't looked at it yet unless it has come to me in some other context, and I am not sure what it is."

"It has," Wales said to the judge. Then he turned to Ashton. "I have been asked by the court and by Ms. Choo to ask you whether you have ever seen that document before?"

"No," Ashton said.

"I am going to ask you if it refreshes," Wales said. "In any way refreshes your recollection of items that you have learned from any source."

"Objection," Choo said, standing up.

"Objection sustained," Judge Kaplan said. "Mr. Wales, you know you can't ask a witness whether something has refreshed her recollection unless the witness has first responded to the question by saying, "I don't remember.""

"You're right, your Honor," Wales said.

"It's not an exception to the hearsay rule," Judge Kaplan said.

"You're right," Wales said. Then he turned back to Ashton. "As far as you know, does the Library of Congress have some methodology when applying loss valuation to theft of heritage items that had been stolen from their institution?"

"Objection, your Honor," Choo said. "This witness is not competent to answer that question."

"I'll let her answer," Judge Kaplan said. "Go ahead, Ms. Ashton."

"Only what I read right now and learned right this minute," Ashton said.

"Apart from this letter," Wales said, "from any other source in the world at any other time, have you learned that the Library of Congress has a certain methodology with regard to evaluating cultural heritage items?"

"Have you learned whether it has a methodology," Judge Kaplan said, to Ashton.

"No," Ashton said.

"No?" Wales said. "Is that to the judge's question or mine?"

"Either one," Ashton said. "I have no knowledge of a method of valuation. I have not learned of a knowledge."

"Let me try it this way," Wales said. "Did you ever learn from any other source, from any source, that the Library of Congress utilized the fair market value of property affected by theft?"

"Mr. Wales, maybe I can save all of us a lot of time," Judge Kaplan said. "I know it was your intention, because you informed me that it was, to call witnesses from the Library of Congress to testify that they used fair market value somehow in connection with thefts. Your witnesses aren't here. I surely would assume that if the issue that the Library of Congress had to deal with was, for example, what claim should be made against any insurance policy we have for economic reimbursement for a loss, that they would use fair market value. I am not prepared to assume in the absence of some proof that it was the Library of Congress' position that the fair market value or the appraised value or some other analogous term is the exclusive relevant factor in determining the harm to the Library of Congress, or to the people of the United States who support it, or to the scholarly community in this world of the loss of materials from that library. Maybe it's so, but it is your burden to produce some evidence on that, and hearsay isn't going to do it on that issue, not that it is not admissible. Of course, I understand strictly the rules of evidence don't apply in this. I am just telling you it will not be persuasive to me. In effect, to have you tell me that that's the way they do it."[93]

So basically what Judge Kaplan said was, the Library of Congress may well have a policy of valuing books strictly based on what they could get on the open market, but that needed to be proven. Wales just saying that that was the case would not constitute proof even though in a technical legal sense, it was admissible.

"Let me put it this way, your Honor," Wales said. "We are not talking about insurance reimbursement, okay? We are talking only in the context of a criminal case. We are also talking about the context of sentence proceeding. Your Honor is sensitive to the fact that we had a witness who disappeared on us, and we are only so informed yesterday. Obviously, we had draft letters. Of course, your Honor did ask me as part of the offer of proof to submit to you letters, and I did, and your Honor had the opportunity to read the record. To read the letters. The letters talk only in terms of criminal proceedings, sentence proceedings, and talk about four specific cases in the US District Court for the District of Columbia, which a defendant, a thief, was prosecuted for stealing items from the Library of Congress. Now, obviously I would love to have my witness here today."

"Right," Judge Kaplan said. "If there really are four cases, they're matters of public record. If there was anything relevant, by God, by this time you have almost a year to get anything relevant out of these court files, and I haven't seen page one. Why Ms. Ashton is being asked to sit here, to be a vehicle for you to try to get her to put in unsubstantiated hearsay I'm not really sure."

"Because I only learned for the first time yesterday—until yesterday we had every reason to believe—we were told she is coming," Wales said. "We had hotel reservations for her."

"Mr. Wales, I am fully sensitive to that," Judge Kaplan said. "I appreciate that you had a problem that burst upon you yesterday."

"That's right," Wales said.

"That is one of the things that happens to trial lawyers," Judge Kaplan said. "It is not Ms. Ashton's problem."

"I understand that," Wales said. "The point is if I don't have Dr. Davenport as a witness, Ms. Ashton, being an expert and being a leading substantial figure in the world of libraries and rare books and manuscripts, many things come to her attention as a major player in this field."

"But she just got finished telling you she doesn't know what the Library of Congress does, if anything," Judge Kaplan said. "Can we please move on?"[94]

And they did move on for a little while. But then the hearing veered right back into another area that Judge Kaplan found outside the scope of the hearing.

"Do you remember Professor Blackner's letters?" Wales said to Ashton.

"Yes," Ashton said.

"Is she a professor of history at Columbia?" Wales said.

"Yes," Ashton said. "She is."

"If necessary, I'll show you copies of these letters and ask you questions," Wales said. "Did professor Blackner—"

"Could you perhaps explain what you're doing here," Judge Kaplan said, "because I gave you the opportunity to ask for the authors of any of these letters to be brought in for cross-examination, and the only one you asked for was Professor Saliba, and when he was not available, I granted your motion to strike his letter. Is what you're trying to do to cross-examine the people you elected not to bring in by cross-examining Ms. Ashton?"

"One or two questions," Wales said. "In fact, I wrote your Honor a letter asking you—if you remember the letter of March 3rd—stating that you have the Columbia letters, I think you have seen them, you can read them as well as I can read them and the witness can read them, and it is a question of whether or not there was any reference not only in Professor Blackner's letter, but any one of the Columbia Professor's letters, any reference to loss of scholarship or impediment of the research efforts of any of the professors, particularly with regard to the Spiegelman theft of material."

"If the burden of what you want to ask Ms. Ashton is to get her to tell you what is and isn't in a half dozen letters we can both read for ourselves," Judge Kaplan said, "I think we can save the time."

"I agree," Wales said.

"It is a matter of argument," Judge Kaplan said.

"I agree," Wales said. "I did suggest that to your Honor. If that be so, of course at the appropriate time I will ask your honor to make a finding to let us say or don't say what I urge; namely, that there was no impediment to any particular professor with regard to any research as to any of the items taken by Daniel Spiegelman."

"I understand that is your position," Judge Kaplan said.[95]
At this point they were more than an hour into the hearing and there was no sense that the judge was becoming more sympathetic to Spiegelman and his defense team. But the fact that Wales had continually been rebuffed by both the judge and Asthon didn't lessen his resolve to continue nor, it seemed, impel him to change his angle of attack. He asked a number of questions about different aspects of the collection and how important photocopies were to scholars. Edison materials, presidential letters, medieval manuscripts—all were subjects visited by Wales in an attempt to show that originals were not better than photocopies. Then he changed tack a bit.

"Let's talk about Papal Bulls for a minute," Wales said. "I think one of the Columbia professors attached a lot of value to Papal Bulls."

"Yes," Ashton said.

"What are Papal Bulls?" Wales said.

"Documents," Ashton said. "Usually legal documents that had judicial force that were written from the Papal throne that had lead seals on them, that is the bull itself. Only the Pope was allowed to use lead."

"During what period of time were Papal Bulls issued?" Wales said.

"Throughout the medieval and renaissance period," Ashton said. "The ones we lost were particularly important because they were 13th Century. There are very few of those."

"During this period of time, let's say the 13th, 14th, 15th, 16th Century, were there thousands of Papal Bulls issued?" Wales said.

"Not to my knowledge," Ashton said.

"Who has the largest repository of Papal Bulls in the world?" Wales said.

"They probably have them in Rome," Ashton said.

"In the Vatican," Wales said. "Is that right?"

"Yes," Ashton said.

"Tell me about the Vatican library," Wales said. "Is that a major library?"

"Of course," Ashton said.

"A major library for documents pertaining to the Catholic Church?" Wales said.

"As far as I know," Ashton said.

"Would you say they have the most important collection of Papal Bulls and other materials relating to the church?" Wales said.

"I don't now that for certain," Ashton said. "But I would assume that's the case."

"Have you ever visited the library?" Wales said.

"I have not been in the Vatican library" Ashton said.

"Would you say that the Papal Bulls that Columbia had is just a drop in the bucket compared to what the Vatican Library has?" Wales said.

"No," Ashton said. "I wouldn't."

"Let's talk about—"

"Papal Bulls are not interchangeable," Judge Kaplan said. "Are they Ms. Ashton?"

"No, they are not." Ashton said. "Each is unique."

"It is not, see one see them all," Judge Kaplan said, "right?"

"Exactly," Ashton said.

"There are thousands of bulls?" Wales said.

"I think that doesn't matter," Ashton said. "I think Professor Somverville's letter addresses this issue."

"As far as you know—"

"I don't know that," Ashton said.

"This is not very profitable," Judge Kaplan said. "There are thousands of millions of oil paintings."

"What?" Wales said.

"Oil paintings," Judge Kaplan said. "It doesn't go to the question of the whether the loss of the Mona Lisa counts."[96]

Wales appeared to change the subject again just after this point, asking about the cataloging efforts of the Edison papers. But he quickly moved back to the idea that there are a lot of rare materials out there and Spiegelman's efforts were merely a drop in the bucket.

"Are there other major libraries in the United States?" he said.

"There are," Ashton said.

"Most Ivy League Schools have major research libraries?" Wales said.

"Yes," Ashton said.

"Is the Morgan Library an important depository for manuscripts?" Wales said.

"It is an important depository," Ashton said.

"In fact, it is the most important one in the United States," Wales said, "with regard to manuscripts, isn't it?"

"It is one of the more important ones," Ashton said.

"Who else is very important," Wales said.

"The Huntington Library in California," Ashton said. "The New York Public Library has some."

"What about Harvard?" Wales said.

"Harvard," Ashton said, "the Ivy League institutions all have collections of medieval and renaissance manuscripts. Princeton has one."

"How about Library of Congress?" Wales said.

"The Library of Congress is—as I said before, I don't know the size of their collection," Ashton said. "My primary contact is with educational institutions."

Wales paused, then continued: "In Europe there are major depositories," he said. "Are there not?"

"Yes," Ashton said.

"That have medieval and—"

"Yes," Ashton said.

"Right," Wales said, pausing. "Okay. The Vatican is one?"

"Yes," Ashton said.

"How do you pronounce the name of the—"

"Biblioteca Nacional," Ashton said. (At several points during the hearing Wales solicited Ashton's advice on pronunciation, most amusingly when he tried to pronounce "incunabula." He asked her if he'd done it right and she replied, simply, "no.")

He continued on with foreign libraries: "British Library?"

"British Library," Ashton said.

"Of course, Oxford and Cambridge are major depositories," Wales said. "Aren't they?"

"Yes," Ashton said.

"Let me ask you about Islamic material," Wales said. "I think [there was] some reference made to Islamic material. Are there major libraries or depositories in the Islamic world with regard to Islamic material?"

"Yes," Ashton said.

"Name me some," Wales said.

"I don't know," Ashton said.

"Let's say in Cairo," Wales said.

"Yes," Ashton said.

"Is that a major center for learning?" Wales said.

"Yes," Ashton said.

"They may have a major library there?" Wales said.

"As far as I know," Ashton said.

"What about Tehran?" Wales said.

"I am not familiar with the major depositories," Ashton said.

"Have you heard Tehran is major?" Wales said.

"I said I am not familiar with these," Ashton said.

"What about Damascus?" Wales said. "Have you heard anything about that?"

"I don't know," Ashton said. "I am not familiar with the depositories of Arabic manuscripts."

"Mr. Wales," Judge Kaplan intervened. "I am giving you a great deal of latitude."

"Yes," Wales said. "Thank you."

"There is a limit," Judge Kaplan said.

"It has been worthwhile, Judge," Wales said, "it really has. Let me see how many more areas, your Honor."

"Maybe you can give us all a time estimate," Judge Kaplan said.

"Just a few more minutes," Wales said.[97] And within a few minutes he was done. But if his cross-examination of Ashton had been, at best, a draw for the defense, the redirect by Katherine Choo would expose the Spiegelman team to be in full retreat.

Just as Wales was finishing up his examination, Judge Kaplan had a question for Ashton before Choo took her turn.

"Are you in a position to shed any light for me on the question of whether there is a relationship between the known or potential scholarly value of a rare book or manuscript and what its appraised or auction value is?" Judge Kaplan said.

"The auction or appraised value is a value that is put on it by people who deal in the buying and selling of manuscripts, and that valuation fluctuates according to what happens to be fashionable at the time," Ashton said. "It may be parallel to what scholars would value it, but scholarly value is entirely separate since a document that is worth $10 on the market may well be the key to an argument that is made by a scholar which influences thousands of people. Conversely, a book that is elaborately illustrated and appears to be extremely valuable and appeal to collectors may have relatively little scholarly value at the time."

Wales was shuffling his papers. He wasn't going to let this go on for very much longer without saying something.

Ashton continued: "Also, scholarly value is calculated in terms of long-term life in a library. In 50 or 60 or a hundred years, things are rediscovered. They gain and lose value in an entirely different way. The market is slow to respond. An example might be women's diaries, papers dealing with slave transactions which were very little valued 50, 60 or a hundred years ago, and now command very high prices in the market, largely because they were rediscovered by scholars at a time when they had low scholarly value, and they were collected by libraries who believed in keeping the artifacts of the past."

"So if I understand what you're saying," Judge Kaplan said, then paused. "Let me see if we can indulge a hypothetical here—I suppose it is my general understanding, which may be right or wrong, the accepted view among historians at the moment Chief Justice Warren was appointed chief justice of the United States by President Eisenhower in connection with the California delegation having sworn from Taft to Eisenhower in the 1952 convention— is that familiar to you?"

"Vaguely," Ashton said.

"Is what you're saying," Judge Kaplan said, "if there appeared a memorandum or manuscript, letter by President Eisenhower or Chief Justice Warren or something that suggested to someone that perhaps the appointment was because Eisenhower foresaw the development that the Warren court would take and wished to bring it about by that appointment, might have a value to scholarship out of all proportion to the value of an Eisenhower or Warren letter considered for itself?"

"Absolutely," Ashton said.

"May I object to that question, your Honor?" Wales said.[98]

But Judge Kaplan had gotten it exactly right. The monetary value of a letter between President Eisenhower and Earl Warren had a particular monetary value that would, at market, be substantial. But the value of a candid letter between the two that introduced to history an idea that had not existed before the letter came to light would be without measure. And the destruction of that letter before anyone had a chance to review it would be far more of a loss than the monetary value that a presidential letter could fetch at market.

With Choo rising to ask some sympathetic questions of Ashton, Spiegelman's *Fatico* hearing was about to take a turn for the worse.

NOTES

1. Federal Bureau of Prisons, FCI Otisville, available at http://www.bop.gov/locations/institutions/otv/index.jsp.

2. *United States v. Spiegelman*, Sentencing Hearing, April 24, 1998, 31.

3. *United States v. Spiegelman*, Notice of Appearance, November 22, 1996.

4. *United States v. Spiegelman,* Order of Detention, November 26, 1996.

5. *United States v. Spiegelman,* Order of Continuance, December 20, 1996.

6. *United States v. Spiegelman,* Order of Continuance, January 21, 1997.

7. *United States v. Spiegelman,* Oral Order of Continuance, February 20, 1997.

8. *United States v. Spiegelman,* Order of Continuance, March 24, 1997.

9. *United States v. Spiegelman,* Plea, April 3, 1997.

10. *United States v. Spiegelman,* Change of Not Guilty Plea to Guilty Plea, April 17, 1997.

11. Interview with Cathy Begley, February 10, 2006.

12. *United States v. Spiegelman,* Plea Agreement Hearing, April 17, 1997.

13. Ibid., 10–11.

14. Ibid.

15. Ibid., 20–23.

16. *Almanac of the Federal Judiciary* (New York: Aspen, 2006), 50.

17. Levin v. McPhee, 917 F. Supp. 230 (S.D.N.Y. 1996).

18. "Corporate Injustice," Wall Street Journal, April 6, 2006, A14.

19. *Almanac* at 51.

20. Susan Galligan interview, March 2, 2005.

21. Galligan interview.

22. Jean Ashton to Jineen Forbes, May 28, 1997.

23. Ibid.

24. Irving Cohen to Judge Kaplan, May 29, 1997.

25. United States v. Spiegelman, Presentencing Report, May 1997.

26. Irving Cohen to Judge Kaplan, June 16, 1997.

27. Ibid.

28. Ibid.

29. United States v. Spiegelman, Hearing, June 18, 1997, 2.

30. Ibid., 3–6.

31. Ibid., 9.

32. Ibid., 9–12.

33. Ibid., 16–19.

34. *United States Sentencing Commission Guidelines Manual,* 5K2.5, November 2003.

35. Hearing at 19–22.

36. Ibid., 24–26.

37. http://www.columbia.edu/cu/lweb/indiv/butler/about2.html.

38. http://www.columbia.edu/cu/lweb/indiv/rbml/about.html.

39. Kenneth A. Lohf, *The Rare Book and Manuscript Library of Columbia University* (New York: Columbia University, 1985), 11.

40. Ibid., 12–31.

41. Ashton interview.

42. *United States v. Spiegelman,* Hearing, July 30, 1997, 3.

43. Ibid., 6–8.

44. Ibid., 9–10.

45. Ibid., 10–11.

46. Ibid., 11–13.

47. Ibid., 11–15.

48. Ibid., 18–21.

49. Ibid., 25–31.

50. H. Elliot Wales to Judge Kaplan, August 12, 1997.

51. H. Elliot Wales to Judge Kaplan, August 14, 1997.

52. Irving Cohen to Judge Kaplan, September 4, 1997.

53. H. Elliot Wales to Judge Kaplan, August 14, 1997.

54. Library of Congress bio of Jean Ashton, available at http://www.loc.gov/bicentennial/bios/preserve/ashton.html.

55. Wales letter.

56. Ibid.

57. *United States v. Spiegelman*, 4 F. Supp. 2d 275, 280 April 24, 1998.

58. Katherine Choo to Judge Kaplan, August 29, 1997.

59. Robert Darnton to Jineen Forbes, October 3, 1997.

60. Ibid.

61. Ibid.

62. H. Elliot Wales to Lewis Kaplan, January 19, 1998.

63. George Saliba to Jineen Forbes, September 29, 1997.

64. Wales Letter.

65. Consuelo Dutschke to Jineen Forbes, October 2, 1997.

66. Roger Stoddard to Jineen Forbes, October 3, 1997.

67. David Scott Kastan to Jineen Forbes, September 26, 1997.

68. Simon Schama to Jineen Forbes, October 27, 1997.

69. See, generally, Kaplan's sentence at 4 F. Supp 2d 275, starting at 279.

70. H. Elliot Wales to Lewis Kaplan, January 19, 1998.

71. Ibid.

72. Ibid.

73. Ibid.

74. Ibid.

75. *Fatico v. United States*, 579 F.2d 707, 709 (1978).

76. Ibid., 712.

77. *United States v. Michael Milken*, (S) 89 Cr. 41 (KMW), Nov. 21, 1990. SDNY.

78. Wales letter to Kaplan, February 3, 1998.

79. Ibid.

80. *United States v. Spiegelman*, Order of February 9, 1998, 97 Crim. 309 (LAK).

81. *United States v. Spiegelman*, Fatico Hearing, March 20, 1998, 2.

82. Begley interview, February 10, 2006.

83. *United States v. Spiegelman*, Notice of Appearance, January 20, 1998.

84. *United States v. Kurtz*, Sealed Complaint.

85. Nancy Davenport interview with author, February 23, 2006

86. Fatico Hearing at 3.

87. Davenport interview.

88. Fatico Hearing at 4.

89. United States v. Spiegelman, 97 Cr 309, Plea Agreement Hearing, April 17, 1997.

90. Ashton interview.

91. Fatico Hearing at 12.

92. Ibid., 13–15.

93. Ibid., 34–38.
94. Ibid., 38–39.
95. Ibid., 46–47.
96. Ibid., 54–57.
97. Ibid., 58–63.
98. Ibid., 63–65.

CHAPTER 6

A Nice Thing for Counsel to Do

When Katherine Choo handed Jean Ashton a pair of white cotton gloves and started to ask her about the scroll she was about to present in the courtroom the trial attorney alarms in Elliot Wales' head started to sound. Choo asked Ashton how the 17-foot manuscript being unfurled in the courtroom compared with the reproduction, a black and white copy that she also produced for everyone to see.

Ashton had been on the defensive for an hour and a half, steadily refuting questions designed to trip her up and get her to say things that were inconsistent with the philosophy behind the departure. If she had come off as ill informed or unsure of herself, that might also have worked against her—that's why she had been nervous. But she had come through the examination relatively unscathed. And now it was time for her side to get aired, not only with her ability to explain the value of the materials that had been stolen but also by showing many of the items themselves.

"Most of the information that is contained in the physical object itself is absent from the photocopy," Ashton said. "The color, the gilt, the size, the annotations on the side which have been pasted on by the original person who used it, the texture of the parchment itself, the glues, the kinds of things that were used, all of these things are evidence that is used and examined by scholars to determine book productions, studies in genealogy. There are many reasons this particular thing would be used. Part of it is the very physical nature of it and part of it is the content. It is the physical nature, in fact, [that is] more important than the context. The artwork, nature of its organizations, this can't be seen on a photocopy."

"How old is that scroll, by the way," Choo said.

But Wales interrupted before Ashton had a chance to answer. He didn't want this to go on any longer.

"Your honor," Wales said. "The defense is willing to stipulate that with respect to manuscripts, the originals are better."

"I can't hear you," Judge Kaplan said.

"The defense is willing to stipulate and concede that with regard to manuscripts, medieval manuscripts, Renaissance manuscripts, the photocopies are not adequate substitutes for the original. I think that the thrust of much of my cross had to do with presidential papers, the Edison papers, and documents of that type. It did not have to do with manuscripts, so I think we have an issue here that is really not relevant."

"Or to put it more precisely," Judge Kaplan said, "an issue here that the defense doesn't contest, though I think it is quite relevant."

The judge indicated for the U.S. Attorney to continue. Choo then mentioned that Columbia had provided ten different items for the court to see in order to rebut some of Wales' claims.

Wales objected again.

"None of these are the Spiegelman documents," Wales said. "These are documents pulled out at random from the Columbia Library."

But Wales had no idea what he was talking about. Almost all of them were Spiegelman documents and those that weren't were not there at random.

"If I may clarify," Choo said, "the materials produced here today are from materials seized by the FBI pursuant to search warrants from locations that Mr. Spiegelman identified to the FBI in a post-arrest statement. In addition, we have brought copies of Nuremberg Chronicles, two copies of which it has in its possession, one of which is missing and Mr. Spiegelman has admitted to selling in Europe. Ms. Ashton, my understanding is, will testify that each of these Nuremberg Chronicles are individual unto themselves and carry distinct cultural value. For that reason, she would like to bring this to the court's attention. Lastly, your Honor, Ms. Asthon has brought one or two volumes of the nine volume Blaeu atlas that was mutilated when maps were cut out of these volumes. She has brought two volumes to show the court how the mutilations occurred. Many of these maps were either recovered in the search warrants or admitted to by Mr. Spiegelman as having been stolen by himself."[1]

Spiegelman had cut more than 250 maps out of these atlases and the razor damage and mutilation was still very much intact.

When Wales and Kurtz saw these atlases they both got to their feet. They were about to give away any last pretensions they had to one of their main lines of defense: that simple copies of the things Spiegelman had stolen were the same as the originals. Wales had just done this vis a vis the Islamic materials and manuscripts, now he was about give over the whole line of argument. The judge recognized him.

"Your Honor," Wales said. "The defense is prepared to stipulate with regard to these manuscripts and with regard to their uniqueness and the fact that photocopies are not an adequate substitute."

"I accept the stipulation," Judge Kaplan said. "But I need to determine a sentence here, and I want the information. I was perfectly prepared to sentence this defendant at least three times, and every time I was met with the assertion that there needed to be a hearing or there are factual issues, and now you've got your hearing, and what I am gathering is you now don't want to hear the case on the other side."

"Well, your honor," Wales said. "I don't think that is a fair statement. I think you have heard an hour and a half from me, and I thank you for that. With regard to some other items that may not really be in dispute, we are willing to stipulate, which I think is a nice thing for counsel to do."

"We all appreciate it," Judge Kaplan said.

"Rather than sit for 20 minutes to hear something really not in dispute," Wales said.

"If that were the test, this would have been a shorter morning, Mr. Wales," Judge Kaplan said and then motioned for Choo to carry on.[2]

What Judge Kaplan discovered over the course of the next hour was exactly how sorry an approximation of the original a copy of many of these items was. Aside from gilt edges and texturing and the marginalia that often wouldn't be adequately picked up by copies, the presence of certain colors could place a document to a particular region.

Choo handed Ashton a photocopy of the Roma de la Rose, the medieval manuscript that Spiegelman had tried to sell to Sebastian Hesselink in the Netherlands. It happened that this particular item was very much in demand in the RBML, being requested about three or four times per year by a particular scholar who very much needed it in his research. ("So there's only one scholar," Wales said later, in an attempt to show that this wasn't actually a loss to scholarship.)

"In your view," Choo said, "why are the photocopies an inadequate replacement for scholarly review and research using the original material?"

"Again they don't show in any detail any depth," Ashton said, "the gilt work, the hand painting. This is a vernacular French poem, very famous in the later middle ages. They don't show the line markings where the scribe lined it, lined up his text, the pin markings where the piece of parchment or leather was pinned to the board. They don't show the texture of the parchment at all and they give a totally inadequate sense of the look and feel of the manuscript and are very hard to read, actually, as well."

"Ms. Ashton," Choo said, "in your view, what do those particular properties of the original manuscript provide to a scholar that is important to research and analysis?"

"Different scholars look at these manuscripts in different ways," Ashton said. "Some analyze the artwork, some analyze the materials that are used, some look at the scribing hand, that is, the hand of the handwriting that is involved to try to determine what area this came from. There are only limited numbers of manuscripts of these poems. There are people who go all over the world looking to see. Each manuscript is unique by different things, and a scholar who is interested in these things will go all over to look at each of these things and record the details."

"What can be learned from the ink or the paint or the parchment that cannot be learned from looking at a photocopy?"

"Well, you can learn a good deal about the artist's abilities, about the part of the country, the country, the part of the world. Certain colors of blue were used in particular Monastic communities. For example, particularly areas of France or Italy specialized in certain kinds of handwriting. So you can locate this particular manuscript in place and in time, and from that you can find something out about the tastes, the economy, the technology of a particular area at a moment in history."

Choo next handed Ashton one of the Euclidean geometry books from the Columbia collection.

"Is that the original Euclid in Columbia's collection?"

"Yes, this is a 13th Century book," Ashton said. "It was written in 1260. It is a textbook of mathematics. There are very few secular, relatively few secular books from the period. This one is very important in part because of the drawings in the margin. We studied modern geometry because of the transmission of Euclid from the past, and it is only in vehicles like this that that can occur or can happen. You can see that it is just like a high school geometry book except that it is—what it is is 1260 to 1998, 630 years old."

The defense team didn't like the way this was going, particularly the fact that Choo seemed to be relishing the opportunity of showing the items to the judge. But whether Wales was tired of being subtly censured by the judge or simply resigned to the fact that an upward departure was inevitable, it was Kurtz who did the talking this time.

"Your honor," Kurtz said, "I must object."

"Of course you're aware, counsel, the rule is the first counsel up on the witness is the one who handles the witness," Judge Kaplan said. "I'll hear you anyway."

"Thank your Honor," Kurtz said. "Yes, I am aware of the rule, and I am sorry. Your Honor, I can appreciate the court's desire to be informed as to the nature of the various art pieces that we have before us and I can appreciate its concern about perhaps viewing the items that were destroyed. However, the government is bound by its plea agreement not to seek an upward departure here. It seems very much to me that what Ms. Choo is doing is presenting a case that there is some scholarly loss; and that, therefore, the court should depart upward. This is contrary to what the agreement is. I can certainly see the court wanting to find this information and may do it sua sponte, but I think it is wholly inappropriate for the government to be taking this position. Moreover, questions about items which are recovered are really not germane. If they're recovered, they're recovered."

Judge Kaplan considered this.

"Are you familiar with my order directing the government, as an officer of the court, to present to me whatever material might be relevant to this?" Judge Kaplan said.

"I am, your Honor," Kurtz said.

"Did you make any objection to that order up to this moment?" Judge Kaplan said.

"No, your Honor," Kurtz said.

"Do you think that order is within my authority?" Judge Kaplan said.

"I do," Kurtz said.

"Do you think I committed legal error by doing that?" Judge Kaplan said.

"No, I certainly do not," Kurtz said.

"Do you think I have to send a probation officer out to do this or to appoint some other private lawyer at government expense to do what Ms. Choo is doing at my order?" Judge Kaplan said.

"No, your Honor," Kurtz said. "My objection is not to the form; my objection is to the tenor. Ms. Choo's questions appear to me to be driven by not a fact-finding mission, as requested by the court in its order, but in my view more toward a position of supporting a loss of scholarly value."

"Mr. Kurtz, I think there is utterly no merit to your position," Judge Kaplan said.

"All right, Sir," Kurtz said.

"However, I am going to ask Ms. Choo to have a seat, and I will ask Ms. Ashton some questions," Judge Kaplan said. "Does that offend you?"

"Not at all, your Honor," Kurtz said.[3]

So Judge Kaplan took over the questioning of Ashton. Within a few minutes of that, he had gotten down from his bench, donned some white gloves and begun inspecting many of the items up close. Having Judge Kaplan—and everyone who handled the material—put on the white gloves was a bit of theatre. Certainly gloves and other protections are central to the preservation of rare materials but Ashton knew that they could have gotten along just fine that day without them; she just wanted to emphasize the importance and delicate nature of the materials being handled.[4]

As Ashton began to instruct the judge on the rudiments of rare book protection and display, Wales commented that "this is like Medieval Manuscripts 101 at Columbia."

In fact, it was far better than that. For a few hours on that March morning, the courtroom held a small collection that would be the envy of most other rare book librarians in the country.

Ashton went through each piece in front of the group, explaining each and responding to whatever questions the judge had as he looked over them.

"This is from the 15th Century," Ashton said of one of the manuscripts. "This is a book of psalms, poems extracted from the Bible. Its small size tells you that it comes from the late middle ages, and the fact that it was made for portability and it's a book of psalms rather than complete Bible means that it was probably made for a lay person or a priest who wished to carry it around with him. The early manuscripts tend to be much larger. By this time in history, things were smaller and more available. These are illuminated manuscripts. [A]s you can see, there is a tremendous amount of gold, and this was made for a rather wealthy person. It has got music in many cases. This is not a work that would be looked at as a treasure for art historians, but it is extremely illuminating for scholars in many other areas. Again, the lines on the page, the nature of the decoration, there is a skin side and a hair side to every manuscript which can be seen in this, and some of these books, I am not sure whether this is, you can see where the scribe has slipped and made a mistake. So you get a sense of the living book itself."

"And address the issue of copies as a substitute," Judge Kaplan said.

"A photocopy again would not give the texture, would not give the color. In some cases, we have photocopied single pages. Maybe we have a photocopy of a single page that is listed in our file, but for scholars, they would need the whole thing to study the variations within it."

"You can see the wooden board in here," she said, picking up another piece, "and the contemporary binding from the 15th Century. You can see the ownership marking in a way, this is a very good example. This book is often used in classrooms to teach graduate students and even undergraduates how books were made in the middle ages because you can see how the leather was bound to the boards and how there are very rough pieces of leather."

"This book is not only important for the particular beauty of its art," Ashton said, "but for the way in which it was made, so that the object itself bears a lot of information as well, and that can't be conveyed by a photocopy. Again, we have the gilt, we have details in the illustrations, you have a depth in the picture that does not come through in copies."[5]

A few minutes later Ashton got to what used to be books full of maps.

"These are two of the 9 Blaeu atlases that were mutilated by the defendant," Ashton said.

The husks of the two books sat on the table before Judge Kaplan.

"These are in the stacks at Columbia," Ashton said, "and I brought them for specific reasons. These are the Blaeu atlases [that were] done in Holland in 1667. They were considered the great glory of Dutch cartography of the golden age. There is only one other known copy of the German edition. Before I can show first the damage that was done to this book, I would like also to point out that this particular copy has a book plate from the Columbia College Library from Dr. Anderson's collection. This makes this a very significant part of New York history because Dr. Anderson graduated from Columbia or got a medical degree from Columbia in 1796. He nursed patients through the yellow fever epidemic of 1796 and 1797. He lost his wife and children in that and became disgusted with the practice of medicine. He became one of the country's foremost practitioners of engraving and illustrations. At Columbia, this was given to the library. I don't know exactly what date it came to use. This particular set of atlases he brought because he was interested in engraving and printing, have a special meaning for scholarship, but also for the history. This particular atlas deals with maps of Britain. As you can see, the title page is removed, it is a very beautiful title page with gilt. This is one of the few things that was recovered."

The judge took a look at the recovered title page that had been razored out.

"Over 250 maps were stolen from these Blaeu atlases," Ashton said, "more than 50 from this volume alone. Most of these have not been recovered, and even if recovered, would take a considerable amount of work to get back into the atlas. One of the things I would like to point out here is that there is a register at the back of this volume that tells us what maps were in it. This old Columbia College Library stamp means it came from the collection in the 19th Century, so we have had it well over a hundred years. This book would ordinarily be stuffed with maps, and you can see in many cases the stubs where they were removed. There are only three maps left in this volume."

Ashton showed one of the remaining maps to the judge.

"This is a sample of the kind of thing that was in here," Ashton said. "Some of them are much more beautiful and elaborate, and some are plainer, but there are, as I say, 250 of them gone. This volume, which had more than 50, only has three and it is unlikely we will ever recover those."

She moved on to the second volume that she had brought.

"This is France," Ashton said. "The title page was left in here and many more maps are here, but I wanted to bring it to illustrate a particular point. These are extra-illustrated volumes. Whether it was Dr. Anderson or someone else, in the 18th century they inserted their own maps in here. These maps do not appear on any index. We can never know exactly what maps were in here. There would have been no reason for us to list them, catalog these separately because they were part of the volume, but we have places where there are stubs, and we know that we have lost not only the maps themselves, but the history of whoever put together this composite atlas, why they put them in, when they put them in.

"This, for example," Ashton said, turning pages as she spoke, "is I think an 18th Century map. A 1712 map of Paris which was added to this atlas."

They were pausing to take in both the beauty and the damage. She slowly turned the page and pointed to another map. "That was 1667. We know it was added 40 or 50 years [later]. Somebody cherishing this in an age of exploration kept it in their own library, and these maps, too."[6]

They moved on to a papal bull then an Illuminated Book of Hours (essentially a prayer book with beautiful and ornate script and illustrations), each time dwelling long enough to get the sense that no black and white reproduction would do it justice. The hearing continued on in this manner for about twenty minutes.

"Finally," Ashton said, "these Nuremberg Chronicles are ones that remain in the Columbia Library, and we brought them to illustrate the fact that although the defense counsel made the point we have duplicates of books, in fact, these two books, both printed in 1483, about 30 years after the invention of printing, are, although they appear the same on the surface, are, in fact, different. They were bound differently, at a different period. The title pages, you can see the title page there is quite different. They were done by the same printer. He customized these for different customers. This one has different handwriting and ownership marks. These have marginal notations that were owned by different people. They were bound by different people. This page that we had open here, as you can see, this was just—they were still in a period of manuscripts. This was illuminated. And this one was, on the other hand, blanks were left for initials here that were filled here and not filled here. The fact they—they're not exactly book ends, which is a point that before the age of machine press, there was really no such thing as a duplicate book, and particularly not in the first 30 years of publishing. This is a wonderful book. It was the most heavily illustrated book of the period and the first book that people could really buy for themselves, like a comic book, tells a history of the world."

She showed the same pages from the two different books side by side.

"Again," she said, "these look similar, but if you can see, the ink registration is very different, which is very important to historians of the book. These prints are reversed. Why, we don't know. If they made a mistake, they decided on the plate book and decided to put it together in a different way. There are drawings. Some of these are done by Duries, master and teacher. There are drawings that exist for this particular drawing, but you can see here the type slip. They didn't know, they were still learning how to deal with typography and handset typing. The ink quality is very different. Anyway, that is the point of illustrating it. Yes, we do have other copies of the Nuremberg Chronicle, but each one is different."[7]

The courtroom was silent for a few minutes as it was clear that the judge was done with questioning Ashton and everyone returned to their respective seats. Ashton went back up to the stand.

"Ms. Ashton," Judge Kaplan said, "is there anything else you would like to bring to my attention?"

"I object to that question, your Honor," Wales said, "to the form. It is too broad."

"Overruled," Judge Kaplan said. "We can have more pointedly-framed questions anytime you want. Ms. Choo is ready to ask them."

Judge Kaplan looked back at Ashton.

"Go ahead, Ms. Ashton," he said.

"There are several points that I think that would be important for the court to understand," Ashton said. "One is, as to the use of these materials, scholarly fashions change. As I said earlier, we calculate use in decades and centuries rather than in weeks or months. Materials are reused and rediscovered every 20 or 30 years. To give an analogy, a diary written by a midwife in Maine in the 18th Century was looked at many times by scholars and ignored as something trivial. A contemporary historian re-examined it and found it a great window into understanding colonial life in the 18th Century and published it and it has become a best seller in the historical community. The fact that something might not have been used in the last three weeks or three years has no merit as to the judgment of its scholarly worth. I think many of the letters from scholars here address that point."

Ashton mentioned the scholars' letters again starting her next point but Judge Kaplan stopped her. He hadn't let Wales talk about them so he couldn't let Asthon, either.

"I want to say one more thing about use, then," Ashton said. "These materials are used not only by scholars for their own research, they're heavily requested and used by scholars who are also teachers to instruct people in the kinds of history that I was just talking about right now. So when they are missing from the collection, students are deprived of learning, and this ranges all the way from such archival letters as the Thomas Edison documents through the medieval manuscripts, even very unexciting modern documents like the Edison stock certificates have been used and used recently in the classroom to help students understand what they can tell from business documents from the past. So you know, there is a kind of use that is not necessarily covered by the term. There has been a resurgence in publication of these lately. These documents have a different meaning in the library than they do in a private collector's house or on the market. A library gives them context and allows them to be used over a period of years, where scholars have access to them. That is all I have to say."

"Mr. Wales," Judge Kaplan said, "is there anything further?"

"I have several questions," Wales said, standing up and walking toward Ashton. "All these items you identified, they've all been recovered, have they not?"

"Well, not the maps from the Blaeu atlas or the Nuremberg Chronicle," Ashton said.

"The Nuremberg Chronicle was recovered, was it not?" Wales said.

"No," Ashton said.

"No?" Wales said. "Okay. Most of the items you identified this morning were recovered items. Is that right?"

"Some of the items were recovered," Ashton said.

"It is just a matter of time before they get back into Butler Hall and part of the Columbia collection. Is that right?"

"I think that is probably correct," Ashton said.

"Then they'll be available to scholars again, right?" Wales said.

"Yes," Ashton said.

"And then they'll be, when they get back to scholars, there will be no loss to scholarship," Wales said. "Isn't that right?"

"There is a five year loss to scholarship," Ashton said, still talking about only those things that had been recovered.

"There is a hiatus, but in the long term they will be there for scholars for this generation or the next generation?"

"The students at Columbia from 1993 to 1998 will not have been able to be exposed to them," Ashton said.

Wales moved on to the Edison papers and then to the Presidential letters that had been stolen.

"Let's talk about a good photocopy," Wales said. "Can it be read?"

"Yes," Ashton said.

"The same with Presidential papers, right, good photocopy, the text can be read?" Wales said. "Isn't that so?"

"It depends on which presidential papers you're speaking about," Ashton said.

"Well," Wales said, "the Washington papers?"

"The text can be read," Ashton said.

"In fact, the papers you showed us," Wales said, "from 1790, the Washington letter to John Jay on the opening of the Supreme Court, you showed us a photocopy. Did you have trouble reading that photocopy?"

"No," Ashton said.

"You read every word of it," Wales said, "right?"

"Yes," Ashton said, "but I didn't show you a photocopy, actually. I showed you the real thing."

"I think you showed us a photocopy, too?" Wales said.

"I didn't see one either, Mr. Wales," Judge Kaplan said.

"Okay," Wales said.

Wales was pretty much done. He continued to ask questions of this sort for the next few minutes and then ended the hearing.[8]

Ashton's more than three hours on the stand was the capstone to almost four years of steady involvement in the Spiegelman saga. At the end, there was nothing else for her to do but wait for her materials to move back uptown to the sixth floor of the Butler Library.

For their part, the defense team asked for ten days so that they could turn in another brief. They submitted it twenty-six days later.[9]

> The enormous time and efforts spent in this proceeding by this Court, defense attorneys, U.S. Attorney and Columbia scholars and witnesses in preparation for and in participation in *Fatico* proceedings illustrates well why upward departures following plea agreements are to be avoided. Nor does the Court of Appeals wish to be burdened with the inevitable appeal. Chief Judge Winter has publicly discussed the "crisis" in the Second Circuit—too many appeals, too few active judges. It is poor policy for a district judge to disregard guidelines and plea agreement, adding to the burdens of this Court, its players, and to the Second Circuit.[10]

So wrote Elliot Wales to Judge Kaplan in a letter dated four weeks after the *Fatico* hearing. The fact that all of the "wasted" time had already been spent by the parties mentioned by Wales would seem to work against his cause; that is, the time would only have been "wasted" if the judge decided the case in exactly the same manner he would have decided it before all those resources were spent. This was practically begging for a nontypical sentence simply to justify the expenditures.

But beyond this simple adverse reasoning, Wales' attempt to cajole Judge Kaplan into shying away from a departure that would further burden the already strained Second Circuit had the feel of a last, blank shot in the defense of a crumbling fort. Whether it was because Judge Kaplan had the sense that such an appeal would never materialize, that even if it did the sentence would be upheld, or that regardless of the outcome of such a procedure he was going to sentence Spiegelman in the way he felt most appropriate, Wales last attempt to preserve a standard sentence fell on deaf ears. The only answer Wales got to his letter came two days later when Judge Kaplan released his sentence. The fact that it came so hard upon the heels of Wales' own last plea should have told him that either he waited too long to send it or it merited almost no consideration by the judge.

Even in this final letter Wales stuck with his theory. It was "Columbia scholars and witnesses" whose time had been wasted, not the time of scholars from any of the myriad schools that had contributed to the cause.

Before Wales sent his letter, Paul Kurtz sent three copies of his Sentencing Memorandum in support of Daniel Spiegelman's position that an upward departure is not permitted to the clerk of the criminal division at the Southern District. It was only a couple of weeks before the sentencing hearing so Kurtz wanted to get the memo in front of Judge Kaplan as soon as possible. There might still be time yet to sway him a bit. By all accounts, Kurtz had done about as good a job as anyone in his position could have; he might yet get the sentence lessened.

The heading on the letter indicated that it was from the National Correctional Counseling Center in Bethesda, Maryland, of which "Paul. C. Kurtz, Esquire," was the executive director. But the letter might have been sent from the regional office—also listed on the letterhead—in Wayne, Pennsylvania. That was a bit further away from where Kurtz lived in Maryland, but it was important that both of his offices appeared to get equal time.

Daniel Spiegelman, aka William Taylor, aka Andreas Kessler, aka Daniel Kikabidze, aka Craig Wesley Hesseltine, aka Martin James Harris, had an arrest warrant issued for him in June 1995.[11] If he had simply pleaded guilty and quietly served his time in prison, he could have been out of incarceration in a couple of years and again selling the stash of rare books and letters that he had stolen from Columbia and squirreled away. Instead, on April 24, 1998, having already spent almost three years in jail and countless dollars on attorney's fees, he was sitting in a New York courtroom ruminating on the knowledge that the judge in front of him was disposed to increase his punishment well beyond the statutory maximum.

Early in that hearing Spiegelman watched as his sentencing expert, Paul Kurtz, began to spar with Judge Lewis Kaplan. It couldn't have been a pleasant experience for him, knowing that since he had already pleaded guilty his sentence was not in the hands of a jury but rather in the hands of the man in a robe behind the bench, arguing frequently with his attorney.

"Does property have an intrinsic value?" Kurtz said to the judge. "The paradox that we believe exists where we have a piece of property that is stolen under the exact same circumstances as Mr. Spiegelman has taken something from Columbia, and he is sentenced and the Court departs upward. Then we have the same piece of property being eventually sold to a private collector. The same piece of property is stolen, same values exist, how can he be sentenced? Should he be sentenced the same way because there's a loss of scholarly value from the private collector?"

But in retort, Judge Kaplan had an example of his own.

"A man steals from a drugstore a $2 vial of penicillin on Third Avenue in Manhattan, case 1," the judge said. "Case 2, someone is dying of a staph infection on an island in the middle of the Pacific. The man steals the only vial of penicillin within 5,000 miles. Same punishment?"

"Same value?" Kurtz said.

"Yes," Judge Kaplan said. "Same value. Same punishment? Same crime?"[12]

Daniel Spiegelman probably wished that he was on a remote Pacific island at that point as it became clear to him that the judge responsible for the next few years of his life saw him as the sort of person who would steal the last bottle of penicillin from someone with a staph infection. He was about to be sentenced by a judge who was actually coming up with on-the-spot hypothetical scenarios that refuted the points Spiegelman's lawyers were trying to make.

During all those late night trips to Columbia years earlier Spiegelman thought he was just stealing books—a commodity to be sold like any other. What Judge Kaplan was about to explain to him was that he had stolen much more than simply a fungible item to be sold on the open market, he had stolen from society its right to learn from the past. That was different than stealing furs or cars. And a slap on the wrist just wouldn't do.

The way the sentence began should have told anyone paying attention all they needed to know about how it was going to end: "Great research libraries are repositories of our social, cultural, and scientific heritage. Their rare books and manuscripts are vital to understanding the world and often are irreplaceable objects of study for scholars who add to our knowledge of ourselves and our environment."[13]

By the time those opening two sentences of the written opinion were released on the afternoon of April 24, Spiegelman already knew his fate. He had already sat and listened to Judge Kaplan earlier that morning offer his stern denunciations and justifications for the sentence. At one point Spiegelman, who was known for his sour temper, almost yelled an answer of "no" back at the judge after his usual sorry first effort hadn't registered with the Court.

"Mr. Spiegelman, your theft of rare books and manuscripts from Columbia certainly inflicted economic harm on Columbia," Judge Kaplan said. "But your theft, quite unlike a theft of money or replaceable objects, did something else as well. And I think given the tradition of public proceeding in criminal matter in this country, it is just appropriate to recount some of the things that you stole.

"You stole 17 medieval and Renaissance manuscripts dating from 1160 A.D. to 1550 A.D., including Euclid's Elementa, three Books of Hours with illumination, dating to the 15th Century, a 14th Century manuscript Roman de la Rose by Guillaume de Lorris and Jean de Meung, and two papal bulls, one 12th Century and one 13th Century.

You stole eight Arabic and Persian manuscripts dating from the 10th Century to 1887. You stole a 1493 edition of the Nuremberg Chronicle, and, as it happens, also a 1493 edition of Seneca's Proverbia.

"You stole 26 medieval, Renaissance and early documents from 1122 to 1789.

"You stole 284 historical maps dating from 1628 to 1891. You razored 237 individual maps out of a 17th Century version of Blaeu's Atlas Major. You stole 26 Presidential letters and documents dating from 1791 to 1918, including six letters by George Washington, eight from John Adams to William Tudor, and 12 letters from other presidents, including John Quincy Adams, Andrew Jackson, Abraham Lincoln and Woodrow Wilson. One of the Washington letters was the letter that Washington wrote to the first chief justice of the United States on the occasion of the first convening of the United States Supreme Court.

"You stole 133 letters and documents from and relating to Thomas Edison, dating from 1860 to 1903, including contracts, patent assignments and correspondence concerning the developments of the telegraph and the expansion of the telegraph network. Many of these items have not been recovered and may never be recovered."

"The philosopher George Santyana once said that 'those who cannot remember the past are condemned to repeat it.' You, Mr. Spiegelman, deprived generations of scholars and students of the irreplaceable raw materials by which they seek to discern the lessons of the past and help us to avoid repeating it. That's what differentiates your offense from a simple theft of money or other easily replaceable property.

"It is no answer to say, as your lawyers have argued, and they have defended you very vigorously and very ably, that there is no specific proof of what discovery would have been made from which stolen item and what that discovery would have been worth in dollars or would have meant to humanity. What is important is that you knowingly risked causing harm of that nature. The fact that your actions, by their very nature, prevent us from knowing exactly what damage you did cannot mitigate your punishment."[14]

The bulk of the written opinion, which runs to eighteen pages in the federal reporter, takes apart the Spiegelman defense piece by piece.

One of Spiegelman's refrains, variously expressed, is the suggestion that there is no proof that there was any specifically identifiable harm to scholarship as a result of his theft of these particular items, especially as some of them were recovered following Spiegelman's arrest. In the very narrowest sense he is right. It is impossible to say with an acceptable degree of confidence that the loss of a particular book or manuscript resulted in an identifiable loss of a specific intellectual insight or historical contribution, much less that the interim loss of those materials ultimately recovered did so during the period in which they were unavailable. It does not lie within human competence to say what would have occurred had the thefts not taken place—any more than we can say what discoveries would have been made or insights achieved but for the loss of knowledge occasioned by the destruction of the Library Alexandria, the rampant looting of European art treasures during World War II, or the infamous book-burnings conducted by the Nazi regime in Germany.

In the last analysis, then, by taking raw materials of importance to scholars and the academic community, Spiegelman knowingly risked causing substantial harm of a kind which is inherently unknowable, unquantifiable, and substantially non-monetary in character. The fact that we cannot know with certainty what new knowledge would have come from which artifact absent Spiegelman's actions, far from supporting Spiegelman's position, supports the view that a monetary measure alone cannot possibly account fully for the seriousness of his offense.[15]

As was typical in the hearing, Judge Kaplan compared the thefts by Spiegelman to those of the notorious or heartless. Like a person stealing the last antibiotic from sick people on a remote island to the destruction of the Mona Lisa to Nazis burning books, the thefts by Spiegelman in the eyes of Judge Kaplan were taken more seriously than even the most hopeful booklover could have expected.

Judge Kaplan quoted liberally from the scholars' letters. Despite the fact that by the end of the *Fatico* hearing, the defense was conceding many of its previously vehemently stated points, the sentencing opinion still noted points of contradiction between Wales' earlier written assertions and those of the scholars' letters. Wales had made a number of statements both in print and in court that didn't seem to be backed up by anything but his own opinions. Judge Kaplan took issue with this practice and quoted a few of the assertions made by Wales side by side with what was written by the scholars, not for the purpose of a detailed refutation but to "demonstrate their vacuity:"

> In each instance, unsubstantiated assertions by [Spiegelman's defense] confront detailed refutation by qualified and, indeed, renowned experts in the relevant fields. The Court credits the experts and rejects Spiegelman's position. The stolen materials have substantial scholarly value.[16]

And that was ultimately Wales' biggest mistake: His insistence at having the *Fatico* hearing at all. Certainly the procedure did nothing to ameliorate Judge Kaplan's desire to depart upward but any fair reading of the sentence demonstrates that it may well have further encouraged him. For instance, while addressing the defense argument that other copies exist of many of the still missing items the judge easily sided with the scholars that mere photocopies or reproductions of the content are nowhere near as valuable to scholars as the originals. But what hadn't been highlighted in the scholars' letters—but was clearly illustrated by Ashton at the hearing—was the fact that even contemporaneous publications of the same materials often contain important differences. Ashton had shown this by bringing in a copy of *Nuremberg Chronicles*, printed by the same printer in the same year as they stolen one, and letting the judge see how they differed and what that meant to the history of printing. He mentioned that in his opinion:

> Nor is the impact of the loss even of those materials which are rare rather than unique eliminated by the existence of other more or less

contemporaneous copies. The mass production of identical books to which we are accustomed in the late twentieth century is a comparatively recent development. As Ms. Ashton demonstrated at the hearing, even two copies of the Nuremberg Chronicles, both printed in 1483 by the same printer, have important differences, and the differences are significant to those who study the development of the book.[17]

Had there been no hearing, the judge would not have had the opportunity to cite to this demonstration as further evidence of the lack of accuracy of the monetary valuation. Nor would the judge then have been able to cite Wales' refutation of his own defenses on those very grounds during the hearing.

There is no question that Wales was a good and able defense attorney. But the *Fatico* hearing was clearly a mistake. Before talk of the hearing surfaced the only thing Judge Kaplan was relying on for his departure ammunition was Ashton's letter. When she and Galligan started gathering their forces in the fall of 1997 for a prolonged battle, that can only have been bad for the defense. The letters from the scholars came only after Spiegelman had fired his first attorney and decided to fight the (then modest) upward departure. Had Spiegelman simply been sentenced in the summer of 1997 it is likely he would not have gotten anywhere near the level of departure that Judge Kaplan finally settled on.

But Wales had little to do with those developments; he signed on to the case after the decision had been made to vigorously fight the departure. Still, by August 1997 the *Fatico* hearing was far from a sure thing. It was not until roughly five months later that Judge Kaplan would agree—reluctantly—to have the hearing.

When time for the hearing came around it was a rout and what happened there can only be laid at Wales' feet. Despite the letters Judge Kaplan had received, by March 1998 he still hadn't seen any of the stolen items in person. It was only after that hearing that he had a full sense, in living color, of the damage that Spiegelman had committed and how roughly he had treated such delicate materials. For the same reason criminal defense attorneys avoid allowing a jury to see graphic pictures of a crime scene, the defense should never have allowed Judge Kaplan to get anywhere near the items that Spiegelman stole and destroyed. The only way to do that would have been to have avoided the *Fatico* hearing altogether.

One of the Spiegelman defense team's arguments had nothing at all to do with the facts of the case and so it merited almost no treatment in the hearings or the letters from the scholars. Rather, it was a point of law. The defense claimed that since there had been a plea agreement in which Spiegelman had agreed to plead guilty to certain charges if the U.S.

Attorneys agreed to certain sentencing recommendations—including not seeking any departures—the judge was forbidden to break that agreement by departing.

The judge had heard from all three of Spiegelman's attorneys during oral arguments on this point, briefly, and had dismissed them each out of hand, sometimes with a bit of humor, as when he wondered aloud to Cohen why the federal system needed judges at all if the prosecution and the defense could simply agree on what should happen to the guilty party in question. In the final oral hearing that April, he addressed the matter more seriously, a preface to what he'd put down in the written opinion.

"Let me say a word about Sentencing Guidelines," Judge Kaplan said, again addressing Spiegelman. "Your counsel certainly are correct in saying that federal judges are obliged by law to adhere to the Sentencing Guidelines in most cases. But Congress never intended the Sentencing Guidelines to constitute blinders, obliging judges to look the other way when faced with extraordinary cases that warrant punishment greater or less than run-of-the-mill cases. They specifically provide that judges may depart from the Guidelines when 'there exists an aggravating or mitigating circumstance of a kind, or to a degree, not adequately taken into account ... in formulating the Guidelines that should result in a sentence different from that described.' The legal arguments your counsel have advanced in support of the argument that I lack authority to depart from the Guidelines in this case are, in my view, entirely without merit. For the most part, they fly in the face of the plain words of the Sentencing Reform Act and the Sentencing Guidelines themselves."

"The Sentencing Guidelines in theft cases measure the seriousness of an offense exclusively by reference," Judge Kaplan said, "at least prior to 1997, to the economic loss inflicted on the immediate victim. Your actions both risked inflicting and, to an important extent, actually inflicted noneconomic losses not only on Columbia University, the immediate victim of your offense, but on countless others who would have used these materials or benefited from the use of them by others, and those are aggravating circumstances in this case of a kind and to a degree not adequately taken into account in the Guidelines."[18]

In his written opinion he treated the matter similarly, but more fully. Since any appeal would consider what was in his written opinion, the justification was quite a bit more formal and well supported than what he'd say to Spiegelman in person:

Having thus determined the facts, the Court ordinarily would proceed to consider the proposed departure. It must pause first, however, to deal with Spiegelman's novel argument that the Court may not depart in this case, no matter what the facts, because it is bound by the plea agreement between Spiegelman and the government—most notably the sentencing stipulations and the agreements that neither the government nor the defendant would seek a departure.[19]

Judge Kaplan then spent almost three pages citing to both statute and case law indicating why this divergence from the plea agreement was not only proper, but clearly stipulated as such by the United States Sentencing Commission.

For the cause of the serious treatment of rare book crimes, this was the most important part of the opinion. While it is certainly true that the relatively novel idea of nonmonetary evaluation of rare materials was important to the wider book community, without this justification for the departure using both statutory law and jurisprudence, that novel approach meant nothing. He may have wanted to sentence Spiegelman to a more appropriate sentence than what was dictated by the Guidelines but without the ability to depart there is no way he could have done so.

On top of that, Judge Kaplan's sentence set a precedent that can be followed by other federal judges who deal with similar crimes. Nonmonetary evaluation of rare materials, after *US v. Spiegelman*, is no longer novel—it is actual precedent. Since this is simply a United States District Court decision, no lower courts are obligated to follow the ruling but these sorts of crimes are rare enough that the likelihood of this question coming up again in the same district very often is slim. The real value of this case to other jurisdictions is that it offers persuasive and sound theory for sentencing. That makes it strong persuasive authority for other similarly situated courts.

The more diffuse and potential impact of *US v. Spiegelman* on the wider federal sentencing system could not have mattered less to Spiegelman. Judge Kaplan's decision had a more immediate and pressing effect on his particular future. Not only was he still in jail a year after he was sure to be out, but it didn't look to him like he was about to get out anytime soon. Cohen had been confident of a thirty month sentence for the thief but Spiegelman knew he was looking at twice that amount. In court that morning, just after the judge had made his ruling, Wales pulled out all the stops.

"You've made your ruling as a matter of law," Wales said. "I'm now asking you as a matter of discretion and as a matter of judgment, please give healthy respect to what the United States Attorney's office does and to what the defense does and what the probation does. To brush it aside—"

"Let me ask you a question in regard to that," Judge Kaplan said. "Suppose that what I were considering here on my own motion after you and the government had agreed on a complete plea agreement was a downward departure. Do you think I should not do that?"

"If there's—" Wales said, then stopped. "Absolutely, that's right. If the defense agrees they're not going to make a motion for downward departure, then absolutely, the defense is bound, you should not downward depart."

"It is done every day in this court," Judge Kaplan said. "Isn't it?"

"I don't think it's done every day in this court, your Honor," Wales said.

"Help me out then," Judge Kaplan said. "One of the provisions of the plea agreements that I see all the time, where there is an agreement that neither side will seek a departure, provides that the defense is at liberty to present to the court any facts concerning sentence and to respond to any inquiries by the court. Isn't one of the customary purposes of defense lawyers insisting on that provision in plea agreements the hope that the court will on its own motion consider a downward departure, even though the defendant has agreed not to seek it, and to leave the defense free to respond in as full a fashion as possible in the hope of getting that downward departure, notwithstanding the agreement not to seek it? Isn't that what this is all about?"

"No. Absolutely not, your Honor," Wales said. "You're wrong. You're wrong. When there's an agreement made, it binds both sides. And defense attorneys, especially those of us who deal regularly with the United States Attorney's office and who value our relationship, we honor scrupulously our agreement, your Honor."

"I would not suggest otherwise," Judge Kaplan said.

"If we make an agreement we are not going to seek downward departure, we do not seek downward departure, your Honor," Wales said. "Because if we gained a slight advantage in one particular case we would just destroy our relationship and our reputation with the office for the rest of our careers. So, your Honor is wrong in that. These agreements we take seriously. We spend hours fashioning them. This one required a lot of research in terms of valuation. What your Honor is really doing is just brushing it aside and seeking to put your own values and your own view on it. And I think you're doing damage to the system."

But Wales had not been party to the valuation sessions and so he was noticeably vague as to how many hours it took to fashion the agreed upon amount. Still, he carried on lecturing the judge in the same manner for almost ten more minutes without break. By the end of that speech Spiegelman and the defense attorneys, it seemed, by rights should have been placed on pedestals outside the courthouse for their continued professional and conciliatory approach to the federal sentencing system.

"So, your Honor," Wales said, in conclusion, "I'm going to ask you to— I accept the fact that you want to upward depart. Okay. We fought that battle and for the moment we lost it. But in terms of five levels and in terms of within the five-level guideline, I'm going to ask you to temper it, your Honor, giving healthy respect to what the United States Attorney and the defense did in this case."

"He did get a three-level downward departure—"

"You wiped it out," Wales said.

"Excuse me," Judge Kaplan said. "For the plea and the cooperation absent which he would be looking this morning at 70 to 87 months, isn't that right?"

"Judge," Wales said, "you've wiped out that three-level adjustment by making a five level. Now, there are—let's put it this way. There really aren't any cases in this court where there's upward departure after a plea of guilty."

"*United States v. Dekjumnon*, 1996," Judge Kaplan said, "Second Circuit, affirmed. That is just one that came immediately to mind when I read that statement in your letter."

"Occasionally there's an upward departure negotiated," Wales said. "From time to time."

"Mr. Wales," Judge Kaplan said, "I was the sentencing judge in that case. I know the facts."

"I can't answer you, Judge," Wales said. "You're just giving me notice of it."

"But you are the one who stands here as a member of the bar and says there has never been an upward departure on a guilty plea and you don't have any idea. You are just saying it."

"Your Honor, I've been practicing in this court for many, many, many years," Wales said. "I've been involved in Sentencing Guidelines. As a matter of fact, when there is a plea agreement, not only do district judges accept it but they always sentence to the lower end of the line. How you feel about this matter, basically the upward departure cases are those after trial but you do not have—when you have a situation where there's a plea agreement and the parties have agreed not to seek upward departure, lower departure, and it's been complete, maybe you're the one instance. But it's not really fair for you to cite yourself in precedence, your Honor."

"It is not fair for you to make a flat, unsubstantiated representation to the Court without having any idea that it is wrong," Judge Kaplan said.

"I could be in error with one case, but I've checked it out with many of my colleagues and thought about it long and hard," Wales said. "I did not make that statement on the spur of the moment. I may be in error."

"I accept your representation of good faith," Judge Kaplan said. "It is the preparation that I question."

"You sprung it on me at the last minute," Wales said. "The system requires when there's a plea agreement they're really not there for departure. That's the practice in the court. You really are doing a disservice to the practice and what we lawyers do, so I'm going to ask you to on that five-level increase tone it down, give the lawyers credit, give Spiegelman credit that he did all these things."

"I am giving Spiegelman credit that he did all these things," Judge Kaplan said.

"That he cooperated and helped Columbia recover, that's right," Wales said. "After all, he could have not helped them recover. Then the loss would have been substantial. We still have a monetary loss which has nothing to do with the recovery and nonrecovery, but in terms of scholarship, more than half the items have gone back to Columbia, so we do not have a loss of scholarship, your Honor."

"You have a smaller one," Judge Kaplan said.

"A substantially smaller loss," Wales said. "Not minimal, substantially. There's a long list of items that he returned. I'm going to ask your Honor to knock down that level five, to make it lower, to give him credit for what he's done and to give the United States Attorney and defense the healthy respect they're entitled to for having resolved this matter without controversy."

"Thank you, Mr. Wales," Judge Kaplan said. "I am not altering my ruling with respect to the extent of the departure. I have immense respect for the United States Attorney's office and for the defense bar that regularly practices in this court and I think that plea agreements ought to be respected most of the time. Nonetheless, it is my view that it is my responsibility, imposed upon me by the Congress of the United States, to decide the sentence in this case."[20]

Judge Kaplan's written opinion ended like this:

> Spiegelman intentionally or knowingly risked inflicting, and inflicted, substantial harm not only upon his immediate victims, Columbia University and its professors and students, but also upon the greater academic community and society as a whole. In callously stealing, mutilating, and destroying rare and unique elements of our common intellectual heritage, Spiegelman did not simply aim to divest Columbia of $1.3 million worth of physical property. He risked stunting, and probably stunted, the growth of human knowledge to the detriment of us all. By the very nature of the crime, it is impossible to know exactly what damage he has done. But this much is clear: this crime was quite different from the theft of cash equal to the appraised value of the materials stolen because it deprived not only Columbia, but the world of irreplaceable pieces of the past and the benefits of future scholarship. To treat Spiegelman's offense as being of the same gravity as the theft of $1.3 million in cash would be to deny the unmistakable importance of the undiscovered knowledge likely buried within the items he stole. Thanks to Spiegelman, that knowledge now may remain forever undiscovered.[21]

With that Judge Kaplan sentenced Spiegelman to sixty months in prison, three years of supervised release, and 300 hours of community service. Judge Kaplan preferred for the community service to be in the aid of adult literacy.

At the time of sentencing Spiegelman had been in custody for thirty-four months; Paul Kurtz asked the judge if he could spend the next two years and two months in Otisville, site of the minimum security prison "camp." Kurtz suggested that he qualified for such treatment.[22]

Spiegelman was also ordered to pay restitution of $314,150. He could pay in monthly increments of $250.

At the end of June 1998, Paul C. Kurtz, Spiegelman's federal sentencing expert, was back in the courtroom before a different judge. He was representing Tohmes Peter in a criminal case in the Southern District of New York involving a scheme to launder millions of dollars in narcotics money.[23] Before a hearing on the sentencing of Peter, Kurtz sent a note to the judge asking for a postponement. He explained "I recently lost my elderly mother and, as a result of attending to personal family business, have fallen behind in attending to client affairs."[24] But Kurtz's mother was alive and well living in Silver Spring, Maryland, not far from where Kurtz himself lived.

The only significance of this defense counsel lie—one in a long string that Kurtz told to judges while representing clients—was that it was his last. On July 7, 1998, almost four years to the day after Consuelo Dutschke had discovered the Columbia thefts and a mere two and a half months after Spiegelman had been sentenced, Paul Kurtz was arrested and charged with forty-four federal criminal counts of making false statements.[25]

Kurtz had been Spiegelman's federal sentencing specialist retained for the sole purpose of lessening his sentence. In that endeavor, of course, he had been spectacularly unsuccessful. (Though Elliot Wales would later say of Kurtz that his sentencing brief was superb. Other people in the courtroom would also say that he was the more talented of the two Spiegelman attorneys.)

Kurtz, it turned out, was not an attorney. The National Correctional Counseling Center—an institute with branches in both Maryland and Pennsylvania that he had claimed to have started solely for the sake of specializing as defense counsel on federal sentencing cases—did not exist except as a front for his bogus practice. A fifty-state search in July 1998 conducted by the FBI showed that Kurtz was not only not licensed to practice in New York, but also not licensed to practice anywhere in the United States.[26]

For a decade Kurtz had represented criminal defendants, mostly those in the sentencing process. On behalf of about 100 clients, he had fooled judges in several jurisdictions along the eastern seaboard. And while in almost all of those cases he was merely brought in to serve along with other counsel as a sentencing expert, his own later plea led to a spate of appeals by former clients.

A subsequent search by the FBI on Paul Kurtz did reveal his qualifications to work with the sentencing guidelines: personal experience. Starting with a misdemeanor conviction for passing bad checks in 1970, Kurtz had racked up felony convictions up and down the east coast for crimes ranging from false statements to larceny to bank fraud to "theft by deception." This goes a long way toward explaining the kinship he felt with criminal defendants like Spiegelman.

The matter of *Unites States v. Kurtz* took a good long while to resolve. From the time of his arrest in 1998 until he surrendered to the Bureau of Prisons in March 2000, the court was treated to a flurry of motions and hearings many, no doubt, aided by Kurtz's own thoughts on his defense. In truth, there can be few people in American legal history who have had as much experience as both defendant and defense counsel as Kurtz. In the end, of course, all that added up to was forty-one months in federal prison.

His experience did not help him out either in his own sentencing or on appeal, where he claimed that his sentence was counter to the Guidelines' intent.[27] Kurtz's stiff sentence of forty-one months in prison, three years probation, $12,800 in restitution, and $5,000 penalty represented its own uniqueness within the Guidelines: The sentencing judge agreed with the prosecution that Kurtz's myriad crimes constituted a higher level of culpability than simply making false statements. It constituted obstruction of justice.

When Kurtz eventually agreed in his plea to three counts of making false statements and one count of credit card fraud he figured on a light sentence. When the prosecution asked for and received a sentence based on obstruction of justice Kurtz found himself staring down the barrel of his second nightmare scenario case in as many years.

The sentencing judge agreed with the prosecution and reasoned that Kurtz's continued lying had jeopardized so many clients for so many years that his was an atypical case, and one that fit the Committee's charge to "use the guideline section most applicable to the nature of the offense conduct charged in the count of which the defendant was convicted."[28] Kurtz appealed the sentence.

The Second Circuit Court of Appeals, which heard his appeal, declined to overturn the lower court's sentence. "Given the nature of Kurtz's conduct, which deprived defendants in criminal cases of their constitutional rights to be represented by bona fide attorneys, there can be no doubt that the obstruction of justice guideline more aptly covered his conduct."[29] Kurtz would have to complete his prison sentence.

In November 2004 he did just that. Kurtz left prison that month and began the supervised release portion of his sentence that was to last three more years. The next month he began paying his restitution—in $250 increments.

Spiegelman, for his part, did not attempt to appeal his sentence based on Kurtz's involvement. In July 1998 Wales spoke with both Spiegelman and his mother and neither wanted to appeal. This may have been because Wales himself, when asked to comment on his former co-counsel, had said that "if all lawyers acted as well and as competently in proceedings as [Kurtz] did, we would have a great bar." Or it may well have been that Spiegelman was not planning on being in prison very long anyway.

NOTES

1. *United States v. Spiegelman*, Fatico Hearing, March 20, 1998, 69–72.
2. Ibid., 72–73.
3. Ibid., 74–81.
4. Ashton interview.
5. Fatico Hearing at 84–86.
6. Ibid., 88–90.
7. Ibid., 92–94.
8. Ibid., 94–99.
9. *United States v. Spiegelman*, Defense Memorandum, April 15, 1998.
10. H. Elliot Wales to Judge Lewis Kaplan, April 22, 1998.
11. *United States v. Spiegelman*, Complaint, June 14, 1995.
12. *United States v. Spiegelman*, Sentencing Hearing, April 24, 1998, 5–6.
13. *United States v. Spiegelman*, 4 F. Supp. 2d 275, 277 (1998).
14. Spiegelman Sentencing Hearing, 12–13.
15. 4 F. Supp., 279–280.
16. Ibid., 281.
17. Ibid., 282.
18. Sentencing Hearing, 13–15.
19. 4 F. Supp. 282.
20. Sentencing Hearing, 19–27.
21. 4 F. Supp. 292.
22. Sentencing Hearing, 28–31.
23. *United States v. Paul C. Kurtz*, Arrest Warrant and Arraignment, 1:98-m-1595, August 6, 1998.
24. Benjamin Weiser, "US Says a Convincing 'Lawyer' Lacked One Thing: His License," *New York Times*, July 15, 1998, A1.
25. Kurtz Arrest Warrant and Arraignment.
26. *United States v. Kurtz*, Sealed Complaint. From testimony of FBI Special Agent.
27. *United States v. Kurtz*, Docket No. 00-1105, January 3, 2001.
28. Ibid.
29. Ibid.

CHAPTER 7

My Deep Apologies to This Court

Spiegelman did his stealing uptown in Morningside Heights. He was sentenced downtown at the Federal Plaza. In September 1999, he was incarcerated in a halfway house in midtown. By that fall his impression of the island of Manhattan can't have been favorable.

So he decided to leave.

A few days before the end of the month, about a year and a half after his sentence began, Spiegelman escaped from the halfway house that had been his home and headed for his mother's house across the river. On Friday, the first day of October, he called Basil Panagopulos, an autograph dealer at Alexander's Autographs in Greenwich, Connecticut, and told him he was a Russian importer/exporter and that he had some rare papers to sell.

This was to be his second sale since leaving jail—he had already unloaded a privateer's commission issued by John Adams and an appointment issued by Abraham Lincoln to a private collector.[1] The materials he wanted to sell to Panagopulos included material with the writing and signatures of Thomas Edison, Thomas Jefferson, and James Monroe.[2] These were all part of the cache of unrecovered Columbia materials that he had claimed he didn't know the location of.

Spiegelman called Panagopulos from a pay phone on a street in New York. That was the first indication that Panagopulos got that the seller might not be legitimate. People selling autographs of the sort that Spiegelman claimed to have didn't usually call from pay phones. This got the dealer's hackles up.[3]

"Can you bring them in?" Panagopulos said. "I'd like to see them."

"Sure," Spiegelman said. "I can be there in an hour and a half."

Sufficiently suspicious, Panagopulos decided to call a friend of his who was also an autograph dealer. Panagopulos was not an expert in the sorts of autographs Spiegelman was offering and the description of these items seemed too good to be true. Something in his head clicked and told him he should check this stuff out in advance of the Russian seller showing up. As it turns out, the whole scenario played out like a condensed version of what had happened to Spiegelman in the Netherlands.

Bruce Gimelson, the dealer friend who Panagopulos thought might have some insight, saved him what would have likely been a bunch of money and certainly a lot of aggravation. Gimelson told Panagopulos that the items sounded like something he had seen in an alert in a trade publication; they reminded him of documents stolen from Columbia some years earlier.

Panagopulos didn't know Jean Ashton but looked up her number and called. Luckily, she was in the office at the time. He asked if she was still missing some of the presidential items.[4] She was surprised to get the call, but surprising calls from people giving information about various items related to the Spiegelman thefts had been trickling in for five years. She consulted the list of missing items and quickly confirmed that some of the things the seller had offered Panagopulos sounded like they might be hers. But the identification of documents was an often difficult process, even when the person doing the identifying had the documents in their presence. Over the phone and counting on the hurried description of a furtive description, Ashton was far from certain the items were Columbia's.[5]

In fact, neither Panagopulos nor Ashton thought the man who called from the street was a thief. Ashton, of course, assumed that Spiegelman was still in jail. And so, if these were Columbia documents, she figured they would simply be ones that Spiegelman had sold to another man before he was captured in 1995. Panagopulos—even after he later confirmed that the items were stolen—also assumed the seller was just the middle man. There was no way he could have committed the crime himself. He seemed like a patsy.

Ashton gave Panagopulos a description of many of the missing presidential papers. He wrote down what he could on a scrap piece of paper—mostly initials and dates—and put the paper in his desk drawer. When the man brought the items in he'd take them to his desk for inspection. From there he'd be able to look at the list he'd jotted on the paper in the drawer.

After talking to Ashton but before Spiegelman arrived Panagopulos called the Greenwich police. Talking to Ashton had made him think there was a better than average chance that what this guy was selling was not on the up and up, even if it wasn't the Columbia stuff. The police, on the other hand, weren't convinced. They refused to send an officer to sit around in his store waiting for Spiegelman to show up on the off chance that some of the items were stolen. They told him to call back when he *knew* the stuff was stolen.

By that time it might be too late, Panagopulos knew. The seller would probably not stick around and wait for the cops to show up. So, as had happened with Hesselink in the Netherlands, it was up to the dealer to come up with a plan and convince the authorities to take the matter seriously.

Spiegelman arrived at Panagopulos' place almost exactly when he said he would. As he had on the phone—and so many previous times with such success—Spiegelman played the role of a Russian importer/exporter, claiming to be a man named Andrew Osharsky. After a few formalities, Spiegelman pulled from his case a military commission signed by Thomas Jefferson. He had no idea how much any of the stuff—the incredibly valuable stuff—he had was worth. And so he just let Panagopulos look at it without even mentioning price. This was a further indication to the dealer that the seller was only a middleman.

Panagopulos inspected the things while quietly looking down into his desk drawer to see if any were on Ashton's list. A couple seemed to be. On cue, while Panagopulos was in the midst of the inspection, one of his employees came into the room. In a perfectly natural voice Panagopulos called out to the man.

"Can you call the accountant and ask about our taxes," Panagopulos said. That was the prearranged signal for the employee to call the police.

This time the police didn't hesitate. Within a few minutes two burly cops were at the door. Spiegelman was promptly arrested. Panagopulos almost felt bad for the man; he was still certain that this Russian exporter was just a guy who had come across some of this stuff and bought it on the cheap. Panagopulos could tell that Spiegelman had no earthly idea what the value of the stuff he was trying to sell was—to him that meant he couldn't be the mastermind of this highly creative Columbia crime.

The documents that Spiegelman had in his immediate possession were confiscated and eventually made their way back to Columbia. It became clear right away that, as Ashton had always suspected, Spiegelman was still in possession of many of the materials that he claimed to have sold. Since his mother lived in the immediate area—and had most likely driven him to Panagopulos' store—it was thought that that was where the cache was. But though the police went to his mother's house, they had no warrant for entry. The house was never searched.

Later that night Panagopulos went down to the police station. He had to give a more formal statement about what had happened. While he was there an officer told him that the guy who had come into his store was the actual thief who had pulled off the heist six years earlier. He had quite a rap sheet, including the recent successful escape and at least two prior attempts. Also, he was to be considered armed and dangerous.

Panagopulos couldn't believe it. The guy who had come into his store didn't seem at all like a criminal mastermind, much less someone who could be considered dangerous. But regardless of what he thought the police had the federal criminal in a cell under surveillance by camera.

When Panagopulos looked at the closed circuit monitor it only confirmed the image he had of the man in his store. Far from planning an escape, Spiegelman was curled up tightly on his cot. Sound asleep.[6]

Six days later Spiegelman was again in downtown Manhattan but this time without the assistance of either Paul Kurtz or H. Elliot Wales. Kurtz was in prison and Wales was out of Spiegelman's price range. Through the month of October Spiegelman retained Barry Fallick as counsel but by the beginning of November he was assigned to a federal public defender, Robert Baum.[7]

By the spring of 2000 Spiegelman must have felt like he was experiencing déjà vu. Katherine Choo was again the United States Attorney prosecuting the case. Cathy Begley was again the FBI Special Agent helping Choo. And, once again, the person helping Spiegelman's lead attorney with this aspect of the case was not a licensed attorney—though, as an NYU law student, she did have more formal training than Kurtz.

There was another similarity to his previous procedure worth noting. Spiegelman was arrested on October 1, 1999. Through various requested extensions, Spiegelman wouldn't be sentenced for almost eight more months. He, with the help of his attorneys, seemed to have a particular knack for delaying final judgment.

At a sentencing conference on April 7, 2000, an even more threatening similarity reared its ugly head: Judge Loretta Preska announced that she was considering an upward departure for Spiegelman's new sentence.[8] Appointed to the federal bench in 1992 by President Bush, Judge Preska couldn't be said to have had a lot in common with Judge Kaplan except the proximity of their offices—they were next door to one another—and the seriousness with which they took Spiegelman's crimes.

"My question is whether or not the criminal history category which we find ourselves in here adequately reflects the seriousness of Mr. Spiegelman's past history and likelihood of recidivism," Judge Preska said. "I am least considering an upward departure on that ground."[9]

This time around Spiegelman was charged not only with the transport of stolen goods interstate but also with escaping from the Le Marquis Community Correction Center in Manhattan. This time around, too, there had been a plea agreement put in place before the parties came before the judge. Spiegelman's attorney informed the judge of the fact.

"I certainly am aware that your Honor is not bound by that agreement but I think it is fair to say that in reaching the plea agreement which we reached the parties considered the criminal history category," Baum said. "I am sure the government was fully aware of it and reached the agreement that we reached. Obviously, if your Honor would like me to address that issue I would be happy to address it but other than that advising you in direct response to your question I think that at least I can say from the plea negotiations many issues were considered."

Not quite Elliot Wales, but the point was the same.

"Thank you," Judge Preska said, then she looked at the U.S. Attorney. "Ms. Choo."

"Your Honor, I believe in light of the plea agreement that we have entered into with Mr. Baum's client that we cannot take a position that the criminal history category underrepresents the seriousness of his prior history," Choo said. "We have stipulated to the history being in category 3 and so I feel that we cannot vary from that in front of the court."

"What is the practice in a situation such as this where the judge is considering a departure from the plea agreement?" Judge Preska said. "It seems to be that both sides, certainly the defense, but both sides would brief it. Yes or no? What is the practice?"

Spiegelman sat quietly though he could have provided helpful information to the judge. Instead, Choo spoke up.

"I must admit that I think it is fairly uncommon in the office for it to happen," Choo said. "This issue, or an analogous one, not based on criminal history but seriousness of the offense, did arise in the prior conviction for the underlying theft of these manuscripts and other documents from Columbia University. The court there acted sua sponte, requested the parties, principally the government, to provide certain evidence to the court so the government acted as a conduit to bring certain witnesses to court for the court's consideration but—"

"It was factual material?" Judge Preska said.

"It was factual material, your Honor," Choo said, "and we did not make any argument to the court because of the fact that we were bound by our agreement."

"All right," Judge Preska said.

"May I just be heard briefly," Baum said.

"Yes sir," Judge Preska said.

"On the factual issue, Mr. Spiegelman has one conviction that wasn't counted," Baum said. "That is a conviction that occurred seventeen years ago. Other than that one conviction which wasn't counted his criminal history category was enhanced for various enhancements having committed this crime. If your Honor is considering an upward departure because it underrepresents, I submit to your Honor that on the facts it clearly does not underrepresent."

"Underrepresents and also the likelihood of recidivism," Judge Preska said. "I think that is an issue that is a glaring one in this case."

"I understand your Honor's concern on that issue," Baum said. "I think that is—the fact jumps out from the facts of the case, but I think that the— when you look—and I was prepared to argue this to the court—when you look at overall the facts and circumstances which is simply this, that if your Honor sentenced him at the top of the guidelines he would have served seven years for this incident basically because he served five previously and if you gave him the top of the guidelines that is two so—"

"It is two different incidents," Judge Preska said, "and my issue is—"

"In some ways it is," Baum said.

"Clearly, I too will sentence Mr. Spiegelman for this incident," Judge Preska said.

"Right," Baum said.

"He has already been sentenced for the other one," Judge Preska said.

"Absolutely correct," Baum said.

"My concern, and the reason I am considering an upward departure, is because of the likelihood of recidivism which has been demonstrated by this incident," Judge Preska said. "It surely related back to the earlier one in that it is recidivist behavior from the earlier incident but it is in no way punishment for the earlier incident."

"It can't be," Baum said.

"Clearly," Judge Preska said.

"I think it would be problematic," Baum said. "I think Ms. Choo articulated some of the potential issues when it is based upon a plea agreement. I am at your Honor's discretion. I would merely urge your Honor that the guidelines itself in light of his criminal background and in terms of recidivism, it is his third conviction going back seventeen years. You are correct that it is a second incident arising from the prior one but I am not sure that with the sentencing enhancements that were attached to this, that it merits further enhancing for this incident, so I most respectfully urge your Honor to consider the facts before you go forward with sentencing today."

"I understand what you say, however, I think I would still like to see your papers on this," Judge Preska said. "I am considering an upward departure, I think, probably more specifically stated, because of the likelihood of recidivism. When would you like to put something in, Mr. Baum? It does not have to be lengthy. It is up to you. Whatever you want."

"I understand," Baum said.

"At your convenience," Judge Preska said.

"May I have two weeks, your Honor?" Baum said.

"Yes sir," Judge Preska said. "Would you like, counsel, for me to give you a date three weeks out?"

"That seems appropriate," Baum said.

"And then if Ms. Choo for some reason wants to put something in, fine," Judge Preska said. "If not, fine."

"That seems appropriate," Baum said.

"Thank you," Judge Preska said.[10]

The court set a date for almost a month later: May 3 at 4 p.m.

On May 24, 2000, the second sentencing hearing for Daniel Spiegelman in the United States District Court for the Southern District of New York got under way. It was supposed to start at 3 p.m. but the proceeding was delayed a bit because Robert Baum had a 2:30 p.m. sentencing hearing that went long.[11]

Judge Preska asked if both parties had had a chance to read the latest presentencing report. They had, and Baum had some objections. The first two were resolved in Spiegelman's favor but then they revisited a familiar charge.

"Your Honor," Baum said, "just one other matter. Paragraph 64, which talks about other arrests for Mr. Spiegelman, it states that he was arrested by United States border patrol officers in San Diego in 1983 and charged with assault on a federal officer. However, it goes on to state that there was no record of this arrest or any record of the defendant in the State of California, and they could not verify that in any way. That being the case, I ask that that be stricken from the record. Mr. Spiegelman was never charged nor arrested for assaulting a federal officer, just that simple."

"Ms. Choo," Judge Preska said.

"Your Honor, Ms. Begley informs me that in fact there is a record of this arrest that the FBI was able to find," Choo said. "I don't believe it was a serious assault, but the charge was one of assault on a federal officer, so we would request that the paragraph remain as is. We do not agree with Mr. Baum's representations."

"Mr. Baum," Judge Preska said.

"May I just have a moment," Baum said.

"Yes sir," Judge Preska said.

Katherine Choo took that time to rise again.

"Your Honor, if I may also note, Mr. Spiegelman's counsel in the prior case before Judge Kaplan raised the same objection," Choo said. "I made the same representation to the court, and the court did not delete the analogous numbered paragraph in the prior PSR, and we would just ask that the court do the same thing here."

"Your Honor," Baum said, "I have the transcript of the proceeding where this was raised before Judge Kaplan, but I don't think Judge Kaplan ever ruled on it. He made a comment about it. I can certainly show it to Ms. Choo, what his comment was. If I may read from the transcript, Mr. Spiegelman's lawyer at the time Mr. Cohen, said the following at page 31 of the sentencing conference on July 30, 1997:

> *Mr Cohen*: Somebody is going to read it later and say: Oh, he was arrested. He probably beat the case or something like that.

> *The Court*: How many people are walking around with disorderly
> conduct convictions sitting at lunch counters at Selma, Alabama? It
> can be misunderstood, there is no question. It is not fair, no question.

The Court went on to say "I don't think that there is anything to be gained
by further hearing on that issue." So I am not sure whether he ruled on it or
whether in a way he was ruling on it. Let's assume that he was detained and
fingerprinted. There is no record of any arrest. There is certainly no record of
any conviction. Being detained and fingerprinted perhaps for investigation
should not be set forth as an arrest, or even as an allegation that he assaulted.
Mr. Spiegelman maintains quite vociferously that he was never arrested and
never assaulted anyone, and there is nothing to support that that, in fact,
happened."

"Ms. Choo," Judge Preska said, "you say you have something to support it."

"May I just have one moment, your Honor," Choo said. "Your Honor, all
I can represent to the court is that there is a record of the arrest, according
to Ms. Begley. The Bureau has a record of this defendant being arrested
after coming across the border from Mexico. He was scratching the officer
in the arrest. He was extradited to New York which I think dates back to
1983. Ms. Begley was not aware of the disposition of the charge back in San
Diego. There clearly is a report of an arrest. This paragraph does not cite to
any conviction, but it does note that there was an arrest, and I believe that
that's accurate."

"Anything else on this, Mr. Baum?" Judge Preska said.

"Nothing further, your Honor," Baum said.

"I decline to delete it, but do not rely upon it in connection with this
sentence," Judge Preska said. She then got on to the subject of the sentence.[12]

In the end there was no upward departure given to Spiegelman on this
second go around. Robert Baum went toe to toe with Judge Preska for almost a half an hour on the subject of recidivism and whether the standard
Guidelines approach to Spiegelman's crime was appropriate or understated
the seriousness. To the knowing observer some of his arguments could have
seemed a bit misplaced—they were certainly repetitive—but to someone not
familiar with Spiegelman, Baum wove a convincing defense against departure. Particularly in light of the fact that Judge Preska seemed determined to
depart upward right from the very beginning.

For her part, Katherine Choo did as capable a job as the plea agreement
would allow. At one point Baum suggested the she was on the cusp of
crossing the line—Choo had been reminding the court that there were still
many missing items and the fact that Spiegelman had lied about them in
the previous trial suggested that he might still have some hidden—but she
never crossed the line. Perhaps if Judge Preska has asked her more pointed

questions the result might have been different, but as it was Choo had no real say in the outcome.

"It is with the greatest reluctance that I decline to depart upwardly," Judge Preska said finally. She then sentenced Spiegelman to another twenty-four months of incarceration and three more years of supervised release.[13]

It was at this point that Spiegelman himself stood to speak. He had never spoken much more than a sentence at one time before in court so this last speech was positively a disquisition.

"I'm sorry, your Honor," Spiegelman said. "I wish to apologize for the trouble that I have brought to this Court and to you personally, your Honor, and to the government, Ms. Choo and Ms. Begley. I have made an error and I hope I can remedy it in the future. Indeed, my deep apologies to this Court."[14]

So he'd apologized to the court for taking up its time. He'd apologized to both Begley and Choo for taking up their time. If he felt at all sorry toward Columbia, there was no mention of it.

The Historical Society of Pennsylvania sits on Locust Street in Philadelphia, Pennsylvania, in an area that has seen more than its share of American history. Founded in 1824, the HSP houses some of the nation's great treasures including more than 600,000 printed items and 19 million manuscript and graphic items. It is a very appealing target for collectors willing to break the law, particularly those with an inside track.

While Daniel Spiegelman was busy peddling his wares in Europe in the fall of 1994, a custodian at the HSP began a little enterprising thievery of his own. He had after-hours access to many of the items not on display at the HSP and started taking advantage of that access. He wasn't personally interested in the stuff he was stealing—if he wanted to appreciate most of it he could see it every day at work—rather he was helping a local collector accrue a personal museum. The collector happened to be an electrical contractor who had done some work for the historical society in the past and became enamored of some of the pieces. He wasn't planning on selling any of the items; he simply wanted to own them.[15]

Over a number of years the custodian, Ernest Medford, acquired about 200 items for the collector, George Csizmazia. The take included a gold snuff box from 1735 that had belonged to Alexander Hamilton, a ring containing a lock of George Washington's hair, the wedding band of Patrick Henry's wife, and a Lancaster County long rifle crafted in 1785. It wasn't until this rifle and several Civil War era swords were discovered to be missing in November 1997 that the Historical Society knew of the thefts. Csizmazia, an electrical contractor who had performed work at the HSP, was quickly questioned and then arrested. He then taped a conversation in which the custodian admitted his own guilt.[16]

Similar to the Spiegelman case, both Medford and Csizmazia pleaded guilty in exchange for an agreement that the government would offer a sentencing recommendation and not pursue an upward departure. Also as in Spiegelman, the government followed through with the agreement. But the sentencing judge departed upward anyway after hearing the statements of Susan Stiff, the President of the Historical Society, and concluding, like Judge Kaplan, that the monetary loss understated the value of the stolen items to the community.[17]

The ordinary Guideline range of the Medford and Czizmazia sentence was similar to that of Spiegelman: twenty-seven to thirty-three months. When the district court departed upward, the increase brought the sentence to forty-eight months. Less than the Spiegelman sentence but at least none of the prison time in this case would have been served outside of the United States. The two thieves immediately appealed.

Writing for the Third Circuit Court of Appeals, Judge (now Associate Supreme Court Justice) Samuel Alito overturned the sentence and sent the matter back down to the district court for further proceedings consistent with his opinion. But Alito, sitting with two other judges, did not overturn the sentence based on the fact that an upward departure was imposed but rather based on several small and technical details about the way the sentence was imposed. In the opinion, Alito actually went out of his way to support Kaplan's theory of departure and reinforce that monetary value should not be the sole basis of value under the Guidelines:

> The price set by the commercial market is insufficient to "fully capture the harmfulness of the [defendants'] conduct." The antiques stolen in this case unquestionably have historical and cultural importance. Moreover, the thefts affected the HSP in ways different in kind from a loss of money or other easily replaceable property, for these thefts damaged the HSP's reputation. In addition, the monetary value of these objects does not adequately take into consideration the real but intangible harm inflicted upon all of the other victims of the offense, including the City of Philadelphia and the general public. Because [the Guidelines] applies to thefts that cause financial harm to the immediate victim of the offense, the non-monetary damage caused here and the harm inflicted upon the public at large justify the District Court's upward departure.[18]

Spiegelman never made it to the Second Circuit Court of Appeals so there is no opinion, other than Judge Kaplan's district court opinion, on which other courts may rely for precedent. In the American federal court system, district courts have limited mandatory precedence value (though the intellectual heft of the theory and written opinion can carry a lot of water). Circuit Courts of Appeals, on the other hand, have great precedence value.

If the Second Circuit Court of Appeals had listened to arguments on both sides of the *Spiegelman* case and then affirmed Judge Kaplan's ruling, the case would have had some real purchase in American law. But that didn't happen.

But what did happen is the next best thing. The Third Circuit gave its imprimatur to the opinion. Not only is the *Medford* opinion binding in the Third Circuit (Pennsylvania, New Jersey, Delaware) but it also offers the rest of the country the heft of a Circuit Court of Appeals opinion. In other words, the opinion has more weight now that it has the stamp of approval of an appeals court. Other district court judges are far more willing to rely on an opinion that has been specifically mentioned as proper by the Third Circuit.

What that means for judges and for United States Attorneys like Bob Goldman, the man who prosecuted Medford and Czizmazia, is a great deal. Kaplan's opinion broke new ground. For that reason alone it was susceptible to being overturned on appeal. It was certainly a legitimate decision based fully on the rules of the Guidelines, but it was still new territory. Given the wrong set of three judges on the Second Circuit, the opinion could have been mooted. But that didn't happen.

When the Third Circuit gave this line of reasoning its stamp of approval, the Kaplan decision entered the realm of serious *stare decisis*. Prosecutors, both state and federal, can now rely on the reasoning of that opinion when prosecuting or making sentencing recommendations for rare book and other cultural criminals. The theory behind the *Spiegelman* decision is no longer simply that of a judge in the Southern District of New York but rather one that has been endorsed by a higher court, and at least one member of the highest court.

But the Guidelines no longer exist as they did when Spiegelman was sentenced; and this was true even before the Guidelines were declared unconstitutional by the Supreme Court. The Guidelines were always a work in progress, changing from one year to the next and one Circuit to the next. The federal sentencing environment that Spiegelman stepped in to in 1998 was different that the one that existed just two years later: decisions were handed down all the time that significantly changed the ways judges could sentence felons. In fact, it is likely that had Spiegelman been sentenced two years later, the way Judge Kaplan considered evidence at the *Fatico* hearing would have been significantly different.

So, in a strange way, the dismantling of the Guidelines may give more weight to the *Spiegelman* decision. Since the Guidelines are no longer mandatory, federal judges have more latitude in their sentencing. They still consider the Guidelines in making their decisions but they are no longer strictly bound by all of the rules associated with them. For that reason judges are more free to consider the theory of Judge Kaplan's opinion.

NOTES

1. *United States v. Spiegelman*, Complaint, October 4, 1999.
2. Benjamin Weiser, "Document Thief's History Repeats Itself, Police Say," *New York Times*, October 7, 1999, B.
3. Basil Panagopulos interview, March 28, 2006.
4. Panagopulos interview.
5. Ashton interview.
6. Panagopulos interview.
7. *United States v. Spiegelman*, Docket, 1:99-mj-01756.
8. *United States v. Spiegelman*, Conference, April 7, 2000.
9. Ibid., 2.
10. Ibid., 2–8.
11. *United States v. Spiegelman*, Sentencing Hearing, May 24, 2000.
12. Ibid., 4–7.
13. Ibid., 14–26.
14. Ibid., 25.
15. *United States v. Medford*, 194 F. 3d 419 (3rd Cir. 1999).
16. *United States v. Medford*, Brief for Appellee, 4.
17. Ibid., 4–7.
18. 194 F.3d, 425–426.

Epilogue

The wound of the Columbia theft has mostly healed but the scar remains. Of the four primary characters from Columbia who factored in this story only Dutschke is still with the school and she still gets visibly upset when she talks about certain aspects of the saga.

Jean Ashton left the RBML in 2005 and now works as director of the library at the New York Historical Society, the place she worked before coming to Columbia. After three decades at Columbia, Rudolph Ellenbogen retired from the school but he still lives in the area. Susan Galligan left Columbia in 1998 and returned to private practice in the same firm she'd worked for before she came to the school. Though the original crime took place more than a decade ago, all four have a very good recollection of the events, right down to some very particular details.

There are questions that remain. Aside from the lingering notion that he had in any way a connection with the Oklahoma City bombing, there are still other mysteries to the Spiegelman saga. Some posited that he had a connection with the Russian mafia in New York; that would explain his ability to employ expensive attorneys. Some persistently thought he had a connection on the inside at Columbia that allowed him floor plans and egress routes. In the end the people who got to know him found that he was monumentally unpleasant; for that reason it was considered unlikely that he would have been able to work with anyone in a conspiracy for very long: No one could stand him. That he was not a nice man was something that everyone involved seemed to be able to agree on.

The only other thing that most seemed to agree on was that he still retains many of the missing items. He had always maintained that he had given over everything he had to the authorities. But that, of course, was before he escaped from the halfway house and tried to sell some of the items he said he'd given back. Both times he was captured the items on him were seized, but there is no indication that the authorities attempted to find the cache of documents he must have had in reserve. Dealers in Europe, where it is speculated that he sold most of the material he was able to get rid of, have not been forthcoming.

In the end a great deal of the Columbia material is still missing. To this day the RBML maintains a list of materials on its website for dealers on the off chance that they come across any of it. Dutschke still holds out hope that a couple of the medieval documents surface at an auction or in a dealer's catalogue. To that end, she keeps an eye out for familiar items.

The major security gap in the RBML's fortress has been plugged and a number of other modern security measures have been taken. No one will ever again take that much material from Columbia's Rare Book and Manuscript Library without notice. In truth, a crime like Spiegelman's is unlikely ever to happen on that scale anywhere again. Certainly book thieves will continue to steal from underprotected collections, but nothing like the amount of material that Spiegelman got out of Columbia could be taken without an incredible confluence of circumstances.

In the end his crime was unique, and will likely remain so. Hopefully, the same won't be true of the sentence Spiegelman received for it. Judge Kaplan was an extremely savvy judge who broke new ground in federal sentencing; judges who are willing to risk being overturned by appeals courts in an effort to do what is right are increasingly rare, particularly when going out on a limb is in the service of something as nebulous as "culture." But now that the path has been tread, it is hoped other judges will follow the lead.

Daniel Spiegelman, inmate 39459-054, was released from federal prison at the age of 42 on July 19, 2001. At that time he had spent a total of a little more than six years in custody.

Author's Note

I have neither attempted to ascertain his whereabouts nor sought to interview Daniel Spiegelman. This story would not have been possible without the unique circumstances of his crime, but there was nothing to be gained from hearing "his side of it." All of the facts of his crime are clear, I don't need to be lied to or told that Spiegelman is really a good man with the best of intentions. The record speaks for itself.

Still, the people I interviewed often asked the question and speculated about the answer. Several people assumed he was still in the United States, periodically selling some of the Columbia stash whenever he needs money. This seems unlikely to me. The risk versus reward of attempting to sell even one more of the Columbia items in the United States would seem fraught with hazard for a man so averse to going back to federal prison.

At least one person in the know thinks he's in Paris. It is certainly true that he seemed to get along better in Europe than in the United States. The market for his Columbia wares would certainly be more hospitable across the ocean than in the United States. For that matter he may well have gone back to eastern Europe, where he was born. While Tblisi is not Manhattan, it is certainly true that rare manuscripts would be a lot less likely to draw attention there.

As for the citations: Nothing in this book is fiction. All dialogue is taken either directly from contemporaneous court transcription, newspaper accounts, or, in a very few instances, from individuals' remembrances of their own words. Nothing that is a direct quote was created by me.

My descriptions of the scene of the crime—the Butler Library and RBML—come both from my own time spent there and interviews with the people who worked there. The way Spiegelman committed the crime was confessed by him as part of his plea agreement and later corroborated by physical evidence. Of course, I've not been in the locked stacks or the vault myself, so all of my descriptions of the interior where the crime was actually committed are based on interviews with the librarians.

In order to bring the crime itself alive somewhat, I've recreated what Spiegelman must have done when he scouted the stacks. Again, there is no film of these actual events so this recreation was a combination of my own "scouting" of the stacks along with information I received through interviews and documents. Some specifics have been left out at the request of interviewees.

In a very few instances there were some discrepancies between what my interviewees said happened and what documents I had in my possession said happened; most often this dealt with times and dates. In those cases I used the information in the written documents. Most of my questions in interviews were confined to filling in the gaps where the written material hadn't gotten. So there was very little overlap and even when there was, very little disagreement of facts.

Index

WITHDRAWN FROM STOCK

About the Author

TRAVIS McDADE is a lawyer and librarian, with experience working with rare manuscripts. He is currently the Legal Research columnist for *Student Lawyer* magazine, an ABA publication for law students. In addition, he is Assistant Professor of Library Administration in the College of Law at University of Illinois at Urbana-Champaign.